AF895801

De Minimis Aid Under EU Law

Ricardo Pedro

De Minimis Aid Under EU Law

ASSER PRESS

Springer

Ricardo Pedro
Faculty of Law: CIDP - Lisbon Centre for
Research in Public Law
University of Lisbon
Lisbon, Portugal

ISBN 978-94-6265-542-3 ISBN 978-94-6265-543-0 (eBook)
https://doi.org/10.1007/978-94-6265-543-0

Published by T.M.C. ASSER PRESS, The Hague, The Netherlands www.asserpress.nl
Produced and distributed for T.M.C. ASSER PRESS by Springer-Verlag Berlin Heidelberg

© T.M.C. ASSER PRESS and the author 2022
No part of this work may be reproduced, stored in a retrieval system, or transmitted in any form or by any means, electronic, mechanical, photocopying, microfilming, recording or otherwise, without written permission from the Publisher, with the exception of any material supplied specifically for the purpose of being entered and executed on a computer system, for exclusive use by the purchaser of the work.
The use of general descriptive names, registered names, trademarks, service marks, etc. in this publication does not imply, even in the absence of a specific statement, that such names are exempt from the relevant protective laws and regulations and therefore free for general use.

This T.M.C. ASSER PRESS imprint is published by the registered company Springer-Verlag GmbH, DE, part of Springer Nature.
The registered company address is: Heidelberger Platz 3, 14197 Berlin, Germany

To Marília, Afonso and João
"The Man Who Killed Don Quixote" is finished!

Foreword

As the old Roman saying goes, "*De minimis non curat praetor*". This book is all about whether, why and to what extent, in the field of State aid, *de minimis* matters.

This concise book has several cardinal virtues: it is concise, it is clear, it is simple, it is complete and it is useful. In addition, it is well-founded and documented in the legislation, the case-law of the Court of Justice and the legal literature. Moreover, not only does it propose a fresh view on an area of EU State aid law that (I hope not to be unfair) has been considerably neglected by the doctrine, but it also offers some creative insights that provide pleasant reading and should be particularly welcomed by practitioners.

The book by Ricardo Pedro helps the reader to understand why a general legal framework such as Regulation (EU) No 1407/2013 on the application of Articles 107 and 108 TFEU to *de minimis* aid may be of a particular practical relevance, provided that it strikes the right balance between the requirements of a sound and effective enforcement by the regulators at the EU and national levels and the overriding need of legal certainty for the undertakings.

In the entirety of its, it also provides a comprehensive overview of the existing *de minimis* schemes and the scope of the *de minimis* regulation, while making interesting contributions to the analysis of relevant legal concepts such as "single undertaking", "firm in difficulty", "quantitative ceilings" and "aid cumulation".

Monitoring *de minimis* schemes, its problems and difficulties have also attracted the author's attention as a crucial step for law enforcement in this field, in the intersection of the Commission's powers and obligations and the Member States' duty of sincere cooperation.

I recommend this book to all those who want to better understand the primary secrets of the old Roman wisdom applied to the modern State aid discipline in an increasingly complex and competitive economic environment.

In particular, those who have to advise their clients on the benefits and risks of applying for and accepting certain aid schemes will find useful guidance here on how to proceed in order to gain the comfort of being on the safe side.

Lisbon, Portugal
May 2022

José Luís da Cruz Vilaça
Professor of EU Law and Lawyer
Former Judge and Advocate General of the Court of Justice of the European Union
Former President of the Court of First Instance of the European Communities (now the General Court of the European Union)

Contents

About the Author

Ricardo Pedro, Ph.D. is a research fellow at the Centre for Research in Public Law of Lisbon's Law School (CIDP). He holds a Master and a Ph.D. in public law (NOVA School of Law—Lisbon). Furthermore, he has been a guest lecturer at several universities and has worked as a lawyer and legal consultant. He is also the author of a number of books, book chapters and scientific articles on public law.

Abbreviations

CAP	Common Agricultural Policy
CF	Cohesion Fund
CFP	Common Fisheries Policy
CJEU	Court of Justice of the European Union
EAFRD	European Agricultural Fund for Rural Development
ECtHR	European Court of Human Rights
EMFF	European Maritime and Fisheries Fund
ERDF	European Regional Development Fund
ESF	European Social Fund
ESIF	European Structural and Investment Funds
GBER	General Block Exemption Regulation
GC	General Court
MS	Member State or Member States
OJ	Official Journal
SGEI	Services of General Economic Interest
SMEs	Small- and Medium-sized Enterprises
TEU	Treaty on European Union
TFEU	Treaty on the Functioning of the European Union

Chapter 1
Introduction and Background

Contents

Abstract This chapter seeks to contextualize *de minimis* aid, and therefore identifies the key questions addressed in this book. *De minimis* aid regimes must be well understood relative to State aid frameworks and insider schemes of notification to the Commission. Bearing in mind that at the time of writing Europe in particular is trying to tackle the fallout from COVID-19, this chapter also deals with the Commission's take on State aid as a tool to address these exceptional circumstances and explores the possibilities that the *de minimis* aid regime could offer. Lastly, bearing in mind that *de minimis* arrangements apply in many Member States as part of the application of European fund frameworks, the chapter outlines the European, Structural and Investment Funds' EU frameworks.

Keywords *De minimis* aid · State aid · COVID-19 · European Structural and Investment Funds · Role of the European Commission · Role of the Member States

© T.M.C. ASSER PRESS and the author 2022

R. Pedro, *De Minimis Aid Under EU Law*,
https://doi.org/10.1007/978-94-6265-543-0_1

1.1 Introduction and Background

Why do *de minimis* aid rules matter? That is the question underpinning this study, and it is relevant from a logical, theoretical and cardinally from a practical perspective.

From a logical perspective, this may seem a *prima facie* paradox, since it is a common rule that matters of a lesser import do not matter in certain areas of the law.

In this context, two meanings have been historically assigned to the *de minimis* rule: (i) a procedural meaning, expressed in the Latin brocard "*de minimis* non curat praetor" and (ii) a substantive meaning, expressed in the maxim "*de minimis* non curat lex".[1]

It often arises within the framework of European Union law namely—besides *de minimis* aidin *agreements between undertakings*[2] and in the *public procurement framework.*[3]

From a *theoretical* perspective, a small-scale aid is presumed not to affect nor threaten to affect competition and the internal market. Therefore, this kind of aid should be *simple and ensure legal certainty to public authorities and recipients.* In other words, in addition to the market perspective, account should be taken of the impact that an aid control framework may have on its main recipients, and consideration should be given to reducing the bureaucratic burden that the aid control procedure would entail.[4]

In a sense, an *appropriateness* judgment must take place whereby small-scale aid—which does not affect nor threaten to affect competition and the internal market—is not reconcilable with a meticulous/bureaucratic control framework, i.e., the *de minimis* aid regime must emerge as a rule that strives to strike a *balance between simplifying and not distorting competition within the internal market*, and which should always be a tool that MS can easily apply. In short and according to the European Commission,[5] *de minimis* aid rules should be *easy to interpret, highly flexible* and *quick to implement*, and have *low administrative costs.* The fact that the *aid need not be notified to the European Commission* is a touchstone of the above characteristics.

In this context, the European legislator has approved four (one general and three special) *de minimis* regulations. These are aid regimes (presumed) compatible with the internal market and competition rules, where no prior notification to the European Commission is required.[6] According to certain Court of Justice *case-law*,

---

[1] See, among others, Hojnik 2013, pp. 26–27.

[2] See, e.g., Communication from the Commission—Notice on agreements of minor importance which do not appreciably restrict competition under Article 101(1) of the Treaty on the Functioning of the European Union (De Minimis Notice) 2014/C 291/01; Vallina 2008, pp. 47–61; de Carvalho 2016, pp. 1163–1208.

[3] See Kalflèche 2007, pp. 6–11; Hojnik 2013, pp. 28–30.

[4] See European Commission 2006 and 2013b.

[5] See European Commission 2013a, p. 6.

[6] Bär-Bouyssière 2005, p. 171.

however, (even) aid below a certain amount *could*—in certain circumstances—distort or threaten to distort competition or affect the internal market between MS.[7] This means that a purely quantitative analysis[8] of *de minimis* aid regulations does not preclude a *substantial analysis* of the *de minimis* regimes as regards distortion of competition. In sum, and by way of introduction, it cannot be stated with absolute certainty that a particular measure complies with EU primary law,[9] even if it complies with the *de minimis* regulations.

For the above reasons, as Advocate General Christine Stix-Hackl warns:[10] "*[…] there is no doubt that the de minimis aid regime must be interpreted strictly because it constitutes a derogation from the obligations arising from Article 88 (2) (3) EC*".[11]

In fact, underlying the configuration of the *de minimis* aid is the understanding of its nature. On the one hand, it is a regime that does not arise from the Treaties or the case-law of the Court of Justice (at least not clearly). On the other hand, it is a regime heavily predicated on State aid policy and Court of Justice's case-law on the positions of the European Commission tends to be balanced.[12]

From a *practical* perspective: if we look closer, we will see that under the *de minimis* regimes *the internal market* and *competition* (and *beyond*)[13] are controlled by the MS and not by the European Commission.

While this option removes the Commission's control of competition as regards small-scale aid (at least in practical terms), it also relieves it of the administrative costs that such control would entail. The costs are passed on to the MS and may involve a large investment in the administrative mechanisms to ensure that the *de minimis* regimes are not breached.

The practical relevance of *de minimis* regimes has also emerged with their mobilisation in times of financial crisis, primarily through the increase in the quantitative ceiling.[14]

A second question that this book seeks to address is, "*how to interpret the* de minimis *aid rules?*" The answer to this question will reveal the main *scope* of this study.

From a negative perspective, *de minimis* aid *is not State aid* under Article 107(1) TFEU[15] because it lacks an essential element of State aid, namely, not to affect nor threaten to affect competition and the internal market. Notwithstanding our attempt

---

[7] Berghofer 2007, p. 15.

[8] Ibid., p. 15.

[9] In the sense that a *substantial analysis* should take place, see Samaniego Bordiú 2004, p. 49; Vilaça 2014, pp. 237 et seq.

[10] Berghofer 2007, p. 15.

[11] Ibid., p. 15.

[12] See Estoa Pérez 2007, pp. 623–636; Pedro 2015, pp. 69 et seq.; Piernas Lopez 2015, pp. 186 et seq.; Van de Casteele 2016, p. 243; Soltész 2016, pp. 230, 231 and 322; Derenne and Verouden 2017, pp. 180 et seq.

[13] See Piernas Lopez 2015, pp. 3 et seq.

[14] See, e.g., Quigley 2015, pp. 463 et seq.

[15] See Consolidated version of the Treaty on the Functioning of the European Union, OJ C 326, 26 November 2012, pp. 47–390 (TFEU).

to gain a better understanding of the *de minimis* concept, the truth is that its practical importance—indeed, as with all laws—results from its framework, in particular from its application by MS when they grant aid to undertakings.

The interpretation of the *de minimis* rules entails considering the four legal regulations presently in force, namely one general and three special regimes. Consequently, one cannot interpret/apply the general *de minimis* regulations without taking account of the special *de minimis* legal aid regulations. On the one hand, this requires determining the material and personal scope of each regime and, on the other hand—considering the common model in place, if several entities are involved in monitoring the different *de minimis* regimes—dictates the necessary coordination between the entities responsible for monitoring the different *de minimis* regimes.[16]

In addition, the operationalization of the scope of *de minimis* regimes is not self-sufficient, but rather requires considering (at least as an auxiliary) the national regulations in connection with the identification of the different economic activities.

The *de minimis* regulations contain a few concepts which are difficult to interpret let alone enforce by the national authorities (some of these difficulties arise *ex novo*, while others already existed in the previous framework) not only because they are poorly consolidated under European Union law, but also because they constitute a derogation to the EU/EEA State aid framework and because the European Commission does not always agree with the Court of Justice, which will require considering the most relevant case-law on this subject.

Lastly, although in practice the general *de minimis* regulation seeks to reduce bureaucratic or transaction costs for the European Commission, MS and the undertakings because of the low aid amounts concerned, in particular as regards the administrative control procedure after the latest reforms to modernize the State aid framework, this rarely happens in the regimes at hand.

The application of the *de minimis* rules entails reviewing Regulation (EU) No 1407/2013 (hereinafter, the "general *de minimis* regulation" or "general *de minimis* regime")[17] together, on the one hand, with other special *de minimis* legal regimes, in particular (i) the regime laid down by Regulation (EU) No 1408/2013 (hereinafter, "the *de minimis* regulation for the agriculture sector" or "*de minimis* regime for the agriculture sector"),[18] (ii) the regime laid down by Regulation (EU) No 717/2014

---

[16] The "special" terminology as referred to is drawn from CJEU, *Spain v Commission*, Judgment of the Court, 19 September 2002, case C-113/00, ECLI:EU:C:2002:507. The terminology used by legal authors varies between "general" or "horizontal" *de minimis* regime and "special" or "specific" regimes. See, among others, Foszczynski and Stobiecka-Kuik 2008, p. 1519 and Walkerova 2008, p. 1568.

[17] Commission Regulation (EU) No 1407/2013 of 18 December 2013 on the application of Articles 107 and 108 of the Treaty on the Functioning of the European Union to *de minimis* aid, OJ L 352, 24 December 2013, pp. 1–8 rectified by the Rectification of Commission Regulation (EU) No 1407/2013 of 18 December 2013 on the application of Articles 107 and 108 of the Treaty on the Functioning of the European Union to *de minimis* aid.

[18] Commission Regulation (EU) No 1408/2013 of 18 December 2013 on the application of Articles 107 and 108 of the Treaty on the Functioning of the European Union to *de minimis* aid in the agriculture sector, OJ L 352, 24 December 2013, pp. 9–17.

(hereinafter "*de minimis* regulation for the fishery and aquaculture sector" or "*de minimis* regime for the fishery and aquaculture sector"),[19] (iii) the regime laid down by Regulation (EU) No 360/2012 (hereinafter the "*de minimis* regulation on financing of undertakings providing SGEI" or "*de minimis* regime on financing of undertakings providing SGEI"),[20] and, on the other hand, with nationals regimes which prove essential for the application of that European aid legal framework.

All in all, the application of *de minimis* regulations raises specific (sub)questions, including: (i) to what economic activity sectors does the general *de minimis* regulation apply; (ii) how to understand the notion of 'single undertaking' provided for *ex novo* in the general *de minimis* regulation (and the special *de minimis* regimes); (iii) how to interpret the legal concept of 'firm in difficulty' for the purpose of including or excluding it in or from the scope of the general *de minimis* regulation; (iv) how to understand the undertakings' mergers, acquisitions and/or spin-off rule provided for in the Regulation on the general *de minimis* aid regime; (v) how to ensure that the incentive is granted at the time when the legal right to receive the aid is granted to the undertaking; (vi) how to monitor compliance with the quantitative ceiling and the time limit in the last three fiscal years; (vii) how to reconcile the general regime for the cumulation of *de minimis* aid with other aid (including *de minimis* aid within the context of SGEI).

A third and last question is, "*what is the role of the Members States in the implementation/monitoring of the* de minimis *regimes ?*"

MS play a crucial role in implementing the de *minimis* regimes, as control is left to them. In other words, unlike State aid that is, as a rule, notified to the European Commission for its review, *de minimis* aid is only controlled by MS. In this regard, it should be noted that monitoring the *de minimis* regulations is one of the most important and most difficult aspects of its practical application, as is often emphasized by the European Commission.

Nevertheless, MS have an obligation to cooperate with the European Commission, in accordance with the provisions of Article 4(3) TEU, and in particular to check (*rectius*, confirm), before granting any *de minimis* aid, that its ceiling will not be exceeded by the new *de minimis* aid.

The *ex-ante* control by MS is particularly important because it does not require the European Commission to be notified of *de minimis* aid, which means that the European method of monitoring *de minimis* aid granted to undertakings to determine whether it affects or threatens to affect competition is based on the administrative control of the MS. This conclusion runs somewhat counter to the Union's understanding of exclusive authority as regards competition policy.

---

[19] Commission Regulation (EU) No 717/2014 of 27 June 2014 on the application of Articles 107 and 108 of the Treaty on the Functioning of the European Union to *de minimis* aid in the fishery and aquaculture sector, OJ L 190, 28 June 2014, pp. 45–54.

[20] Commission Regulation (EU) No 360/2012 of 25 April 2012 on the application of Articles 107 and 108 of the Treaty on the Functioning of the European Union to *de minimis* aid granted to undertakings providing services of general economic interest, OJ L 114, 26 April 2012, pp. 8–13.

Lastly, the control entrusted to MS shows that they have a margin of discretion in accordance with the principle of procedural and organisational autonomy. However, this discretion is limited by the principle of effectiveness of European Union law (*maxime, de minimis* regulations). There are thus two options: (i) MS must obtain from the undertaking concerned a written or electronic statement regarding the existence of any other *de minimis* aid to which the *de minimis* regulations apply during the two previous fiscal years and the current fiscal year or (ii) MS must set up a central *de minimis* aid register containing full information on all *de minimis* aid granted by an authority of that MS over a period of three fiscal years.

1.2 *De Minimis* and State Aid

For a better understanding of the regimes that will be addressed later, and by way of introduction only, *de minimis* aid regimes must be put in context regarding State aid. It is as such essential to consider the main rules of primary European law on State aid.[21]

Very briefly, account should first be taken of the *principle of relative prohibition of State aid* laid down in Article 107(1) TFEU, secondly of the admissibility of aid *automatically consistent* with Union law set out in Article 107(2) TFEU and, lastly of the admissibility of *aid which may be consistent* with Union law set out in Article 107(3) TFEU.

Within the general framework of primary European law on State aid, two other provisions should also be mentioned:

(i) Article 108 TFEU establishing the rules on the *permanent examination of State aid by the European Commission in cooperation with Member States* and
(ii) Article 109 TFEU on the *power to adopt regulations.*

Lastly, it should be borne in mind that, according to Article 3(1)(b) TFEU, *the European Union has exclusive authority* as regards competition, particularly as regards State aid.

For the proper legal understanding of the State aid regime provided for in Article 107(1) TFEU, its constituent elements must first be identified, which are cumulative and focus on the grant of (i) an *economic advantage to an undertaking through* (ii) *public resources, such measures being (broadly speaking) attributable to the State,* (iii) *being selective,* (iv) *distorting or threatening to distort competition* and *being liable to affect trade between Member States.*[22]

[21] See, e.g., Quigley 2015, pp. 3 et seq.; Hofmann 2016, pp. 39 et seq., and CJEU, *Italy v Commission,* Judgment of the Court, 29 April 2004, case C-372/97, ECLI:EU:C:2004:234; *Überseering,* Judgment of the Court, 5 November 2002, case C-208/00, ECLI:EU:C:2002:632.

[22] See, among others, Quigley 2015, pp. 53 et seq.; Arhold 2016, pp. 82 et seq.; Conte and Kavanagh 2017, pp. 65 et seq.

Let us take a closer look at each of these elements.[23]

A first element of the notion of State aid concerns the *economic advantage granted to an undertaking*, i.e., an economic benefit which an undertaking would not have obtained under normal market conditions without the State's intervention.[24] There is therefore an advantage every time a company's financial situation improves as a result of State intervention.

To assess the existence of the advantage, the company's financial situation after the measure must be appraised and compared with the prevailing financial situation had the measure not been introduced.[25]

The advantage can be *directly* or *indirectly* granted to a recipient undertaking (in the latter case, whenever the measure is designed to channel its secondary effects towards identifiable undertakings or groups of undertakings).[26]

It should also be taken into account that economic transactions (directly or indirectly) carried out by public authorities, whatever their form, fall under the Union State aid rules.[27] To determine whether such economic transactions take place under normal market conditions or whether, on the contrary, State aid is being granted (*maxime*, an economic advantage), the market economy operator test ("MEOT")[28]

---

[23] See the perspective of the European Commission in this matter in the Commission Notice on the notion of State aid as referred to in Article 107(1) of the Treaty on the Functioning of the European Union (2016/C 262/01), OJ C 262, 19 July 2016, pp. 1–50.

[24] See, *inter alia*, CJEU, *Spain v Commission*, Judgment of the Court, 29 April 1999, case C-342/96, ECLI:EU:C:1999:210.

[25] See *Italy v Commission*, Judgment of the Court, 2 July 1974, case 173/73, ECLI:EU:C:1974:71.

[26] See Commission Notice on the notion of State aid as referred to in Article 107(1) of the Treaty on the Functioning of the European Union (2016/C 262/01), OJ C 262, 19 July 2016, p. 26.

[27] See Quigley 2015, pp. 153 et seq.; Arhold 2016, pp. 108 et seq.; Conte and Kavanagh 2017, pp. 70 et seq.

[28] Which, according to case-law, may take several concrete forms/variations, depending on the economic operation in question, namely:

(i) *the market economy investor principle*: mobilised to determine whether an investment by a public body constitutes State aid—in order to identify the presence of State aid in cases of public investment (notably capital injections), it being necessary to assess whether, in similar circumstances, a private investor of comparable size operating under normal market economy conditions could have been prompted to make the investment in question [e.g., CJEU: *Belgium v Commission* ('*Tubemeuse*'), Judgment of the Court, 21 March 1990, case C-142/87, ECLI:EU: C:1990:125; *Italy v Commission* ('*ALFA Romeo*'), Judgment of the Court, 21 March 1991, case C-305/89, ECLI:EU: C:1991:142];

(ii) *the private creditor test*: in order to examine whether debt renegotiations by public creditors involve State aid, by comparing the behaviour of a public creditor with that of hypothetical private creditors who are in a similar situation (e.g., CJEU: *Spain v Commission*, Judgment of the Court, 22 November 2007, case C-525/04 P, ECLI:EU:C:2007:698; *Frucona v Commission*, Judgment of the Court, 24 January 2013, C-73/11 P, ECLI:EU:C:2013:32; *DMTransport*, Judgment of the Court, 29 June 1999, case C-256/97, ECLI:EU:C:1999:332);

(iii) *the private seller test*: in order to assess whether a sale by a public body involves State aid, by analysing whether a private seller, under normal market conditions, could have obtained an equal or better price (e.g., GC, *Land Burgenland and Austria v Commission*, Judgment of the Court, 28 February 2012, joined cases T-268/08 and T-281/08, ECLI:EU:T:2012:90).

applies, which is a consequence of the principle of neutrality with regard to the system of property ownership (Article 345 TFEU).

Another element relates to the *public nature of resources*, i.e. *only* state-origin funds are relevant, on the one hand, and *all* public resources are relevant, on the other,[29] whether these funds are *positively transferred* (e.g. direct or indirect incentives) or through the *State's waiver of revenue* (e.g. loss of tax, social security revenue[30] or the granting of access to the public domain or natural resources or the granting of special or exclusive rights without adequate compensation in line with market rates applied). In addition to the situations mentioned above, it should be borne in mind that the creation of a specific risk imposing an additional burden on the State in the future, namely through a guarantee,[31] may also constitute State aid.

The European or national origin of resources is irrelevant if MS have *discretionary powers*[32] in their application/administration, as is the case with the ESIF.[33] Conversely, the resources are not deemed to be State resources when it comes to the application/administration of European funds by MS under *tied* powers, as is the case with the Horizon 2020 framework program.[34]

Measures are attributable to the State (or broadly speaking to any public entity)[35] if a public authority grants an advantage to a recipient, even if the authority in question enjoys legal autonomy relative to other public authorities or if the public authority appoints a public-law or a private-law body to administer the measure conferring an advantage.

As the CJEU states: "*It is settled case-law that no distinction is to be drawn between cases where the aid is granted directly by the State and those where it is granted by public or private bodies which the State establishes or designates with a view to administering the aid (…). [C]ommunity law cannot permit the rules on*

---

[29] See GC, *Air France v Commission*, Judgment of the Court, 12 December 1996, case T-358/94, ECLI:EU:T:1996:194.

[30] See CJEU, *France v Ladbroke Racing and Commission*, Judgment of the Court, 16 May 2000, case C-83/98 P, ECLI:EU:C:2000:248.

[31] See CJEU, *Residex Capital v Gemeente Rotterdam*, Judgment of the Court, 8 December 2011, case C-275/10, ECLI:EU:C:2011:814, para 39.

[32] See CJEU, *Commission v Ireland and others*, Judgment of the Court, 10 December 2013, case C-272/12 P, ECLI:EU:C:2013:812.

[33] See European Commission Decision of 22 November 2006 on State aid N 157/06, OJ C 80, 13 April 2007, p. 2.

[34] Regulation (EU) No 1291/2013 of the European Parliament and of the Council of 11 December 2013 establishing Horizon 2020—the Framework Programme for Research and Innovation (2014–2020) and repealing Decision No 1982/2006/EC, OJ L 347, 20 December 2013, pp. 104–173.

[35] However, as already outlined, a measure is not attributable to the MS if it arises from a *binding obligation under Union law*. See CJEU, *Puffer*, Judgment of the Court, 23 April 2009, case C-460/07, ECLI:EU:C:2009:254, para 70.

State aid to be circumvented merely through the creation of autonomous institutions charged with allocating aid".[36]

Another key element of the notion of State aid is the *selectivity of the measure*,[37] i.e., favouring certain undertakings or certain productions: giving priority to one undertaking or group of undertakings, or one or certain products. Selective measures achieve the opposite of general measures, i.e., those which are equally available to all undertakings operating in an MS.

On the one hand, the selectivity of the measure may be *material in nature*, meaning that it applies only to certain undertakings (groups) or certain sectors of the economy in a given MS, *legal* (as a direct result of the legal criteria for granting a measure formally reserved for certain undertakings only), or *de facto* (although the formal criteria for the application of the measure are formulated in general and objective terms, the structure of the measure shows that its effects significantly favour a specific group of undertakings).[38]

On the other hand, selectivity may be *regional in nature*, i.e., the measures are *regional* in *scope.*[39]

Yet another essential element of the notion of State aid is that of *distortion of competition and the ability to affect the trade between MS.* A measure granted by the State distorts or threatens to distort competition if it is likely to improve the recipient's competitive position relative to other undertakings with which it competes.[40]

The European Commission assumes that there is a distortion of competition where the State grants a financial advantage to an undertaking in a liberalized sector where there is, or could be, competition. For such purpose, it is, as a rule, deemed sufficient that the aid affords an advantage to the recipient, which releases it of costs which it would typically have had to bear in its day-to-day management or regular activities.[41]

Concerning *the ability to affect the trade between MS*, the European Commission assumes that an advantage granted to an undertaking operating in a market open to competition will distort competition and may also affect trade between MS. Moreover, according to case-law, the European Commission is not required to prove that the aid in question affects the market, but only to examine the extent to which

---

[36] See CJEU, *France v Commission*, Judgment of the Court, 16 May 2002, case C-482/99, ECLI:EU:C:2002:29, para 23.

[37] See Vilaça 2014, pp. 237 et seq.

[38] See CJEU, *Commission and Spain v Government of Gibraltar and United Kingdom*, Judgment of the Court, 15 November 2011, joined cases C-106/09 P and C-107/09 P, ECLI:EU:C:2011:732.

[39] See CJEU, *Portugal v Commission*, Judgment of the Court, 6 September 2006, case C-88/03, ECLI:EU:C:2006:511.

[40] See GC, *Alzetta and others v Commission*, Judgment of the Court, 15 June 2000, joined cases T-298/97, T-312/97, T-313/97, T-315/97, T-600/97 to T-607/97, T-1/98, T-3/98 to T-6/98 and T-23/98, ECLI:EU:T:2000:151.

[41] Such an assertion appears, namely in the CJEU, *Wolfgang Heiser v Finanzamt Innsbruck*, Judgment of the Court, 3 March 2005, case C-172/03, ECLI:EU:C:2005:130.

that aid is liable to affect the market,[42] which indicates a broad approach to this requirement.[43]

If State financial aid strengthens the position of an undertaking relative to other competitors in intra-Community trade, the latter must be deemed to be affected by the aid.[44] The European Commission's understanding is that it is not necessary to define the market or to investigate the impact of the measure on the competitive position of the recipient and its competitors in detail.[45]

But an effect on trade between MS cannot be purely hypothetical or presumed: the European Commission must examine the foreseeable effects on competition and intra-Community trade at the time the aid is granted.[46]

Conversely, if a measure has a purely local impact,[47] i.e., if the recipient provided goods or services in a limited area within a MS and was not likely to attract customers from other MS, the measure has, in principle,[48] no effect on trade between MS.

1.3 State Aid and *De Minimis* in the Context of COVID-19

1.3.1 State Aid in Exceptional Circumstances

The recent social and economic impact of COVID-19 shone the spotlight anew on State aid.

To put it very briefly, at issue is, on the one hand, the admissibility of aid *automatically compatible* with Union law referred to in Article 107(2) TFEU and, on the other hand, the admissibility of aid which *may be compatible* with Union law set out in Article 107(3) TFEU.

---

42 See CJEU, *Eventech v The Parking Adjudicator*, Judgment of the Court, 14 January 2015, case C-518/13, ECLI:EU:C:2015:9, para 65.

43 See Derenne and Verouden 2017, p. 178.

44 Such an assertion appears, namely in GC, *Regione autonoma Friuli-Venezia Giulia v Commission*, Judgment of the Court, 4 April 2001, case T-288/97, ECLI:EU:T:2001:115 and case C-518/13, para 66.

45 See GC, *Italy v Commission*, Judgment of the Court, 4 September 2009, case T-211/05, ECLI:EU:T:2009:304.

46 See GC, *AITEC and others v Commission*, Judgment of the Court, 6 July 1995, joined cases T-447/93, T-448/93 and T-449/93, ECLI:EU:T:1995:130, para 141.

47 See, e.g., European Commission Decisions: SA.37963 (United Kingdom—Alleged state aid to Glenmore Lodge), OJ C 277, 21 August 2015, p. 3; SA.34576 (Portugal—Jean Piaget/Nordeste continuous care unit), OJ C 73, 13 March 2013, p. 1; SA.39403 (The Netherlands—Investment in the Port of Lauwersoog) OJ C 259, 7 August 2015, p. 4.

48 See CJEU, *Altmark Trans GmbH and Regierungspräsidium Magdeburg v Nahverkehrsgesellschaft Altmark GmbH, and Oberbundesanwalt beim Bundesverwaltungsgericht*, Judgment of the Court, 24 July 2003, case C-280/00, ECLI:EU:C:2003:415, paras 77 and 78.

Considering the very significant economic and social impact of the COVID-19 pandemic, it is important to highlight the legal hypotheses that can cater to exceptional situations such as the pandemic.

It should be noted at the outset that some of the possible aid measures and schemes that MS may develop can be framed in the context of the aid provided for in Article 107(2)(b) TFEU, which states that "*aid to make good the damage caused by natural disasters or exceptional occurrences shall be compatible with the internal market*".

In other words, as better detailed below, the COVID-19 outbreak should be qualified as an "*exceptional, extraordinary and unforeseeable occurrence*", with a very significant economic impact, which means that exceptional interventions by MS to offset the damages associated with that outbreak should be deemed warranted.

Neither the TFEU nor any other Union legislation provides an accurate definition of the notion of "*exceptional occurrence*". As exceptional occurrences derogate from the general prohibition of State aid in the internal market laid down in Article 107(1) TFEU, the European Commission has consistently held that the notion of "*exceptional occurrence*" set out in Article 107(2)(b) TFEU should be interpreted restrictively, in accordance with Union settled case-law.[49]

MS have submitted various State aid schemes to the European Commission over the years to address exceptional circumstances and the European Commission has consistently held that they comply with European State aid rules.[50] The European Commission characterizes an event as an exceptional occurrence on a case-by-case basis, taking into account its own previous practice. In this sense, the following requirements must be cumulatively met: (i) *unpredictability or difficulty to predict*;[51] (ii) *significant scale/economic impact*;[52] and (iii) *extraordinary nature*.[53]

In order to be compatible with Article 107(2)(b) TFEU, the compensation measure must also (i) have a *causal link between the notified scheme and the harmful event* (*in casu*, COVID-19), (ii) *be proportionate to* the damage caused by the exceptional occurrence. The aid must not result in overcompensation for damage; it must remedy only the damage caused by the exceptional occurrence and (iii) the aid provided for under this scheme *cannot be cumulated with other State aid granted to address the same costs*.

---

[49] See CJEU: *Spain v Commission*, Judgment of the Court, 11 November 2004, case C-73/03, ECLI:EU:C:2004:711; *Giuseppe Atzeni and others v Regione autonoma della Sardegna*, Judgment of the Court, 23 February 2006, joined cases C-346/03 and C-529/03, ECLI:EU:C:2006:130.

[50] Orzan 2016, pp. 236 et seq.

[51] In this context, see Commission Decision: S.A. 32163 - 2010/N (Slovenia—Rectification of consequences of the damage caused to air carriers and airports by earthquake activity in Iceland and the resulting volcanic ash in April 2010 3) OJ C 135, 9 May 2012, p. 1.

[52] In this context, see Commission Decision: State Aid No SA.33487 (2011/N) Agricultural and fisheries aid to compensate for damage due to exceptional occurrence (red sludge "Aluminium accident"), OJ C 120, 25 April 2012, p. 1.

[53] See European Commission Decision of 19 May 2004 on the aid scheme which Italy is planning to implement for poultry undertakings–AIMA programme for the poultry sector C 59/2001 (ex N 97/1999) (notified under document number C(2004) 1802), OJ L 32, 6 February 2007, pp. 14–22.

The European Commission's practice has been to accept the following situations as "*natural disasters*"[54] and to bring them under the notion of "*exceptional occurrence*": *earthquakes, avalanches, landslides, and floods.* It has moreover accepted the following situations according to the development under the State Aid Modernisation initiative, which also allows exempting certain categories of natural disasters: *tornadoes, hurricanes, volcanic eruptions, and fires of natural origin.* Exceptional occurrences which have so far been accepted by the European Commission in compliance with these concepts also include: *war, internal disturbances or strikes, and, with certain reservations and depending on their extent, major nuclear or industrial accidents and fires which result in widespread loss.* The European Commission has not accepted, for instance, that *a fire at a single processing plant covered by normal commercial insurance could be considered an exceptional occurrence.*[55]

The European Commission made an interesting application of the concept of "*exceptional occurrence*" in the aftermath of the 9/11 New York and Washington attacks,[56] in that it considered that the events of 11 September 2001 could be described as "*exceptional occurrences*" under the legal framework, given their unforeseeable nature, the number of victims, the extent of the damage, and their impact on the world's economy.

In short, a case methodology is followed whereby the European Commission must assess proposals to grant State aid under Article 107(2)(b) TFEU on a case-by-case basis, taking account of its previous practice.

The tangible threat of a pandemic, coupled with the public health risk arising from the absence of therapeutics or vaccines for COVID-19, are exceptional circumstances.

The rapid spread of the disease can have tremendous consequences, such as fatal outcomes in high-risk groups and economic and social disruption.

COVID-19 therefore qualifies as an "*exceptional occurrence*", as it was unforeseeable, is clearly distinguishable from ordinary events, both in its character and in its effects on the affected undertakings and the economy as a whole, and is consequently *outside the normal functioning of the market.* In short, COVID-19 can be considered an "*exceptional occurrence*" within the meaning of Article 107(2)(b) TFEU.

It is in this context that the European Commission has approved a *Danish aid scheme* worth €12 million to compensate event organisers for the damages caused by the

---

[54] In the context of and for the purposes of the application of Commission Regulation (EU) No 651/2014 of 16 June 2014, declaring certain categories of aid compatible with the internal market in application of Articles 107 and 108 of the Treaty, OJ L 187, 26 June 2014, pp. 1–7, may constitute a natural disaster exempted by this Regulation: "*earthquakes, landslides, floods, in particular floods caused by flooding from river or lake shores, avalanches, tornadoes, cyclones, volcanic eruptions and wildfires of natural origin must be regarded as events constituting a natural disaster. Damage caused by adverse weather conditions such as frost, hail, ice, rain or drought, which occur on a more regular basis, should not be considered a natural disaster within the meaning of Article 107(2)(b) of the Treaty*".

[55] See European Union Guidelines for State aid in the agriculture and forestry sectors and rural areas for 2014–2020 (2014/C 204/01), OJ C 204, 1 July 2014, pp. 1–97.

[56] See European Commission 2001.

cancellation of major events with more than 1000 participants between 6 and 31 March 2020 due to the outbreak of COVID-19, in accordance with Union State aid rules—Commission Decision: *State Aid SA.56685 (2020/N) - DK - Compensation scheme for cancellation of events related to COVID-19.*[57]

The compensation may cover up to 100% of eligible costs if they are not covered by the organiser's insurance. However, companies that have received previous unlawful aid declared incompatible by a European Commission decision are debarred from this scheme.

This is the first of several COVID-19 outbreak-related State aid measures notified by a MS to the European Commission, and the Danish authorities have fulfilled their obligation under Article 108(3) TFEU by notifying the aid measure before implementing it.

The compensation provided for by the Danish scheme will be paid from the State budget and is therefore granted through State resources within the meaning of Article 107(1) TFEU. The compensation decision is made after the State authorities examine the application, which means that the measure is attributable to the State. Since the compensation will relieve the recipients from costs they would otherwise have to bear as a result of their business, will not be granted to all operators in a comparable factual and legal situation, but only to those organising specific events (large events or events), and targets a specific public, the measure is selective and confers an advantage (the advantage corresponds to the amount of compensation paid under the scheme) that may distort or threaten to distort competition. Lastly, as the scheme covers a competitive sector and undertakings engaging in trade between MS, there is a risk that the aid might distort or threaten to distort competition and affect such trade. In sum, the proposed aid measure constitutes State aid within the meaning of Article 107(1) TFEU.

Several State-aid measures have been later approved under Article 107(2)(b),[58] in the context of COVID-19.

Article 107(3)(c) TFEU, which states, "*The following may be considered compatible with the internal market: (c) aid to facilitate the development of certain economic activities or of certain economic areas, where such aid does not adversely affect trading conditions to an extent contrary to the common interest*", provides yet another regulatory framework on State aid that could serve as a basis to support companies in distress due to the COVID-19 outbreak.

In this context, MS may, e.g., set up dedicated support schemes for SMEs, notably to cover their liquidity needs for a period of up to 18 months.[59]

The European Commission's practice has been to approve these support schemes. According to information provided by the European Commission, some MS already have such schemes in place. For instance, in February 2019, the Commission

[57] See OJ C 125, 17 April 2020, p. 8.

[58] See European Commission 2020a.

[59] See European Commission Decision SA.56685 (2020/N), OJ C 125, 17 April 2020, p. 8.

approved a €400 million support scheme requested by Ireland to cover acute liquidity needs, rescue and restructure SMEs, in preparation for *Brexit.*[60]

Some State aid measures have been later approved under Article 107(3)(c) TFEU,[61] in the context of COVID-19.

Lastly, support may also be provided under Article 107(3)(b) TFEU, which states that, "*The following may be considered compatible with the internal market: (b) aid to promote the execution of an important project of common European interest or to remedy a serious disturbance in the economy of a Member State*".

It should be borne in mind that this is a derogation from Article 107(1) TFEU and, therefore, the concept of "*serious disturbance in the economy of a Member State*" must be interpreted restrictively.[62]

The situation must be serious, i.e., the disturbance must affect the entire economy of the MS concerned, and not just that of one of its regions or parts of its territory.

It should also be noted that the European Commission enjoys *a broad discretion* in the implementation of this provision, whose exercise involves economic and social assessments that must be made in a Community context. Consequently, when reviewing the lawfulness of the exercise of that freedom, European Union Courts cannot make their own assessment in lieu of that of the proper authority, but must confine themselves to examining whether there is manifest error in the authority's assessment or whether the authority misused its powers.[63]

It is for the MS to demonstrate that the aid measures notified to the European Commission under this framework are necessary, appropriate and proportionate to remedy the "*serious disturbance in the economy of the MS*" concerned and that all conditions are fully met.

In the light of the severity of the 2008 economic and financial crisis and its impact on the overall economy of the MS, the European Commission considered that certain categories of State aid could be warranted for a limited period of time to overcome these difficulties and that such aid could be declared compatible with the internal market on the basis of Article 107(3)(b) TFEU.

More recently—in the context of this public health pandemic—the European Commission noted that the seriousness of the economic and financial impacts caused by the COVID-19 outbreak in certain countries might warrant adopting aid to "*remedy a serious disturbance in the economy of a Member State*".

More recently, in the context of COVID-19, several State aid measures have already been approved under Article 107(3)(b) TFEU.[64] Moreover, as will be detailed

---

[60] See European Commission 2019.

[61] See European Commission 2020a.

[62] See CJEU, *Freistaat Sachsen and Others v Commission*, Judgment of the Court, 30 September 2003, joined cases C-57/00P and C-61/00P, ECLI:EU:C:2003:510; GC, *Banco Privado Português, SA and others v European Commission*, Judgment of the Court, 12 December 2014, case T-487/11, ECLI:EU:T:2014:1077.

[63] See, to that effect and by analogy, CJEU, *Unicredito Italiano SpA v Agenzia delle Entrate, Ufficio Genova 1*, Judgment of the Court, 15 December 2005, case C-148/04, ECLI:EU:C:2005:774.

[64] See European Commission 2020a.

below, the temporary framework under analysis was based on the provisions of that Article.

1.3.2 Temporary Framework for State Aid Measures to Support the Economy During the Current COVID-19 Outbreak

Exceptional situations call for exceptional measures. This framework is indicative of that since it was especially designed to address the "crisis" caused by COVID-19 and approved in just a few days. On 13 March 2020, the Executive Vice-President of the Commission, Margrethe Vestager, issued a Declaration stating that a proposal for a Temporary framework for State aid measures to support the economy in the context of the COVID-19[65] outbreak was in the pipeline. On 19 March 2020, the framework had already been approved.

The proposed temporary framework was, in a nutshell, announced to be based on Article 107(3)(b) TFEU and to include four types of aid: (i) direct incentives and selective tax benefits; (ii) bank loans with state guarantees; (iii) public and private loans with subsidised rates; and (iv) guarantees for banks channelling support to the real economy.

Broadly speaking, a key notion of the temporary framework is that such aid should target the banks' customers rather than the banks themselves. The framework also provides guidance on how to minimise any undue residual aid to banks, in line with EU rules.

The European Commission Communication—*Temporary framework for State aid measures to support the economy in the context of the COVID-19 outbreak*—was published on 19 March 2020.[66]

Before we move on to discussing how the framework works, it is important to bear in mind that it is not a *European support intervention*, as was claimed by some,[67] but a legal framework that allows MS to address the difficulties businesses are currently facing, while maintaining the integrity of the EU's internal market and ensuring a level playing field. In sum, this framework seeks a balance between ensuring that competition is not distorted and that the market is not affected, and immediately addressing the adverse effects of the COVID-19 outbreak on the European and global economy, i.e., a balance between *competition policy* and *emergency policy*.

It is a *soft law* and not a *hard law* framework, which means that it does not establish directly applicable rules but is an instrument whereby the European Commission

---

[65] See Vestager 2020.

[66] C (2020) 1863 final, OJ C 91I, 20 March 2020, pp. 1–9.

[67] See CESUE 2020. Therefore, as this is not a *radical solution either*—as would be the case with the proposal to suspend the State aid regime during COVID-19 and as has even been suggested by Austria, see Competition Policy International 2020.

clarifies the conditions for authorizing State aid to support the economy in the context of the COVID-19 outbreak.

The temporary framework under analysis sets out the options available to MS under EU rules to provide liquidity and access to finance to companies, in particular SMEs, facing a sudden shortage in this period to allow them to recover from the present situation.

The framework builds on Article 107(3)(b) TFEU, which states that, "*The following may be considered compatible with the internal market: (b) aid to promote the execution of an important project of common European interest or to remedy a serious disturbance in the economy of a Member State*".

The eventual compatibility is justified by the need to remedy a serious disturbance in the economy of a MS.

In order to benefit from the Temporary and exceptional State aid framework created in the context of the COVID-19 outbreak, the MS should demonstrate that the State aid measures notified to the European Commission under the Communication being assessed *are necessary, appropriate, and proportionate to remedy a serious disturbance in the economy of the MS concerned* and that all the conditions of this Communication are fully satisfied.

MS have five types of measures available to establish schemes to grant aid: (i) aid in the form of direct grants, repayable advances or tax advantages, (ii) aid in the form of loan guarantees, (iii) aid in the form of subsidised interest rates on loans, (iv) aid in the form of guarantees and loans channelled via credit or other financial institutions, (v) short-term export-credit insurance, provided that the conditions specifically provided for by the European Commission are satisfied.

This framework is temporary and should be in force between 19 March and 31 December 2020, according to its original version.

At the time of writing, the temporary and exceptional State aid framework created to address the COVID-19 outbreak has already been amended six times.

The first amendment[68] authorised aid to accelerate research, testing and production of relevant products to combat COVID-19, to protect employment and to continue to support the economy during the current crisis. It was justified by the need to identify further temporary State aid measures that the Commission considered consistent with Article 107(3) TFEU in the context of the COVID-19 outbreak, and because it had been shown that further clarifications and amendments to certain provisions were needed. Five types of aid measures allowed under the temporary framework were added: (i) aid for research and development activities in the context of COVID-19; (ii) investment aid for testing and optimisation infrastructure (*upscaling*); (iii) investment aid for the production of products relevant to tackle COVID-19; (iv) aid in the form of tax and/or social security contribution deferrals; (v) aid in the form

[68] Communication from the Commission Amendment to the Temporary Framework for State aid measures to support the economy in the current COVID-19 outbreak, 2020/C 112 I/01, C/2020/2215, OJ C 112I, 4 April 2020, pp. 1–9.

of wage subsidies for workers in order to avoid furloughs during the COVID-19 outbreak.

The second amendment[69] sought to further streamline crisis-hit companies' access to capital and liquidity. It was justified by the need to identify other temporary State aid measures that the Commission considered consistent with Article 107(3)(b) TFEU in the context of the COVID-19 outbreak and to make drafting amendments, as well as to clarify and amend certain provisions further.

The third amendment[70] sought to extend the support to micro, small and start-up businesses and encourage private investment. Its purpose was to clarify and modify the conditions of the temporary State aid measures which the European Commission considered consistent with Article 107(3)(b) and (c) TFEU in the context of the COVID-19 outbreak.

The purpose of the fourth amendment[71] was to extend the measures provided for in the Temporary Framework until 30 June 2021 and its Section 3.11 until 30 September 2021; to identify other temporary State aid measures (aid in the form of support for unpaid fixed costs); and to clarify and amend the conditions of certain temporary State aid measures which the Commission considered consistent with Article 107(3)(b) TFEU in the context of the COVID-19 outbreak. The communication also aimed to amend the list of countries classified as marketable risk countries set out in the Annex to the communication from the Commission to the MS on the application of Articles 107 and 108 TFEU to short-term export-credit insurance.

The purpose of the fifth amendment[72] was to extend the measures provided for in the Temporary Framework until 31 December 2021; to adapt the aid ceilings of certain measures in order to address the prolonged economic effects of the current crisis; and to clarify and modify the conditions of certain temporary State aid measures which the European Commission considered consistent with Article 107(3)(b) TFEU in the context of the COVID-19 outbreak. The communication also aimed to amend the list of countries classified as marketable risk countries in the Annex to the Communication from the Commission to the Member States on the application of Articles 107 and 108 TFEU to short-term export-credit insurance.

---

[69] Communication from the Commission Amendment to the Temporary Framework for State aid measures to support the economy in the current COVID-19 outbreak 2020/C 164/03, C/2020/3156, OJ C 164, 13 May 2020, pp. 3–15.

[70] Communication from the Commission Third amendment to the Temporary Framework for State aid measures to support the economy in the current COVID-19 outbreak 2020/C 218/03, C/2020/4509, OJ C 218, 2 June 2020, pp. 3–8.

[71] Communication from the Commission 4th Amendment to the Temporary Framework for State aid measures to support the economy in the current COVID-19 outbreak and amendment to the Annex to the Communication from the Commission to the Member States on the application of Articles 107 and 108 of the Treaty on the Functioning of the European Union to short-term export-credit insurance 2020/C 340 I/01, C/2020/7127, OJ C 340I, 13 October 2020, pp. 1–10.

[72] Communication from the Commission Fifth Amendment to the Temporary Framework for State aid measures to support the economy in the current COVID-19 outbreak and amendment to the Annex to the Communication from the Commission to the Member States on the application of Articles 107 and 108 of the Treaty on the Functioning of the European Union to short-term export-credit insurance 2021/C 34/06, C/2021/564, OJ C 34, 1 February 2021, pp. 6–15.

Lastly, at the time of writing, a sixth amendment to the Temporary Framework for State Aid has been adopted.[73] It seeks in a nutshell to prolong the measures provided for therein until 30 June 2022, as the Commission considers this extension appropriate to ensure that national support measures effectively help the affected companies during the pandemic while maintaining the integrity of the internal market and ensuring a level playing field, and to introduce two new measures to create direct incentives for future-oriented private investment and solvency support measures for a further limited period.

Some of these measures were adopted between 24 and 48 hours after notification ("*astonishing speed*"),[74] establishing a flexible temporary framework.

The flexibility—"*full flexibility*"[75]—of the temporary framework is not without its disadvantages, in that it enables the violation of competition and internal market rules—making the "*fair distribution of State aid between the Member States*"[76] more difficult.

Legal authors were therefore quick to stress that, in practice, "*this framework tends to benefit, for the most part, the Member States with the means and budget to spend the most resources*" and "*massive capital injections from some Member States may lead to massive distortions of competition*".[77]

Since the COVID-19 outbreak started, several MS have already notified and secured the Commission's approval of State aid measures in various Commission decisions.[78] As mentioned, the temporary framework is based on Article 107(3)(b) TFEU and is an add-on to the options available to MS to mitigate the social and economic impact of the coronavirus outbreak in line with EU State aid rules, which include the option afforded by Article 107(2)(b) TFEU to compensate specific companies or specific sectors for the damages directly caused by exceptional events, such as the coronavirus outbreak.

In sum, and despite the high relevance of the temporary and exceptional State aid framework (*soft law*) created in the context of the COVID-19 outbreak since the beginning of the coronavirus outbreak, State aid measures have also been adopted directly under Article 107(2)(b), Article 107(3)(b) and Article 107(3)(c) TFEU.

---

[73] Communication from the Commission Sixth Amendment to the Temporary Framework for State aid measures to support the economy in the current COVID-19 outbreak and amendment to the Annex to the Communication from the Commission to the Member States on the application of Articles 107 and 108 of the Treaty on the Functioning of the European Union to short-term export-credit insurance 2021/C 473/01, C/2021/8442, OJ C 473, 24 November 2021, pp. 1–15.

[74] Hornkohl and Van't Klooster 2020.

[75] Buendia Sierra and Dovalo 2020, pp. 3 et seq.

[76] Hornkohl and Van't Klooster 2020.

[77] Buendia Sierra and Dovalo 2020, p. 7.

[78] See European Commission 2020a.

1.3.3 De Minimis *in Exceptional Circumstances*

In terms of background, bear in mind that the recently approved temporary State aid framework has so far not followed the 2008 option of increasing the quantitative ceiling of the general *de minimis* regime to €500,000 or to another quantitative ceiling that would presumably not affect the internal market.

The *de minimis* option followed by the European Commission during the 2008 crisis[79] was to consider that the abovementioned financial crisis affected not only structurally weak companies, but also companies that found themselves facing a sudden shortage or even unavailability of credit. The European Commission therefore found it necessary to temporarily authorize the granting of a limited amount of aid, even though it falls under Article 107(1) TFEU in that it exceeds the ceiling laid down in the *de minimis* regulation. To this end, the European Commission considered that this type of aid would be compatible with the internal market under Article 107(3)(b) TFEU.

The European Commission clarified that several conditions should be cumulatively satisfied. Given the brevity of this text, the following should be highlighted for illustrative purposes only: the aid must not exceed a cash grant of €500,000 per company and should be granted by way of an aid scheme.

As far as the *de minimis* regimes are concerned, the solution adopted by the Temporary and exceptional State aid framework created in the context of the COVID-19 outbreak was to maintain its ceilings. Other than stated below, it did not offer any interpretation of the frameworks—which somehow may mean that the European Commission intends to keep control (even if very flexible) over any measures with impact on the competition and internal market framework that the MS intend to approve.

In other words, the European Commission chose to indicate the conditions for certain support measures that the MS could design to address the effects of COVID-19 in a relatively detailed manner. To this end, it designed typologies of measures (the MS can also combine these measures) that the MS could choose from (according to their reality and needs) and subsequently submit to the European Commission for approval—"*plug-in measures*". In abstract terms, this option would allow fair competition; however, there are many doubts that a 24-h analysis allows the European Commission carefully to consider the measures and, consequently, that it allows for the effective control that the rules on State aid impose.[80]

On the other hand, this option caters to the European Commission's responsibility to take control of State aid—its exclusive competence—instead of leaving this control to the MS, as would happen with the maximisation of the *de minimis* regimes.

Lastly, the only clarification set out in the temporary and exceptional State aid framework created in the context of the COVID-19 outbreak regarding *de minimis* regimes is that the temporary aid measures covered herein *may be* cumulated with aid under

[79] See Quigley 2015, pp. 463 et seq.

[80] On the impact of these measures, see Van Hove 2020.

the *de minimis* regulations, provided that the provisions and rules on cumulation laid down in those regulations are abided by.

1.4 Procedural and Implementation Regulation

As already mentioned, one of the most relevant aspects of the State aid framework is the *obligation to notify the European Commission* for its Union law consistency analysis/assessment. According to the Court of Justice, the notification obligation is one of the fundamental elements of such monitoring, and the MS are therefore obliged both to notify the European Commission of each measure intended to introduce or change aid and not to put that measure into effect until the European Commission has taken a final decision on it.[81]

This obligation, which arises from Article 108 TFEU, is currently[82] developed in Council Regulation (EU) No 2015/1589 of 13 July 2015 laying down detailed rules for the implementation of Article 108 of the Treaty on the Functioning of the European Union.[83]

For the sake of a complete background, it should be noted that this act sets out the rules for a *permanent examination of State aid* granted in four types of procedures: (i) notified aid procedure; (ii) illegal aid procedure; (iii) misused aid procedure; (iv) procedure concerning existing aid schemes.

Considering that Article 33 of the current Regulation empowers, as did the previous Regulation, the European Commission to adopt detailed rules on aid notification, Regulation (EC) No 794/2004 of the European Commission of 21 April 2004 on the application of Council Regulation (EC) No 659/1999 was adopted laying down rules for the implementation of Article 93 of the EC Treaty: provisions on the form, content and other aspects of notifications, the annual reports set out in the Regulation, the computation of time limits in State aid processes and the interest rate on recovery of unlawful aid.[84]

---

[81] See, among others, CJEU, *Eesti Pagar AS v Ettevõtluse Arendamise Sihtasutus and Majandus- ja Kommunikatsiooniministeerium*, Judgment of the Court, 5 March 2019, case C-349/17, ECLI:EU:C:2019:172.

[82] Which replaced and revoked the Council Regulation (EC) No 659/1999 of 22 March 1999 laying down detailed rules for the application of Article 93 of the EC Treaty, OJ L 083, 27 March 1999, pp. 1–9.

[83] OJ L 248, 24 September 2015, pp. 9–29. This regulation was subject to rectification.

[84] OJ L 140, 30 April 2004, pp. 1–134. This act was subject to several changes.

1.5 Aid for Financing Undertakings Providing SGEI

To have the bigger picture of the *de minimis* aids rules it is important to offer an overview of the planned regulation for aid for the *financing of undertakings providing SGEI.*[85]

First of all, it should be noted that SGEI must be understood as an *autonomous concept*[86] resulting from European Union law which, on the one hand, "*is an evolving notion that depends, among other things, on the needs of citizens, technological and market developments and social and political preferences in the Member State concerned*" and the Court of Justice, on the other hand, "*has established that SGEI are services that exhibit special characteristics as compared with those of other economic activities*".[87]

In short, it is a concept that swings between the objective of *market efficiency*, on the one hand, and the *equity* objectives identified at the national level, on the other hand.

Very briefly put, it is a concept consisting of four elements: (i) an objective or material *public service*, i.e., regardless of who provides it; (ii) of *collective interest* or *public interest*; (iii) of *economic interest*, that is, of industrial and commercial character; and (iv) an *essential* and *universal service* (a service directed to the public in general).

With regard to the financing of undertakings providing SGEI, it should be borne in mind that a set of conditions are laid down which, once met, establish a *presumption of consistency* of "public service compensation"[88] with European Union law on State aid [which is therefore not classified as State aid under Article 107(1) TFEU]. To apply the regulation in question, a primary requirement must therefore be fulfilled, namely there must be a SGEI at stake.[89]

Thus, for certain SGEI to operate on the basis of principles and conditions enabling them to fulfil their mission—as required under Article 14 TFEU[90]—financial support for SGEI providers may be necessary,[91] notably when revenues from the provision of the service do not cover the specific costs resulting from public service obligations.

It is in this context that *Article 106(2) TFEU* stipulates that undertakings entrusted with the operation of services of general economic interest or having the character

---

[85] For other developments, see Wolf 2016, pp. 295 et seq.

[86] Autonomous, first and foremost, from the concepts provided for by national legislation. Naturally, by imposing the principle of the primacy of Union law, national regimes must respect Union law regimes.

[87] Communication from the Commission on the application of the European Union State aid rules to compensation granted for the provision of services of general economic interest. OJ C 8, 11 January 2012, pp. 4–14.

[88] See Met-Domestici 2006, p. 1881.

[89] Bacon 2017, pp. 114 et seq.

[90] In this context, it is still relevant the Protocol to the TFEU (No 26) on services of general interest and Article 36 of the Charter of Fundamental Rights of the European Union.

[91] Under the terms of Article 345 TFEU, as interpreted by the Court of Justice, it is immaterial whether these services of general economic interest are provided by public or private undertakings.

of a revenue-producing monopoly are subject to the rules contained in the Treaty, in particular to the rules on competition, in so far as the application of such rules does not prevent the legal or *de facto* performance of the particular tasks assigned to them.

This should not, however, affect the development of trade in a way that is contrary to the interests of the Union. In short, the article seeks to strike a balance between competition rules and the effective performance of public service-related tasks.

In addition to those Articles—and secondary EU law—it should be borne in mind that a proper understanding of the framework of financing aid for undertakings providing SGEI also requires an examination of Court of Justice case-law.

Altmark[92,93] is the *preeminent case* in this matter, laying down *four cumulative criteria* which, once fulfilled, remove the economic advantage element in the State aid concept. In other words, it is understood that State intervention should be considered as a remuneration of the services provided by the recipient undertakings to fulfil public service obligations.

The following criteria must be considered:

(i) "*the recipient undertaking must actually have public service obligations to discharge, and the obligations must be clearly defined*";
(ii) "*the parameters on the basis of which the compensation will be calculated must be established in advance in an objective and transparent manner*";
(iii) "*the compensation cannot exceed what is necessary to cover all or part of the costs incurred in the discharge of public service obligations, taking into*

---

[92] See case C-280/00.

[93] Earliest case-law can be seen in CJEU: *Procureur de la République v ADBHU*, Judgment of the Court, 7 February 1985, case C-240/83, ECLI:EU:C:1985:59; *Ferring SA v Agence centrale des organismes de sécurité sociale (ACOSS)*, Judgment of the Court, 22 November 2001, case C-53/00, ECLI:EU:C:2001:627. Notably, these two earlier judgments adopt the "compensatory theory" [aid does not constitute State aid under Article 107(1) TFEU]. Focusing on the *Ferring* judgment, as a judgment that took a decisive role in the debate between consideration of the "compensatory theory" or the "State aid theory". The case concerns the wholesale distribution of medicines by wholesaler-distributors and laboratories. A French law required wholesalers to hold a minimum permanent stock of medicines to enable them to supply pharmacies in the territory allocated to them within a short period. Laboratories could also distribute those products to pharmacies but were exempt from that obligation. That is why, in 1997, a levy was imposed on laboratories in order, first, to make up for the competitive disadvantage suffered by wholesaler-distributors and, second, to finance the Caisse Nationale d'Assurance Maladie, which would be the recipient of the revenue. According to the Court of Justice: "*It must therefore be replied that Article 92 of the Treaty must be interpreted as meaning that a measure such as that provided for by Article 12 of Law No 97-1164, which is levied solely on direct sales of medicines by pharmaceutical laboratories, does not constitute State aid to wholesale distributors unless the advantage obtained by them through not being liable to that tax exceeds the additional costs which they bear in discharging the public service obligations imposed on them by the national rules*". In summary, the Court of Justice considered that the fact that certain obligations were imposed on wholesale distributors was decisive in order to escape the principle of incompatibility laid down in Article 107(1) TFEU. Therefore, according to the *Ferring* judgment, the compensation necessary to ensure the operation of a service of general economic interest does not constitute State aid. Further the compensation approach was embraced and elaborated in the Altmark case.

account the relevant receipts and a reasonable profit for discharging those obligations";

(iv) "*where the undertaking which is to discharge public service obligations, in a specific case, is not chosen pursuant to a public procurement procedure which would allow for the selection of the tenderer capable of providing those services at the least cost to the community, the level of compensation needed must be determined on the basis of an analysis of the costs which a typical undertaking, well run and adequately provided with means of transport so as to be able to meet the necessary public service requirements, would have incurred in discharging those obligations, taking into account the relevant receipts and a reasonable profit for discharging the obligations.*"[94]

If any of the requirements of the *Altmark* judgement[95] are not met, compensation must be deemed to be State aid. However, in addition to Altmark, the *internal market compatibility test* under 106(2) should still be taken into account [there may still be compatibility with the internal market provided that the above requirements of Article 106(2) of TFEU are met].[96]

That is to say, if the requirements of the *Altmark* judgement are not met and the amount (in excess of the quantitative ceiling established under the *de minimis* regime) is included in the State aid framework, it must also be assessed whether the requirements of Article 106(2) TFEU are met to determine whether such aid can be considered compatible with the internal market.[97]

For this purpose, the following requirements need to be considered: (i) *existence of a SGEI;* (ii) *existence of a public service "mandate";* (iii) *need for the compensation measure;* (iv) *proportionality of the measure;* (v) *the measure should not be considered incompatible with the internal market in a manner that is contrary to the interests of the Union.*[98]

In summary, checking whether the conditions or the so-called "*Altmark test*" are met serves to determine the existence of State aid within the meaning of Article 107(1) TFEU, while Article 106(2) TFEU is applied to determine whether a certain aid measure constituting State aid is compatible with the internal market.[99]

The reform undertaken by the European Commission in 2011 through the publication of several documents ("*SGEI Package /Altmark*") is also worth considering.

---

94 See, for instance, Quigley 2015, pp. 235 et seq.

95 One of the consequences of *Altmark* case-law was exactly to reduce the scope of the regime provided for in Article 106(2) TFEU.

96 See, among others, Quigley 2015, p. 248.

97 See, among others, GC: *TF1 v Commission*, Judgment of the Court, 16 October 2013, case T-275/11, ECLI:EU:T:2013:535, and *Viasat Broadcasting UK v Commission*, Judgment of the Court, 24 September 2015, case T-125/12, ECLI:EU:T:2015:687.

98 Bacon 2017, pp. 114 et seq.

99 Caoimh and Sauter 2016, p. 94.

Regulation (EU) No 360/2012 is of particular import for the matter at hand.[100] In addition to this specific framework, the following should be considered:

(i) *Communication from the Commission on the application of the European Union State aid rules to compensation granted for the provision of services of general economic interest (2012/C 8/02),*[101] which aims to clarify the key concepts underlying the application of State aid rules to public service compensation. To summarize, on the one hand, the Communication goes back to the Altmark case-law, which stipulates in which conditions public service compensation does not constitute State aid, namely the absence of an economic advantage and, on the other hand, already announces the adoption of a future specific *de minimis* regulation on SGEI;

(ii) *2012/21/EU: Commission Decision of 20 December 2011 on the application of Article 106(2) of the Treaty on the Functioning of the European Union to State aid in the form of public service compensation granted to certain undertakings entrusted with the operation of services of general economic interest (2012/21/EU),*[102] laying down the conditions under which State aid in the form of public service compensation granted to certain undertakings responsible for the management of services of general economic interest is compatible with the internal market and exempt from the notification obligation, and identifying the exempt categories;

(iii) *Communication from the Commission - European Union framework for State aid in the form of public service compensation (2011) (2012/C 8/03),*[103] which specifies how the European Commission will examine cases that are not immediately covered by the Decision and should therefore be notified to it.

1.6 Aid in the Agriculture Sector and in the Fishery and Aquaculture Sector

1.6.1 In General

To offer an overview of *de minimis* aid rules, it is important to make a brief reference to aid in the agriculture, fishery, and aquaculture sectors. A broad reference to these rules is made for a better understanding of the position of *de minimis* rules and their relationship with other aid regulations within specific sectors such as the agriculture and fishery sectors.

[100] Commission Regulation (EU) No 360/2012 of 25 April 2012 on the application of Articles 107 and 108 of the Treaty on the Functioning of the European Union to *de minimis* aid granted to undertakings providing services of general economic interest, OJ L 114, 26 April 2012, pp. 8–13.

[101] OJ C 8, 11 January 2012, pp. 4–14.

[102] OJ L 7, 11 January 2012, pp. 3–10.

[103] OJ C 8, 11 January 2012, pp. 15–22.

Agriculture and fishery have always had special treatment, which is now enshrined in Articles 38 through 44 TFEU. Article 42 stipulates that the provisions of the Chapter on competition rules apply to the production and trade of agricultural products only to the extent determined by the European Parliament and by the Council, in the context of Article 43(2), in accordance with the procedure laid down therein, and having regard to the objectives set out in Article 39.

Agricultural products are, on the one hand, as defined in Article 38(1) TFEU, namely products of the soil, of stock farming and of fisheries, and products of first-stage processing directly related to these products, and, on the other, the products listed in Annex I to the TFEU.

It should be borne in mind that the definition provided for in Article 38 TFEU goes beyond the products included in that List and that the Court of Justice has already decided in this respect that in certain circumstances the provisions of the List prevail in the event of conflict.[104]

Although this definition and the List include fishery products, it should be borne in mind that the rules on aid applicable to agriculture are substantially different to those applicable to fisheries, and therefore aid in the agriculture sector, on the one hand, and in the fishery and aquaculture sector, on the other, will be addressed separately.

1.6.2 Aid in the Agriculture Sector

In view of the *objectives of the common agricultural policy* provided for in Article 39(1) TFEU, it should be noted that the fulfilment of those objectives does not mean that the aid involved cannot be characterized as State aid, as the General Court has pointed out.[105]

These objectives can be found through the *two pillars* on which the common agricultural policy is built. In terms of State aid and under Article 42 TFEU, Regulation (EU) No 1308/2013 of the European Parliament and of the Council of 17 December 2013[106]—on the first pillar—and Regulation (EU) No 1305/2013 of the European Parliament and of the Council of 17 December 2013[107]—on the second pillar—develop rules for the application or exclusion of the general State aid regime.

[104] See CJEU, *CILFIT*, Judgment of the Court, 29 February 1984, case C-77/83, ECLI:EU:C:1984:91.

[105] See GC, *Italy v Commission*, Judgment of the Court, 13 September 2012, case T-379/09, ECLI:EU:T:2012:422.

[106] Regulation (EU) No 1308/2013 of the European Parliament and of the Council of 17 December 2013 establishing a common organisation of the markets in agricultural products and repealing Council Regulations (EEC) No 922/72, (EEC) No 234/79, (EC) No 1037/2001 and (EC) No 1234/2007, OJ L 347, 20 December 2013, pp. 671–854.

[107] Regulation (EU) No 1305/2013 of the European Parliament and of the Council of 17 December 2013 on support for rural development by the European Agricultural Fund for Rural Development (EAFRD) and repealing Council Regulation (EC) No 1698/2005, OJ L 347, 20 December 2013, pp. 487–548.

Lastly, and very broadly speaking, the specific rules on aid in the agriculture sector that can be found in various secondary European law should also be considered, with emphasis on: (i) the *de minimis* regime for the agriculture sector—to which Article 107(1) TFEU does not apply, its notification to the European Commission not being, in particular, required; (ii) the regime provided for in Commission Regulation (EU) No 702/2014 of 25 June 2014,[108] which also allows for exemption from notification if the substantive and procedural rules provided for therein are complied with. In view of their practical relevance, the European Union Guidelines for State Aid in Agriculture and Forestry and Rural Areas 2014–2020,[109] which establish a set of support measures to be notified to the European Commission, are also to be taken into account.

1.6.3 Aid in the Fishery and Aquaculture Sector

Although some fishery and aquaculture products are listed in Annex I to the TFEU, for the purposes of aid, the general definitions are as set out in Article 5 of Regulation (EU) No 1379/2013 of European Parliament and of the Council of 11 December 2013.[110,111]

Under subparagraphs (a) and (b) of that Article 5, "*Fishery products*" mean aquatic organisms resulting from any fishing activity or products derived therefrom, as listed in Annex I, and "*Aquaculture products*" mean aquatic organisms at any stage of their life cycle resulting from any aquaculture activity or products derived therefrom, as listed in Annex I.

As stated above, Article 42 TFEU stipulates that the provisions of the Chapter on competition rules apply only to the production and trade of agricultural products, to the extent determined by the European Parliament and the Council. In this sense, Article 8 of Regulation (EU) No 508/2014 establishing the European Maritime Affairs and Fisheries Fund[112] regulates that Articles 107 through 109 TFEU apply

[108] Commission Regulation (EU) No 702/2014 of 25 June 2014 declaring certain categories of aid in the agricultural and forestry sectors and in rural areas compatible with the internal market in application of Articles 107 and 108 of the Treaty on the Functioning of the European Union, OJ L 193, 1 July 2014, pp. 1–75.

[109] OJ C 204, 1 December 2014, pp. 1–97. These Guidelines were modified by the Commission Notice amending the European Union Guidelines for State aid in the agricultural and forestry sectors and in rural areas 2014–2020, OJ C 390, 24 November 2015, pp. 4–9.

[110] Regulation (EU) No 1379/2013 of the European Parliament and of the Council of 11 December 2013 on the common organisation of the markets in fishery and aquaculture products, amending Council Regulations (EC) No 1184/2006 and (EC) No 1224/2009 and repealing Council Regulation (EC) No 104/2000, OJ L 354, 28 December 2013, pp. 1–21.

[111] See Bacon 2017, p. 431.

[112] Regulation (EU) No 508/2014 of the European Parliament and of the Council of 15 May 2014 on the European Maritime and Fisheries Fund and repealing Council Regulations (EC) No 2328/2003, (EC) No 861/2006, (EC) No 1198/2006 and (EC) No 791/2007 and Regulation (EU) No 1255/2011 of the European Parliament and of the Council, OJ L 149, 20 May 2014, pp. 1–66.

as a rule to support granted by MS in the fishery and aquaculture sector, but *shall not apply* to payments made by MS pursuant to and in accordance with that Regulation which fall within the scope of Article 42 TFEU.

Lastly, under secondary European law the specific aid regimes for fishery and aquaculture are: (i) the *de minimis* regulation for the fishery and aquaculture sector; (ii) Commission Regulation (EU) No 1388/2014 of 16 December 2014.[113] Account should also be taken of the Communication from the Commission—Guidelines for the examination of State aid to fisheries and aquaculture given its practical relevance.[114]

1.7 Aid Exempt from Notification

As already mentioned, one of the main features of *de minimis* aid is that *it is not required to be notified to the European Commission for its analysis.*

In addition to the *de minimis* regulations, Union law allows for other aid regimes not subject to notification, i.e., aid can be exempted from notification if any of its characteristics show that it is compatible with the internal market. The law no longer refers to its *amount* (small) in this case, as is the case with the *de minimis* regulations, but above all to the category of aid in question.

In summary, and for the sake of a better understanding of the specific (sectoral) exemption regimes referred to below, the general block exemption regulation in force should be identified.[115]

Before going any further, it should be borne in mind that the framework immediately referred to is predicated on the existence of the so-called *enabling regulation.*

Given that Article 109 TFEU empowers the Council to adopt all appropriate regulations for the implementation of Articles 107 and 108 and in particular to lay down the conditions for the application of Article 108(3) and the categories of aid which are exempt from this procedure, the Council adopted Council Regulation (EC) No 994/98 of 7 May 1998 on the application of Articles 107 and 108 of the Treaty on the Functioning of the European Union to certain categories of horizontal State aid. Meanwhile this regulation was *repealed* by Council Regulation (EU) No 2015/1588 of 13 July 2015[116] empowering the European Commission to declare, by means of regulations, areas in which it has sufficient experience to define general compatibility

[113] Commission Regulation (EU) No 1388/2014 of 16 December 2014 declaring certain categories of aid to undertakings active in the production, processing and marketing of fishery and aquaculture products compatible with the internal market in application of Articles 107 and 108 of the Treaty on the Functioning of the European Union, OJ L 369, 24 December 2014, pp. 37–63.

[114] OJ C 217, 2 July 2015, pp. 1–15.

[115] From a practical point of view, this regime is of enormous relevance, since, according to the European Commission, 90% of State aid measures (with a combined annual expenditure of more than EUR 33 billion) are implemented by the MS under the General Block Exemption Regulation.

[116] Council Regulation (EU) 2015/1588 of 13 July 2015 on the application of Articles 107 and 108 of the Treaty on the Functioning of the European Union to certain categories of horizontal State

criteria, that certain specific categories of aid are compatible with the internal market in accordance with one or more of the provisions of Article 107(2) and (3) TFEU, and exempt from Article 108(3) TFEU.

Under the enabling regulation, the European Commission then adopted block exemption regulations and *de minimis* regimes.

The current *General Block Exemption Regulation* was approved by Commission Regulation (EU) No 651/2014 of 16 June 2014 declaring certain categories of aid compatible with the internal market in application of the Articles 107 and 108 of the Treaty,[117] entered into force on 1 July 2014[118] and expires on 31 December 2020. Later the Commission Regulation (EU) 2020/972 of 2 July 2020 amending Regulation (EU) No 1407/2013 as regards its extension and amending Regulation (EU) No 651/2014 as regards its extension and relevant adjustments.[119] The purpose is to provide predictability and legal certainty, while preparing for a possible future update of the State aid rules adopted as part of the State Aid Modernisation initiative. The European Commission should act in two phases. Article 59, second paragraph, of the Commission Regulation (EU) No 651/2014 was consequently amended and replaced with the following: '*It shall apply until 31 December 2023.*'

Compared to the immediately preceding framework,[120] the existing framework goes far beyond regional and horizontal aid, covering various types of sectoral aid and exempting other categories of horizontal aid.[121]

This framework applies directly in MS whose aid referred to therein may benefit from the notification exemption provided for in Article 108(3) TFEU provided that such aid satisfies all the conditions laid down in Chapter I, as well as the specific conditions for the relevant category of aid laid down in Chapter III of the GBER.

As already mentioned, the obligation to notify aid is excluded in the block exemption regulations and *de minimis*, provided that all the requirements imposed by those regulations are met. The question that must be asked is whether, in the event of failure

aid, OJ L 248, 24 September 2015, pp. 1–8, amended by Council Regulation (EU) 2018/1911 of 26 November 2018 amending Regulation (EU) 2015/1588 on the application of Articles 107 and 108 of the Treaty on the Functioning of the European Union to certain categories of horizontal State aid, OJ L 311, 7 December 2018, pp. 8–9.

[117] OJ L 187, 26 June 2014, pp. 1–78.

[118] It may apply to individual aid granted before its entry into force; provided that such aid complies with all the conditions set out therein, with the exception of Article 9 [see Article 58(1) of the GBER].

[119] OJ L 215, 7 July 2020, pp. 3–6.

[120] Commission Regulation (EC) No 800/2008 of 6 August 2008 declaring certain categories of aid compatible with the common market in application of Articles 87 and 88 of the Treaty (General block exemption Regulation), OJ L 214, 9 August 2008, pp. 3–47.

[121] The application of the GBER takes on a relevant complexity, whose analysis goes far beyond what is allowed and required by this study. As an example, in the area of regional aid, other acts should be called upon, as is the case with the Guidelines on regional aid for the period 2014–2020, OJ C 209, 23 July 2013, pp. 1–45 (meanwhile amended), in which the European Commission sets out the conditions under which regional aid can be considered compatible with the internal market, defining the criteria for the identification of regions which fulfil the conditions set out in Article 107(1) and (3) point a) and point c) TFEU.

to comply with any mandatory requirement of the block exemption regulations and *de minimis*, the obligation to notify is still excluded or if it applies.

The Court of Justice has already addressed the issue in connection with an exemption regulation, i.e., in connection with the GBER 2008 (Regulation No 800/2008),[122] and clarified that the relevant MS only becomes a party to the GBER if an aid measure adopted by a MS fulfils the relevant conditions laid down in Regulation No 800/2008. It further explained that the relevant MS can only avail itself of the notification obligation exemption provided for in Article 3 of that regulation if an aid measure adopted by a MS meets the relevant conditions of Regulation No 800/2008. Conversely, State aid which is not covered by that regulation remains subject to the notification obligation provided for in Article 108(3) TFEU.

The Court of Justice recalled that Article 108(3) TFEU establishes a preventive review of new aid projects. The objective of the preventive review is ensuring that only compatible aid is implemented. To achieve that objective, the implementation of an aid project is deferred until the Commission's final decision[123] clears any doubts as to its compatibility. Consequently, if aid has been granted pursuant to Regulation No 800/2008 when the conditions laid down for exemption under that Regulation were not met, that aid has been granted in breach of the obligation to notify and must therefore be considered unlawful. It has been stressed that, to the extent that [exemption regimes] relax the general notification obligation rule, Regulation No 800/2008 and the conditions laid down therein must be interpreted strictly.[124]

De minimis regulations, like the GBER regulation, benefit from a notification exemption and must therefore be interpreted restrictively. The *ratio decidendi* should therefore also be applied to the *de minimis* regime, i.e., as soon as the mandatory requirements imposed by the *de minimis* regulations are not met, they should be notified to the European Commission for the latter to assess their validity.

1.8 European Structural and Investment Funds

A brief reference needs to be made to *another block of rules* to properly understand the subject we are dealing with, namely the ESIF framework, which can be deemed

---

[122] See CJEU, *Dilly's Wellnesshotel GmbH v Finanzamt Linz*, Judgment of the Court, 21 July 2016, case C-493/14, ECLI:EU:C:2016:577, and case C-349/17.

[123] See *Deutsche Lufthansa AG v Flughafen Frankfurt-Hahn GmbH*, Judgment of the Court, 21 November 2013, case C-284/12, ECLI:EU:C:2013:755, paras 25–26 and case-law referred to therein.

[124] See case C-493/14. Clarifying in para 38: "*Such an approach finds support in the objectives pursued by the general block exemption regulations as referred to in recitals 4 and 5 to Regulation No 994/98. Indeed, if the Commission is authorised to adopt such regulations, in order to ensure effective control of the competition rules in respect of State aid and to simplify administrative management without weakening the Commission's control in this area, those regulations also aim to increase transparency and legal certainty. Compliance with the conditions laid down in those Regulations, including therefore Regulation No 800/2008, ensures that those objectives are fully met.*"

as upstream or downstream of the *de minimis* aid regime according to the point of view.

Regardless of how one looks at it, the truth is that granting financial incentives in the context of the ESIF[125] entails complying with the aid regime, namely State aid and *de minimis* aid, in addition to the ESIF (national and European) framework.

As regards the ESIF, it should first be noted that the European Union has implemented several policies since its creation with one common *fundamental element, namely the granting of subsidies from the European budget*. In other words, financing from European funds is essential. Without those funds, key policies such as agriculture or economic, territorial[126] and social cohesion[127]—all fundamental objectives of the Union[128]—cannot be understood and implemented.

Financing from the EU budget has proved to be *one of the most attractive aspects of European integration*,[129] especially for countries with certain not so competitive sectors and/or certain regions with serious development problems, and at the same time an essential instrument to build the single European market.[130]

At the time of writing, EU funding is guided by the "Europe 2020 Strategy"[131] which sets out three mutually reinforcing priorities: (i) smart growth: developing an economy based on knowledge and innovation; (ii) sustainable growth: promoting a more resource-efficient, greener and more competitive economy; (iii) inclusive growth: fostering an economy with high levels of employment that ensures social and territorial cohesion.

The priorities of the "Europe 2020 Strategy" have been translated into thematic objectives in the Common Strategic Framework (CSF),[132] which aims to promote the Union's smooth, balanced, and sustainable development. It is basically a strategic document providing direction on the programming process towards smart, sustainable and inclusive growth, and on the Fund-specific missions in accordance with their objectives based on the TFEU, including economic, social and territorial cohesion. Each ESI Fund should support thematic objectives.[133]

---

[125] These financial incentives can be direct or indirect. On the need for consistency between indirect incentives, financial instruments in particular, with the *de minimis* regime, see Nicolaides 2013b.

[126] See Article 3(3) TEU.

[127] See Cappello 2014, pp. 22 et seq.

[128] See Pantazatou 2016, p. 187.

[129] About European integration see, among many others, Bernard 2002, pp. 99–145.

[130] See Mento 2007, p. 136.

[131] See European Commission 2020b.

[132] See Annex I to Regulation (EU) No 1303/2013 of the European Parliament and of the European Council of 17 December 2013 laying down common provisions for the European Regional Development Fund (ERDF), the European Social Fund (ESF) and the Cohesion Fund, the European Agricultural Fund for Rural Development (EAFRD) and the European Maritime and Fisheries Fund (EMFF), which are necessary to ensure the effectiveness of the ESI Funds and the coordination of the Funds with one another and with other Union instruments, OJ L 347, 20 December 2013, pp. 320–469 ("Regulation (EU) No 1303/2013").

[133] These objectives are: "*1) Strengthening research, technological development and innovation; 2) Improving access to ICTs; 3) Enhancing the competitiveness of SMEs, of the agricultural sector*

The current ESIF, like their predecessors,[134] are an expression of the various EU policies, each policy having its own funds as a rule. The ERDF, the ESF and the CF are used for cohesion policy; EAFRD is used for rural development policy and the EMFF for maritime and fisheries policies.

Lastly, it should be noted that the ESIF consist of two structural funds: ERDF, ESF and three investment funds: CF, EAFRD and EMFF.

It is also important to make a brief reference to the primary European Union law dedicated to the legal framework of the ESIF to better understand it. The ESIF arise because one EU objective is to build the single market, which entails minimizing or altogether removing, if possible, economic and social asymmetries between the MS and their regions, and seeking the balanced development of the EU territory and the reduction of structural differences between regions. These European *instruments*[135] or *bodies*[136] are aimed at minimizing the various regions' different levels of socio-economic underdevelopment, in order to promote the growth of the more disadvantaged ones and strengthen the EU's economic and social cohesion,[137] and the seamless growth of the economy. This aspiration naturally informs the Treaty of Lisbon.

Article 174 TFEU accordingly states that the EU must promote its overall harmonious development in order to strengthen economic, social and territorial cohesion, and Article 175 TFEU establishes that "*the Union shall also support the achievement of these objectives by the action it takes through the Structural Funds (European Agricultural Guidance and Guarantee Fund, Guidance Section; European Social Fund ; European Regional Development Fund), the European Investment Bank and the other existing financial instruments*".

It should also be borne in mind that, under the first paragraph of Article 177 TFEU, "*the European Parliament and the Council shall define the tasks, priority objectives and the organisation of the Structural Funds, which may involve grouping the Funds. The general rules applicable to them and the provisions necessary to*

(for the EAFRD) and of the fishery and aquaculture sector (for the EMFF); 4) Supporting the shift towards a low-carbon economy in all sectors; 5) Promoting climate change adaptation, risk prevention and management; 6) Preserving and protecting the environment and promoting resource efficiency; 7) Promoting sustainable transport and removing bottlenecks in key network infrastructures; 8) Promoting sustainable and quality employment and supporting labour mobility; 9) Promoting social inclusion, combating poverty and any discrimination; 10) Investing in education, training and vocational training for skills and lifelong learning; 11) Enhancing institutional capacity of public authorities and stakeholders and efficient public administration". See Article 9 of Regulation (EU) No 1303/2013.

[134] For an historical approach to the configuration of the structural funds, see, among others, Gallizioli 1992, pp. 1 et seq., Ordoñez Solís 1997, pp. 17 et seq., and Evans 1999, pp. 2 et seq.

[135] Evans 1999, p. 2, and Mento 2007, p. 136.

[136] Campos 2014, pp. 134 et seq.

[137] The TFEU does not define cohesion. On the multiple perspectives of the concept of cohesion (political, social, and economic), see Evans 1999, pp. 21–24. The most common perspective is *the economic perspective*, which can be defined as enabling all regions to compete on the internal market and the monetary union, by providing them with the necessary infrastructure and capacities. On the doubts raised by the term "territorial cohesion", see Ferreira 2012, pp. 731–734.

ensure their effectiveness and the coordination of the Funds with one another and with the other existing financial instruments shall also be defined in accordance with that procedure".

The TFEU establishes specific rules concerning structural and investment funds, with a focus on:

(i) The *European Social Fund* (Article 162 TFEU), which aims "to *improve employment opportunities for workers in the internal market and to contribute thereby to raising the standard of living*", with the objective of "*facilitating employment and geographic and occupational mobility of workers within the Union, and facilitating adaptation to industrial changes and to changes in production systems, in particular through vocational training and retraining*".[138] According to some legal authors,[139] this fund is the best instrument in that it enables the EU to achieve the strategic objectives of its employment policy by improving the education and qualification levels of its citizens. The concern that financing from the ESIF should ensure the promotion of equality between men and women, as required under Article 8 TFEU, and of the fight against discrimination, as required under Article 10 TFEU[140,141] is also worth highlighting.

(ii) The *ERDF* (Article 176 TFEU) is "*intended to help redress the main regional imbalances in the Union through participation in the development and structural adjustment of regions whose development is lagging behind and in the conversion of declining industrial regions*". It should also be noted that this fund needs to take account of the outermost regions' specific handicaps, in accordance with Article 349 TFEU.[142]

(iii) The *CF* (second paragraph of Article 177 TFEU) is designed to provide a financial contribution "*to projects in the fields of environment and trans-European networks in the area of transport infrastructure*". Lastly, the CF must also contribute to actions designed to achieve the Union's environmental objectives, in accordance with Articles 11[143] and 191 TFEU,[144] in particular energy

[138] For further developments on the mission, intervention regime, financing, and management of this fund, see Campos 2014, pp. 134 et seq.

[139] See Bastos 2012, p. 696.

[140] More than an ESIF principle, it is a fundamental principle of European Union law. For further developments, among others, see Lopes 2012, pp. 223 et seq.

[141] According to legal authors, this provision should be read together with the provisions of the Charter of Fundamental Rights of the European Union, see Lopes 2012, p. 229. On the "innovative" legal force of this Charter, see Pedro 2014, pp. 286 et seq.

[142] On these regions, see Neves 2012, pp. 1223 et seq.

[143] The idea of sustainable development is embraced. For further developments, see Gomes and Antunes 2011, pp. 205–233, and Rocha 2012, p. 232. In the context of the ESIFs, see Gomes and Saraiva 2019, pp. 73 et seq.

[144] On environmental policy within the Union, see Pimenta and Lemos 2012, pp. 758–762, and Aragão 2012, pp. 764 et seq.

efficiency[145] and renewable energy and, in the field of transport which is not part of the trans-European networks, rail, inland waterway and maritime transport, intermodal transport systems and their interoperability, road, maritime and air traffic management, clean urban transport and public transport.

(iv) Pursuant to Articles 38 to 44 TFEU on the agriculture and fisheries policy, the *EAFRD* takes into account that rural development cannot be sufficiently achieved by the MS due to the links between rural development and the other instruments of the CAP,[146] the disparities between different rural areas and the financial constraints on MS in an expanded Union, but can be better achieved at Union level because Union finance is a multiannual guarantee and because the Union is better equipped to focus on its priorities.

The Union is further required to take heed of sustainable development and promotion and of the objective of protecting and improving the environment as set out in Article 11 TFEU, in line with the polluter-pays principle,[147] when pursuing Union priorities for rural development.

(v) The *EMFF* is supported by several articles of the TFEU, namely Articles 42, 43(2), 91(1), 100(2), 173(3), 175, 188, 192(1), 194(2), 195(2) and 349, and aims to promote the CFP. Moreover, it should be borne in mind that its financial support is predicated on MS and operators complying with CFP rules—a requirement that reflects the Union's public interest task[148] to ensure the conservation of marine biological resources under the CFP, pursuant to Article 3(1) (d) TFEU.

Since it is a challenge to carry on fishing activities in the outermost regions of the Union, notably because of their remoteness and particular climatic conditions, it should be possible for the EMFF to take into account the specific constraints of those regions, recognised in Article 349 TFEU.

The destination of European funds has been governed by European regulations or EU decisions, whereby a more or less intense European programming procedure has been established. As already mentioned, it has the participation of the European Commission and national authorities and focuses on investment in growth and increase of employment in MS and regions.[149] Several European regimes regulating the various ESIF were approved[150] pursuant to this primary law.

The normative *corpus* of the ESIF—at the time of writing—includes a general regulation, which is further fleshed out for each specific fund.[151] Regulation (EU) No 1303/2013 of the European Parliament and of the Council of 17 December 2013 lays down the common provisions applicable to the European Regional Development

[145] See Pedro 2018, pp. 36–45.

[146] On the CAP, see Campos 2014, pp. 680 et seq.

[147] Drawing attention to the importance of direct support for agricultural income, see Cunha 2012, p. 302.

[148] On this exclusive power of the Union, see Soares 2012, p. 210.

[149] See Pantazatou 2016, p. 197.

[150] See Belicka 2014, pp. 116–125.

[151] See Cappello 2014, p. 62.

Fund (ERDF), the European Social Fund (ESF) and the Cohesion Fund, the European Agricultural Fund for Rural Development (EAFRD) and the European Maritime and Fisheries Fund (EMFF) and the provisions necessary to ensure the effectiveness of the ESI Funds and that they are aligned with one another and with other Union instruments.

In addition to Regulation (EU) No 1303/2013, "Fund-specific Regulations" are to be taken into account, namely: (i) Regulation (EU) No 1301/2013;[152] (ii) Regulation (EU) No 1304/2013;[153] (iii) Regulation (EU) No 1300/2013;[154] (iv) Regulation (EU) No 1299/2013;[155] (v) Regulation (EU) No 1305/2013;[156] (vi) Regulation (EU) No 508/2014.[157]

At the time of writing, a draft European regulation to succeed Regulation (EU) No 1303/2013 is (still) *under discussion.* The draft regulation—the European Common Provisions Regulation[158]—is similar to the regulation in force in that it has several rules with impact on a future organisational and procedural regime for the management of ESIF, which should be supplemented by specific regulations for each fund.

The regulation seeks, in short, to establish common provisions for seven funds under shared management: the Cohesion Fund; the European Maritime and Fisheries Fund; the European Regional Development Fund; the European Social Fund Plus;

---

152 Regulation (EU) No 1301/2013 of the European Parliament and of the Council of 17 December 2013 on the European Regional Development Fund and laying down specific provisions concerning the Investment for growth and jobs goal and repealing Regulation (EC) No 1080/2006, OJ L 347, 20 December 2013, pp. 289–302.

153 Regulation (EU) No 1304/2013 of the European Parliament and of the Council of 17 December 2013 on the European Social Fund and repealing Council Regulation (EC) No 1081/2006, OJ L 347, 20 December 2013, pp. 470–486.

154 Regulation (EU) No 1300/2013 of the European Parliament and of the Council of 17 December 2013 on the Cohesion Fund and repealing Council Regulation (EC) No 1084/2006, OJ L 347, 20 December 2013, pp. 281–288.

155 Regulation (EU) No 1299/2013 of the European Parliament and of the Council of 17 December 2013 on specific provisions for the support from the European Regional Development Fund to the European Territorial Cooperation goal, OJ L 347, 20 December 2013, pp. 259–280.

156 Regulation (EU) No 1305/2013 of the European Parliament and of the Council of 17 December 2013 on support for rural development by the European Agricultural Fund for Rural Development (EAFRD) and repealing Council Regulation (EC) No 1698/2005, OJ L 347, 20 December 2013, pp. 487–548.

157 Regulation (EU) No 508/2014 of the European Parliament and of the Council of 15 May 2014 on the European Maritime and Fisheries Fund and repealing Council Regulations (EC) No 2328/2003, (EC) No 861/2006, (EC) No 1198/2006 and (EC) No 791/2007 and Regulation (EU) No 1255/2011 of the European Parliament and of the Council, OJ L 149, 20 May 2014, pp. 1–66.

158 European Commission 2018. This proposal was later transformed into the Regulation (EU) 2021/1060 of the European Parliament and of the Council of 24 June 2021 laying down common provisions on the European Regional Development Fund, the European Social Fund Plus, the Cohesion Fund, the Just Transition Fund and the European Maritime, Fisheries and Aquaculture Fund and financial rules for those and for the Asylum, Migration and Integration Fund, the Internal Security Fund and the Instrument for Financial Support for Border Management and Visa Policy, OJ L 231, 30 of June 2021, pp. 159–706.

the Asylum and Migration Fund; the Border and Visa Management Instrument;[159] the Internal Security Fund. Its main purpose is to substantially reduce unnecessary administrative burdens for recipients and managing authorities, while maintaining a high level of assurance of legality and regularity.

The ESIF are guided by four principles: *shared management, additionality, complementarity,* and *partnership.*

Most funds have been managed by the national authorities[160] in tandem with the programming and control powers of the European Commission,[161] i.e., through a "shared", "decentralized",[162] "mixed"[163] or "co-administration"[164] by the European Commission and the MS[165] interacting in different tasks of the administrative procedure of administration and control of the granting of ESIF-financed financial support.[166]

MS are largely tasked with implementing administrative measures to comply with EU law according to the principle of loyal cooperation between the Union and the MS [Article 4(3) TEU].[167] National administration materialises in an administrative implementation of EU law [Article 291(1) TFEU]. In addition, the European Commission may have delegated powers to adopt non-legislative acts of general application to supplement or amend certain non-essential elements of the legislative act (Article 290 TFEU).

In the context of the implementation of the European budget, the European Commission is responsible for implementing the Union's budget in cooperation with the MS, and the (public law)[168] principle of sound financial management of the funds must be ensured (Article 317 TFEU).[169] To that end, the regulations should provide for specific rules which, among other things, enable the European Commission to

---

[159] From a conditionality perspective, see Neves 2019, pp. 10 et seq.

[160] The main role of the MS in the implementation of the ESIF should be highlighted, as, moreover, recognised by the GC, *United Kingdom of Great Britain and Northern Ireland v European Commission*, Judgment of the Court, 4 September 2015, case T-245/13, ECLI:EU:T:2015:595: "*In fact, the management of the financing of the Fund falls primarily to the national administrations responsible for ensuring strict compliance with Union rules and is based on trust between the national authorities and the Union authorities. Only the Member State is in a position to know and determine precisely the data required to draw up the Fund's accounts, and the Commission does not have the necessary proximity to obtain the information it needs from economic operators*".

[161] Ordóñez Solís 2011a, pp. 124 et seq.

[162] Guillem Carra 2018, pp. 296 et seq.

[163] Roque 2011, pp. 99–101.

[164] Franchini 1993, pp. 174 et seq.

[165] Mento 2007, pp. 135–172, and Bernard 2002, pp. 99–145.

[166] These are fertile grounds for applying the so-called European Administrative Law in which national authorities, when applying European Union law, are subject to the principles of the European legal system.

[167] For a brief characterisation of this principle, see de Quadros 2012, p. 35; Klamert 2014.

[168] Porras Gómez 2015, pp. 354 et seq.

[169] The justification for this shared management is, of course, that in practice the MS implement 80% of the Union's funds. See Porras Gómez 2015, pp. 420 et seq.

satisfy itself that MS are using ESIF in a lawful and regular manner and in accordance with the principle of sound financial management within the meaning of Regulation (EU, Euratom) No 966/2012 of the European Parliament and of the Council, *repealed in the* meantime by Regulation (EU, Euratom) 2018/1046 of the European Parliament and of the Council.[170]

Although shared management may be a source of unease for the European Commission, considering that it remains politically responsible for the implementation of the EU budget, which is mostly implemented by the MS in effect (*EU meta-governance*),[171] the truth is that after the Treaty of Lisbon this is assumed at the level of the Union's primary law.[172]

According to the *principle of additionality*, Union support should not lead MS to relax their cohesion efforts, rather the Union's efforts should add to the efforts of MS[173,174]—as stated in recital 87 of Regulation (EU) No 1303/2013: "*In order to ensure a genuine economic impact, support from the Funds should not replace public or equivalent structural expenditure by Member States under the terms of this Regulation*".

The *principle of complementarity*[175] is designed to prevent any moral hazards arising from the support afforded by ESIF. European funds should preferably not be used for projects where the risks for national entities are very low. This is how recital 105 of Regulation (EU) No 1303/2013 should be read, which states: "*it is necessary to determine the elements that allow modulating the co-financing rate of the Funds for priority axes, in particular, in order to increase the multiplier effect of Union resources. It is also appropriate to establish the maximum co-financing rates by category of region in order to ensure respect of the principle of co-financing through an adequate level of national support, both public and private.*"

Lastly, the *partnership principle* requires the involvement of the different national and supranational actors at all stages of the procedure for granting and monitoring the ESIF ("*the urban authorities and other competent public authorities; the economic and social partners; and relevant bodies representing civil society, namely environmental organisations, non-governmental organisations and bodies responsible for promoting social inclusion, gender equality and non-discrimination*").[176] Partnership Agreements must be signed between the MS and the European Commission regarding the priorities for financing with European structural funds, pursuant to the above European normative block. Article 2.20 of Regulation (EU) No 1303/2013

---

170 Regulation (EU, Euratom) 2018/1046 of the European Parliament and of the Council of 18 July 2018 on the financial rules applicable to the general budget of the Union, amending Regulations (EU) No 1296/2013, (EU) No 1301/2013, (EU) No 1303/2013, (EU) No 1304/2013, (EU) No 1309/2013, (EU) No 1316/2013, (EU) No 223/2014, (EU) No 283/2014, and Decision No 541/2014/EU and repealing Regulation (EU, Euratom) No 966/2012, JO L 193, 30 July 2018, pp. 1–222.

171 Porras Gómez 2015, p. 474.

172 Pacheco 2012, p. 1123.

173 Article 95 of Regulation (EU) No 1303/2013 and Annex X to the same Regulation.

174 Bernard 2002, pp. 5 et seq.

175 Articles 60 and 120 of Regulation (EU) No 1303/2013.

176 Article 5(1) of Regulation (EU) No 1303/2013.

defines Partnership Agreements as "*a document prepared by a Member State with the involvement of partners in line with the multi-level governance approach, which sets out that Member State's strategy, priorities and arrangements for using the ESI Funds in an effective and efficient way so as to pursue the Union strategy for smart, sustainable and inclusive growth, and which is approved by the Commission following assessment and dialogue with the Member State concerned*".

The meeting of ESIF regimes with aid regulations[177] is indicative of the need to cover the *complementary nature* that results from the pursuit of the cohesion policy and the competition policy.[178,179] Regulation (EU) No 1303/2013 repeatedly highlights the need for the ESIF regime to comply with aid rules. Article 37, para 1, second subparagraph of that act is quite telling: "*When applying this Title, the managing authorities, the bodies implementing funds of funds, and the bodies implementing financial instruments shall comply with applicable law, in particular on State aid and public procurement*".

Incidentally, the Regulation refers to aid in several Articles. Article 6 requires operations supported by the ESIF to comply with EU law, including State aid law. Explicit references to aid are also found in recitals 36, 38, 58, 64, and in Articles 2,[180] 37, 38, 44, 61, 62, 65, 71, 131, 137, 140 and 146. In addition, Annex XI sets out *ex-ante* conditions for the effective application of State aid legislation.

---

[177] It should be noted that if there is a need to comply with the aid regime in the application of the ESIF regime, other issues may emerge, which may be included in a broader topic, that is, the *intersection* between *State Aid Law* and *Public Procurement Law*. In broad terms, the issue at stake is *whether a competitive awarding procedure automatically rules out the presence of State aid*. In this context, several topics deserve attention, in particular the following situations, which lead to the *question whether State aid is at stake*:

(i) When the contractual conditions allow a contractor to receive overpayments or when the contracting authority does not have a genuine need for the contracted services;
(ii) Where award criteria not strictly economic are concerned, which aim to achieve public policies concerning the environment or social dimensions;
(iii) When there is a question of a bid submitted with an abnormally low price, in situations where the economic operator in question has benefited from support that the others have not.

The most common answer is that the existence of a procurement procedure of a competitive nature and in compliance with public procurement rules creates the *(rebuttable) presumption that there is no State aid* within the meaning of Article 107(1) TFEU. For all, and among many, see Hughes 2009, p. 5; Arrowsmith 2014, pp. 302 et seq. (and the vast literature cited therein); Sánchez Graells 2015, pp. 124 et seq. (and the vast literature cited therein); Bovis 2016, pp. 161 et seq.

[178] See Pantazatou 2016, p. 187. For an overview of the relationship between the two policies, see Wishlade 2003, pp. 145 et seq.

[179] Strictly speaking, the legal regime is supposed to bring together competition policy, European cohesion policy and national regional policy.

[180] It should be noted that this Article [*maxime* 2(13)] also includes *de minimis* aid in the "State aid category, for purely operative rather than theoretical reasons".

In turn, Union Courts' case-law has already addressed structural fund support in the context of State aid frameworks.[181]

On top of the framework foreseen for the implementation of the ESIF, the European legal framework foreseen for the (non-distortion of) competition guarantee cannot be disregarded, as the financing of the ESIF is often made by way of support to entities (undertakings) operating in the European market.[182,183]

Markets do not always function optimally,[184,185] sometimes for social or political reasons.[186]

Whenever this support is granted to undertakings, the framework foreseen in the Treaties regarding State aid must necessarily be considered[187] to ensure the proper functioning of the internal market.[188] In other words, ESIF rules must be consistent with aid rules, to ensure the required compliance with two European legal frameworks: on the one hand, the ESIF frameworks and, on the other hand, the State aid frameworks (if the recipients are undertakings).

The first is a framework designed to implement certain public policies based on the European budget, and the second is a framework designed to achieve competition by ensuring that aid (therefore State aid and *de minimis* aid) does not affect nor has the potential to affect competition, irrespective of whether it involves national or European funding.[189]

References

Aragão A (2012) Art. 191(2)(3) TFEU In: Lopes Porto M, Gonçalo A (eds) Tratado de Lisboa: anotado e comentado [Treaty of Lisbon: annotated and commented]. Almedina, Coimbra, pp 763–769

---

181 See CJEU: *Nerea SpA v Regione Marche*, Judgment of the Court, 6 July 2017, case C-245/16, ECLI:EU:C:2017:521; *Italy v Commission*, Judgement of the Court, 24 November 2005, case C-138/03, ECLI:EU:C:2005:714; and CG, *ARAP v Commission*, Judgement of the Court, 17 June 1999, case T-82/96, ECLI:EU:T:1999:127.

182 In other words, there should be a control of the ESIF regime and the State Aid regime. On the discussion as to whether this is a situation of complementarity or conflict, see Pantazatou 2016, pp. 187 et seq.

183 Of great interest from a contextual point of view, see Campos 2013, pp. 213–244.

184 See de Almeida 2012, pp. 29–62.

185 See Campos 2014, pp. 943–974.

186 See Nicolaides 2013a, p. 41.

187 For further developments, among many, see Heidenhain 2010, p. 22.

188 See Pesaresi and Van Hoof 2008, p. 4.

189 See Ordónez Solís 2011b, p. 166.

Arhold C (2016) The definition of State aid. In: Säcker FJ, Montag F (eds) European State Aid Law: A Commentary. Verlag C.H. Beck, Munich, pp 82–154

Arrowsmith S (2014) The law of public and utilities procurement: regulation in the EU and UK, 3rd edn. Sweet & Maxwell, London

Bacon K (2017) European Union law of State aid, 3rd edn. Oxford University Press, Oxford

Bär-Bouyssière B (2005) Les règlements d'exemption en matière d'aides d'Etat [State aid exemption regulations]. In: Dony M, Smits C (eds) Aides d'État. Éditions de l' Université de Bruxelles, Brussels, pp 170–193

Bastos R (2012) Art. 162 TFEU. In: Lopes Porto M, Gonçalo A (eds) Tratado de Lisboa: anotado e comentado [Treaty of Lisbon: annotated and commented]. Almedina, Coimbra, pp 694–696

Belicka D (2014) Unification and Simplification of European Structural and Investment Funds Management. European Structural and Investment Funds Journal 2: 116–125

Berghofer M (2007) The New *De Minimis* Regulation: Enlarging the Sword of Damocles? European State Aid Law Quarterly 6: 11–23

Bernard N (2002) Multilevel governance in the European Union. Kluwer Law International, The Hague, 99–145

Bovis C (2016) Public procurement and State Aid. In: Hofmann HCH, Micheau C (eds) State Aid Law of the European Union. Oxford University Press, Oxford, pp 161–186

Buendia Sierra L, Dovalo A(2020) A State Aid Versus COVID-19: The Commission Adopts a Temporary Framework. European State Aid Law Quarterly 19: 3–7

Campos M F (2013) A concessão de ajudas públicas até à IIª Guerra Mundial [The granting of public aid until World War II]. Boletim de Ciências Económicas 6: 213–244

Campos M F (2014) Fundamentos económicos da concessão de ajudas públicas no mercado nacional [Economic rationale for granting public aid in the national market]. Boletim de Ciências Económicas 57: 943–974

Caoimh O A, Sauter W (2016) Criterion of Advantage. In: Hofmann HCH, Micheau C (eds) State Aid Law of the European Union. Oxford University Press, Oxford, pp 84–128

Cappello M (2014) Guida ai fondi strutturali europei 2014-2020 [Guide to European Structural Funds 2014-2020]. Maggioli Editore, Rome

Cesue (2020) A European answer to the coronavirus threat to prove that the EU is a true community with a shared future. http://www.cesue.eu/en/appeal Accessed 20 April 2020

Competition Policy International (2020) Austria Wants Rule Suspension of EU State Aid During COVID-19. www.competitionpolicyinternational.com. Accessed 20 April 2020

Conte G, Kavanagh J (2017) Advantage. In: Werner P, Verouden V (eds) EU State Aid Control: Law and Economics. Kluwer Law International, The Netherlands, pp 65–86

Cunha A (2012) Art. 38-44 TFEU. In: Lopes Porto M, Gonçalo A (eds) Tratado de Lisboa: anotado e comentado [Treaty of Lisbon: annotated and commented]. Almedina, Coimbra, pp 299–303

de Almeida J N (2012) O sentido da atribuição de auxílios de Estado numa economia de mercado: a impossibilidade lógica da existência dos auxílios de Estado numa economia de mercado funcionando de acordo com o regime da concorrência perfeita [The case for State aid in a market economy: the logical impossibility of the existence of State aid in a market economy operating under perfect competition]. In: Avelãs Nunes A J, Cunha L P, de Oliveira Martins M I (eds) Estudos em Homenagem ao Prof. Doutor Aníbal de Almeida. Coimbra Editora, Coimbra, pp 29–62

de Carvalho S (2016) Algumas reflexões acerca do efeito da recente comunicação *de minimis* no tratamento jusconcorrencial das restrições verticais na União Europeia [Reflections on the effect of the recent *de minimis* communication on competition law treatment of vertical restrictions in the European Union]. In: Piton A P, Carneiro A T (eds) Liber amicorum: Manuel Simas Santos. Rei dos Livros, Lisbon, pp 1163–1208

de Quadros F (2012) Art. 4 TUE. In: Lopes Porto M, Gonçalo A (eds) Tratado de Lisboa: anotado e comentado [Treaty of Lisbon: annotated and commented]. Almedina, Coimbra, pp 33–35

Derenne J, Verouden V (2017) Distortion of Competition and Effect on Trade. In: Werner P, Verouden V (eds) EU State Aid Control: Law and Economics. Kluwer Law International, The Netherlands, pp 169–189

Estoa Pérez A (2007) La regulación de las ayudas de MINIMIS en el derecho comunitario: comentario al reglamento (CE) No 1998/2006 [Regulation of de MINIMIS aid in EU law: commentary on regulation (EC) No 1998/2006]. Revista de derecho comunitario europeo 11: 623–636

European Commission (2001) Communication from the Commission to the European Parliament and the Council - The repercussions of the terrorist attacks in the United States on the air transport industry /* COM/2001/0574 final */. EUR-Lex - 52001DC0574 - EN - EUR-Lex (europa.eu). Accessed 20 April 2020

European Commission (2006) IP/06/1765. https://ec.europa.eu/commission/presscorner/detail/en/IP_06_1765 Accessed 20 April 2020

European Commission (2013a) Commission Staff Working Document Impact Assessment - accompanying the document - commission regulation (EU) no .../... - on the application of articles 107 and 108 of the Treaty on the Functioning of the European Union to *de minimis* aid - {c(2013a) 4448 final} {swd(2013a) 522 final} - Brussels, 18 July 2013, swd(2013) 521 final. untitled (europa.eu). Accessed 20 April 2020

European Commission (2013b) IP/13/1293. https://ec.europa.eu/commission/presscorner/detail/en/IP_13_1293 Accessed 20 April 2020

European Commission (2019). State aid: Commission approves €12 million Danish scheme (europa.eu). Accessed 15 March 2020

European Commission (2020a). https://ec.europa.eu/competition-policy/state-aid/coronavirus_en. Accessed 20 April 2020a

European Commission (2020b) EUROPE 2020 A strategy for smart, sustainable and inclusive growth/* COM/2010/2020 final */. EUR-Lex - 52010DC2020 - PT - EUR-Lex (europa.eu). Accessed 20 April 2020

Evans A (1999) The EU structural funds. Oxford University Press, Oxford

Ferreira E (2012) Art. 174-175 TFEU. In: Lopes Porto M, Gonçalo A (eds) Tratado de Lisboa: anotado e comentado [Treaty of Lisbon: annotated and commented]. Almedina, Coimbra, pp 731–734

Foszczynski A, Stobiecka-Kuik F (2008) Chapter 15 - Part 4. In: Mederer W, Pesaresi N, Van Hoof M (eds) EU Competition Law: Volume IV: Book Two, State Aid. Claeys and Casteels, Leuven, pp 1511–1558

Franchini C (1993) Amministrazione italiana e amministrazione comunitaria: la coamministrazione nei settori di interesse comunitário [Italian administration and Community administration: the co-administration in areas of Community interest], 2nd edn. CEDAM, Padova

Gallizioli G (1992) I fondi strutturali delle Comunità Europe. Cedam

Gomes C A, Antunes T (2011) O ambiente e o Tratado de Lisboa: uma relação Sustentada [Environment and the Lisbon Treaty: a sustainable relationship]. In: Nuno Piçarra et al (eds) A União Europeia segundo o Tratado de Lisboa: aspectos centrais. Almedina, Coimbra, pp 205–233

Gomes C A, Saraiva R (2019) O quadro europeu de apoio 2014-2020 para o Ambiente, o compromisso da União Europeia com a luta contra as alterações climáticas e a resposta nacional: lições aprendidas e perspetivas futuras [The 2014-2020 European Support Framework for Environment, the European Union's commitment to fighting climate change and the national response: lessons learned and prospects]. https://www.icjp.pt/sites/default/files/publicacoes/files/ebook_dirpublicopoliticacoesaofundoseuropeus_icjpmaio2019.pdf. Accessed 31 October 2020

Guillem Carra J (2018) Las correcciones financieras en materia de fondos estructurales [Financial corrections to Structural Funds]. Revista Argonesa de Administración Pública 51: 281–319

Heidenhain M (2010) The Concept of State Aid. In: Heidenhain M (ed) European State Aid Law. Verlag C.H. Beck, Munich, pp 22–60

Hofmann H C H (2016) The Legal Rule of Subsidies and State Aid Review. In: Hofmann HCH, Micheau C (eds) State Aid Law of the European Union. Oxford University Press, Oxford, pp 36–62

Hojnik J (2013) *De Minimis* Rule within the EU Internal Market Freedoms: Towards a More Mature and Legitimate Market?". European Journal of Legal Studies 6: 26–27

Hornkohl L, Van't Klooster J (2020) With Exclusive Competence Comes Great Responsibility: How the Commission's Covid-19 State Aid rules Increase Regional Inequalities within the EU, VerfBlog. https://verfassungsblog.de/with-exclusive-competence-comes-great-responsibility/. Accessed 20 April 2020

Hughes D M (2009) The Inter relationship between the European State Aid and Public Procurement Rules: When does a government contractor gain an 'economic advantage'? EIPA 1: 5

Kalflèche G (2007) De minimis curat Europae consilium: à propos de la communication interprétative de la communication relative au droit communautaire applicable aux passations de marchés non soumises ou partiellement soumises aux directives "marchés publics" du 23 juin 2006 17, 7: 6–11

Klamert M (2014) The Principle of Loyalty in EU Law. Oxford University Press, Oxford

Lopes D (2012) Art. 10 TFEU. In: Lopes Porto M, Gonçalo A (eds) Tratado de Lisboa: anotado e comentado [Treaty of Lisbon: annotated and commented]. Almedina, Coimbra, pp 228–231

Mento S (2007) Poteri amministrativi della Commissione Europea in materia di fondi strutturali. Rivista trimestrale di diritto pubblico 1: 135–172

Met-Domestici A (2006) Aides d'Etat, service public et droit communautaire: eléments de clarification sur la validité des compensations de service public [State aid, public service, and EU law: clarifications on the validity of public service compensation]. Droit administratif. L'actualité juridique 34: 1881

Neves A F (2019) O quadro normativo e as vinculações gerais da política de coesão [The legal framework and general obligations of cohesion policy]. https://www.icjp.pt/sites/default/files/publicacoes/files/ebook_dirpublicopoliticacoesaofundoseuropeus_icjpmaio2019.pdf. Accessed 31 October 2020

Neves C C (2012) Art. 349 TFEU. In: Lopes Porto M, Gonçalo A (eds) Tratado de Lisboa: anotado e comentado [Treaty of Lisbon: annotated and commented]. Almedina, Coimbra, pp 1223–1225

Nicolaides P (2013a) Structural Funds and Regional State Aid. European Structural and Investment Funds Journal 1: 41–45

Nicolaides P (2013b) An Assessment of the State Aid Consistency of Financial Instruments Supported by Structural and Investment Funds" (Regulation 1303/2013b). https://www.lexxion.eu/en/stateaidpost/an-assessment-of-the-state-aid-consistency-of-financial-instruments-supported-by-structural-and-investment-funds-regulation-1303-2013b/. Accessed 4 April 2018

Ordóñez Solís D (1997) Fondos estructurales europeos: régimen jurídico y gestión Administrative [European Structural Funds: legal framework and administrative management]. Marcial Pons, Madrid

Ordóñez Solís D (2011a) La gestión de los fondos europeos [The management of European funds]. Revista de Derecho de la Unión Europea 20: 117–149

Ordóñez Solís D (2011b) El derecho de las subvenciones en la Unión Europea [Subsidy law in the European Union]. In: Garcés Sanagustín M, Palomar Olmeda A, Arteagabeitia Gómez I M (eds) Derecho de las subvenciones y ayudas Públicas [Public subsidies and aid Law]. Editorial Aranzadi, Pamplona (Navarra), pp 165–212

Orzan M F (2016) De Jure Compatible Aid under 107(2) TFEU. In: Hofmann HCH, Micheau C (eds) State Aid Law of the European Union. Oxford University Press, Oxford, pp 234–239

Pacheco J L (2012) Art. 317 TFEU. In: Lopes Porto M, Gonçalo A (eds) Tratado de Lisboa: anotado e comentado [Treaty of Lisbon: annotated and commented]. Almedina, Coimbra, pp 1122–1124

Pantazatou K (2016) European Structural and Investment Funds and State Aid Control: Two Policies at Odds with Each Other? In: Hofmann HCH, Micheau C (eds) State Aid Law of the European Union. Oxford University Press, Oxford, pp 187–218

Pedro R (2014) Notas sobre o direito a uma decisão judicial em prazo razoável na União [Notes on the right to a judicial decision within a reasonable time in the Union].In: Marques A, Barcelos P (eds) Direitos fundamentais e soberania na Europa: história e atualidade. IFILNOVA - Instituto de Filosofia da Nova da Universidade Nova de Lisboa, Lisbon, pp 275–302

Pedro R (2015) Auxílios *de minimis* 2014-2020: Notas à luz do Regulamento (UE) n.º 1407/2013 [De minimis aid 2014-2020: Notes regarding Regulation (EU) No 1407/2013]. Revista de Concorrência e Regulação 17: 65–95

Pedro R (2018) Eficiência energética dos edifícios: brevíssimas notas sobre alguns dos principais instrumentos legislativos europeus e portugueses [Building energy efficiency: very brief notes on the main European and Portuguese legislative instruments]. https://www.apden.pt/sites/default/files/publicacoes/pdf/2018-05/Ebook_Anais_de_Sustentabilidade.pdf. Accessed 5 July 2021

Pesaresi N, Van Hoof M (2008) Introduction and Context Part 1 – Chapter 1. In: Mederer W, Pesaresi N, Van Hoof M (eds) EU Competition Law: Volume IV: Book One, State Aid. Claeys and Casteels, Leuven, pp 1–17

Piernas Lopez J J (2015) The Concept of State Aid Under EU Law: From Internal Market to Competition and Beyond. Oxford University Press, Oxford

Pimenta C, Lemos P (2012) Art. 191(1) TFEU. In: Lopes Porto M, Gonçalo A (eds) Tratado de Lisboa: anotado e comentado [Treaty of Lisbon: annotated and commented]. Almedina, Coimbra, pp 758–762

Porras Gómez A M (2015) La gobernanza multinivel del gasto público Europeo [Multi-level governance of European public spending]. Centro de Estudios Políticos y Constitucionales, Madrid

Quigley C (2015) European State Aid Law and Policy, 3rd edn. Hart Publishing, Oxford/Portland, Oregon

Rocha M M (2012) Art. 11 TFEU. In: Lopes Porto M, Gonçalo A (eds) Tratado de Lisboa: anotado e comentado [Treaty of Lisbon: annotated and commented]. Almedina, Coimbra, pp 232–234

Roque M P (2011) Direito processual administrativo europeu: a convergência dinâmica no espaço europeu de justiça administrativa [EU procedural administrative law: dynamic convergence of administrative justice in the European area]. Coimbra Editora, Coimbra

Sánchez Graells A (2015) Public procurement and the EU competition rules, 2nd edn. Hart Publishing, Oxford

Samaniego Bordiú, G (2004) Fundamentos económicos de los efectos de las ayudas en la Competencia [Economic rationale for the effect of aid on competition]. Gaceta Jurídica de la Unión Europea y de la Competencia 233: 49

Soares A G (2012) Art. 4 TFEU. In: Lopes Porto M, Gonçalo A (eds) Tratado de Lisboa: anotado e comentado [Treaty of Lisbon: annotated and commented]. Almedina, Coimbra, pp 209–211

Soltész U (2016) The definition of State aid. In: Säcker FJ, Montag F (eds) European State Aid Law: A Commentary. Verlag C.H. Beck, Munich, pp 228–243

Vallina R (2008) De minimis lex non curat o de minimis praetor non curat? Gaceta jurídica de la Unión Europea y de la Competencia 2: 47–61

Van de Casteele K (2016) De minimis aid. In: Hancher L, Ottervanger T, Slot PJ (eds) E.U. State Aids, 5th edn. Sweet & Maxwell, London, pp 235–244

van Hove J (2020) Impact of state aid on competition and competitiveness during the COVID-19 pandemic: an early assessment, Study for the Committee on Economic and Monetary Affairs, Policy Department for Economic, Scientific and Quality of Life Policies, European Parliament. http://www.europarl.europa.eu/RegData/etudes/STUD/2020/658214/IPOL_STU(2020)658214_EN.pdf. Accessed 5 July 2021

Vestager M (2020) Draft proposal for a State aid Temporary Framework to support the economy in the context of the COVID-19 outbreak. https://ec.europa.eu/commission/presscorner/detail/en/STATEMENT_20_479. Accessed 20 April 2020

Vilaça J L C (2014) EU Law and Integration Twenty Years of Judicial Application of EU Law. Hart Publishing, Oxford/Portland, Oregon

von Donat C (2010) Rescue and Restructuring Aid. In: Heidenhain M (ed) European State Aid Law. Verlag C.H. Beck, Munich, pp 211–240

Walkerova K (2008) Chapter 16 - Part 4. In: Mederer W, Pesaresi N, Van Hoof M (eds) EU Competition Law: Volume IV: Book Two, State Aid. Claeys and Casteels, Leuven, pp 1559–1577

Wishlade F G (2003) Regional state aid and competition policy in the European Union. Kluwer Law International, The Hague

Wolf M (2016) Services of General Economic Interest. In: Säcker FJ, Montag F (eds) European State Aid Law: A Commentary. Verlag C.H. Beck, Munich, pp 295–381

Chapter 2
De Minimis Aid: Growing Pains

Contents

Abstract This chapter addresses the main issues arising from the evolution of the *de minimis* rules, which are a dynamic reality with their own growing pains. It particularly seeks to understand how a regime that arises in the context of State aid but is not State aid due to its negligible value, has gained such relevance and momentum. Deals with the relevance afforded to the *de minimis* regime by the European Commission and with how the CJEU understands the recognition of a *de minimis* rule. Lastly, the role of Member States in the application of the *de minimis* regimes is brought into relief, as are the contradictions that the practical application of *de minimis* regimes with different characteristics sometimes entails.

Keywords *De minimis* principle · Bagatelle nature · State aid · European Courts · Member States · *De minimis* control system

2.1 In General

This chapter aims to clarify how the *de minimis* regimes put a minor aid on display that is grappling with growing pains. Although *de minimis* aids emerge as one of the exceptions within the scope of State aids (not to be confused with the State aid framework, as the MS are under no obligation to notify it to the European Commission—and therefore should be interpreted in a restrictive way) they are still of great practical importance because of the small but necessary aids granted to SME (and also to large companies).

As already mentioned, this is a paradigm that has been evolving at various levels, namely the degree to which the instrument mobilised is binding—from a Communication to a Regulation, and there are presently *de minimis* rules for different sectors or types of activities (besides the general *de minimis* regime, there are special *de*

© T.M.C. ASSER PRESS and the author 2022

R. Pedro, *De Minimis Aid Under EU Law*,
https://doi.org/10.1007/978-94-6265-543-0_2

minimis regimes: (i) for the agriculture sector, (ii) for the fisheries and aquaculture sectors and (iii) for enterprises providing SGEI). The regime proper has developed and become more sophisticated, as an analysis of Regulation (EU) 1407/2013 clearly shows.

This evolution should, on the one hand, be understood in the context of the European Union's legal system as regards the sources of law; on the other hand, it should be understood in the light of its nature, that is, its minimal character. In practical terms, the *de minimis* regimes indicate a reinforcement of MS's role of checking the requirements of such aid and of recovering illegal aid.

Considering this context, we will address the main thorny problems resulting from the application of the general *de minimis* regime.

In short, this is the background to the growing pains of the *de minimis* regimes discussed below.

2.2 *De Minimis* Communications, Regulations and Case-Law

The *de minimis* regimes can, to some extent, be framed in a more general context wherein attention is given to the *bagatelle nature*, which in turn requires considering the application of the general rule as such or rather the need of a cost/benefit test. In other words, the Law, and Competition Law specifically, is not unaware of the idea of proportionality in the definition of frameworks, namely aid regimes.

Both the legal systems of the MS and the legal system of the Union[1] (in certain fields of the law) have an underlying *de minimis* principle, i.e., a principle that imposes an adequate evaluation of the situations in order to frame them in an adjusted regime. Consequently, whenever situations prove to be of *lesser value*, either in the light of the values of a given legal Community, the general principles of the law, or from an economic and financial point of view, the framework to be applied should convey that lesser or *de minimis* value—as the brocard "*de minimis* non curat praetor"[2] and/or "*de minimis* non curat lex"[3] generally indicates.

If one focuses on the (context of) State aid frameworks, the valuation of the *de minimis* idea emerges as the principle that forced the European legislator to create autonomous regimes for low-value aid, thereby admitting that such aid will theoretically not affect the internal market and competition. The consequence drawn by the European legislator was that if the internal market and competition are not affected, at least *a priori*, the aid does not require the European Commission's *ex-ante* control, thus

[1] On the sense that the "*de minimis* rule is recognised world-wide", see Hojnik 2013, p. 27.

[2] Regarding procedural context, see e.g. ECHR judgments: *Korolev v Russia*, 1 April 2010, case 5447/03, and *Bock v Germany*, 16 February 2010, case 22051/07.

[3] The law concerns itself only with matters of broader community relevance.

setting aside the obligation to notify low-value aid to the European Commission for analysis and validation purposes.

As will be seen below, the exemption from the European Commission's control does not mean that the issue is not regulated; on the contrary, the issue continues to be regulated, but control is no longer within the European Commission's remit, monitoring obligations falling to the MS. In other words, the law (*in casu*, secondary law) is still concerned with monitoring *de minimis* aid. However, it tasks the MS with checking that the requirements foreseen in the *de minimis* regimes for granting this type of aid are fulfilled.

The European Commission, not the MS, is the "*praetor*" exempted from minor aid control in this instance. Although MS are not tasked with controlling competition—that is within the European Commission's exclusive purview—they are tasked with controlling compliance with the legal requirements set out in the relevant regulations.[4]

Despite the European legislator's option, the application of a *de minimis* rule should arguably not exempt the MS from any control/monitoring: the bagatelle nature imposes that consequence and the (control) rules regarding this type of aid should not apply, since we are not dealing with State aid.

This principle[5] led to several concrete achievements, as denoted by the various *de minimis* regimes approved. The European Commission has been authorised by the Council to adopt *de minimis* regulations establishing legal rules applicable to the Commission, the MS and business.[6]

Despite these developments, it is still not easy to understand this issue clearly, particularly given the European Commission and the EU Courts' lack of consensus regarding the *de minimis* rule in the context of State aid. This lack of consensus could be explained by the fact that the TFEU does not expressly support the *de minimis* rule. In other words, although the element of the rule affecting competition and the internal market in particular falls within the scope of interpretation of Article 107(1) TFEU, the truth is that it does not expressly result from this Article.

Even if the Article were to be interpreted a *contrario sensu*, the fact that competition and the internal market are not affected removes the prohibition on the grant of aid (since State aid is not involved). On the one hand, *de minimis* aid is only a type of the *genus* and the Article does not imply that the aid in question is not State aid. On the other hand, the Article does not express what requirements make it possible to assert (without a case-by-case examination) that competition and the internal market will not be affected, or will be affected only to a negligible extent, by the grant of a particular aid.

This absence of rules in the Treaties could explain why the European Courts are "shy" to expressly admit a *de minimis* rule in the scope of State aid or "to deny

---

[4] On the one hand, the *ex-post* control allowed to the European Commission is very limited and on the other hand it is predicated on the data collected by the MS. In short, in practical terms, it depends on the MS's monitoring.

[5] An explicit reference to this principle can be found in Estoa Pérez 2007, p. 625.

[6] Berghofer 2007, p. 14.

such rule" offhand. On the other hand, after the European Commission provided guidelines and, above all, regulations on the requirements to be considered for the admission of *de minimis* rules, there is case-law that does not fail to decide based on them.

Therefore, the evolution of the European Court's case-law seems not to be indifferent to the (consolidated) evolution, experience and regulation of the subject by the European Commission. While this does not mean that the two institutions "evolve in tandem", it also does not mean that the European Courts are indifferent to the rules foreseen in the *de minimis* regulations.

The *de minimis* rule has evolved a great deal, from a Communication to a Regulation. It can be said, in practice, that the European Commission has long accepted that minor aids do not affect competition and the internal market.[7]

The 1992 Community guidelines on State aid for Small- and Medium-sized Enterprises (SMEs),[8] although only in the context of SMEs,[9] provide for the *de minimis* rule, with a view to streamlining the administrative process for SMEs and clarifying that it is desirable that aid below a certain absolute amount should not be notified to the European Commission.

Subsequently, the Commission 1996 notice on the *de minimis* rule for State aid,[10] removed the *de minimis* rule from the context of SMEs on the one hand, and, on the other hand, modified the regime of the previous guidelines since they did not cover certain aid that clearly did not threaten to distort competition and trade between MS in a discernible manner and took into account that the conditions attached to it could prove difficult to monitor, particularly in the event of cumulation with aid schemes approved by the European Commission.

The European Commission has to abide by the "guidelines"[11] that it adopts in relation to the control of State aid, insofar as they do not deviate from the rules of the Treaty and are accepted by the MS.[12] In this sense, the Court of Justice has already clarified that "*the European Commission may not refuse to apply the* de minimis *rule to aid granted to undertakings belonging to sectors which are not excluded from the application of that rule by the various legal texts applicable*".[13]

The Court of Justice has ruled on several occasions on the scope of State aid control related guidelines, stating that "*the Commission may impose on itself guidelines for the exercise of its discretion by means of acts such as guidelines, in so far as those*

[7] Zuleger 2010, p. 61; Quigley 2015, p. 95.

[8] OJ C 213, 19 August 1992, pp. 2–8.

[9] Although there is no limit regarding the size of the company that can benefit from this *de minimis* option.

[10] OJ C 068, 6 March 1996, pp. 9–10.

[11] On the different designations mobilised, see Hofmann 2016, pp. 49 et seq.

[12] See CJEU, *IJssel-Vliet Combinatie BV v Minister van Economische Zaken*, Judgment of the Court, 15 October 1996, case C-311/94, ECLI:EU:C:1996:383, para 43.

[13] See CJEU, *Spain v Commission*, Judgment of the Court, 26 September 2002, case C-351/98, para 53.

acts contain rules indicating the approach to be followed by the Commission and do not depart from the rules of the Treaty".[14]

Moreover, the formulation of such guidelines by the European Commission creates a situation in which the Commission is bound by them. In that regard, and according to the Court of Justice, "*It also follows from the judgment in CIRFS and Others v Commission that the Commission is also bound by the guidelines which it adopts*".[15] In other words, even in those matters regarding which the European Commission enjoys discretionary powers, from the moment it adopts a position on its understanding, as soon as it takes a position on its action, it becomes self-bound and it must follow that system, otherwise the principle of equal treatment will be violated.[16]

As already mentioned, the regulation of *de minimis* aid has evolved from a Communication to a Regulation, changing the Community act mobilized by going from using "soft law" to using "hard law" instruments. This change seems to underpin the criterion of the Commission's "considerable experience" in applying exemption arrangements.

Commission Regulation (EC) No 69/2001 of 12 January 2001 on the application of Articles 87 and 88 of the EC Treaty to *de minimis* aid[17] Commission Regulation (EC) No 1998/2006 of 15 December 2006 on the application of Articles 87 and 88 of the EC Treaty to *de minimis* aid,[18] and Regulation (EU) No 1407/2013 were approved[19] in addition to the Communications already mentioned.

It should be underlined that the *de minimis* rule has been consolidated in a regulation for about two decades now.

As already mentioned, European Courts' case-law is not very "consensual/consistent";[20] is "contradictory"[21] or, more broadly speaking, "evolving towards admissibility". This case-law evolution—which will hardly fit the simplistic formula that there is no *de minimis* case-law rule—should be understood in the light of the absence of an express reference in the Treaties to the *de minimis* rule and the evolution of the *de minimis* regimes as envisaged by the European Commission.

For a better understanding, account should be taken of several passages in the case-law of the European Courts concerning their understanding of *de minimis* rule.

Thus, the aforementioned contradictory case-law seems to result from:

---

[14] See CJEU: *Germany v Commission*, Judgment of the Court, 5 October 2000, case C-288/96, ECLI:EU:C:2000:537, para 62; *Italy v Commission*, Judgment of the Court, 7 March 2002, case C-310/99, ECLI:EU:C:2002:143, para 52.

[15] See case C-311/94, para 43.

[16] Hofmann 2016, pp. 50 et seq.

[17] OJ L 10, 13 January 2001, pp. 30–32.

[18] OJ L 379, 28 December 2006, pp. 5–10.

[19] OJ L 352, 24 December 2013, pp. 1–8.

[20] Quigley 2015, p. 91.

[21] Hojnik 2013, pp. 28 and 29.

(i) a batch of rulings to the effect that the Court of Justice does not recognise a *de minimis* aid rule:

– "as regards the effect of the measure at issue on trade between Member States, it is settled case-law that the relatively small amount of aid or the relatively small size of the undertaking which receives it does not as such exclude the possibility that trade between Member States might be affected";[22]

– "aid of relatively small amount may also be capable of affecting trade between Member States, in particular where the sector concerned is characterised by strong competition";[23]

– "there is no ceiling or percentage below which it may be considered that trade between Member States is not affected";[24]

– "where the sector is characterised by a large number of small enterprises, aid, even if relatively small in scale individually, but potentially open to all or a large proportion of the undertakings in the sector, may affect trade between Member States.[25]

(ii) and the judgments which show that the Court of Justice recognises a *de minimis* aid rule:

– "(...) the small amounts of aid granted to an undertaking over a given period of time mean that, in a number of economic sectors, trade between Member States is not affected";[26]

– "The Commission was therefore entitled to reach the view, in the exercise of its discretion to assess the possible economic effects of aid, that, other than in certain sectors where competitive conditions are of a particular kind and except in respect of export aid, aid in amounts falling below those laid down in the Community guidelines on State aid for SMEs, and subsequently in its Notice on the *de minimis* rule for State aid (OJ 1996 C 68, p. 9), does not affect trade and is therefore not caught by Articles 92 and 93 of the Treaty".[27]

Trying to go beyond the claim that the case-law is "inconsistent" or "contradictory", it should be recalled that the main argument against the admission of the *de minimis* rule has precisely resulted from Union Courts' case-law, namely *that low value aid can also affect competition and the internal market.*

This is, above all, a statement of principle—naturally valid—but it does not deny the existence of low-value aid; which, for that very reason, tends not to affect competition and the internal market. Moreover, the Union Courts have been called upon

[22] See CJEU: *Belgium v Commission*, Judgment of the Court, 21 March 1990, case C-142/87, ECLI:EU:C:1990:125, para 43; *Spain v Commission*, Judgment of the Court, 14 September 1994, joined cases C-278/92, C-279/92 and C-280/92, ECLI:EU:C:1994:325, para 42; *Federal Republic of Germany v Commission of the European Communities*, Judgment of the Court, 19 September 2000, case C-156/98, ECLI:EU:C:2000:467, paras 32 and 39; case C-280/00, para 81; case C-172/03, para 32.

[23] See CJEU: *Italy v Commission*, Judgment of the Court, 21 March 1991, case C-303/88, ECLI:EU:C:1991:136, para 27; case C-298/00 P, para 54.

[24] See CJEU: case C-280/00, para 81; *Enirisorse SpA v Ministero delle Finanze*, Judgment of the Court, 27 November 2003, joined cases C-34/01, C-35/01, C-36/01, C-37/01 and C-38/01, ECLI:EU:C:2003:640, para 28; case C-172/03, para 32.

[25] See CJEU: *Spain v Commission*, Judgment of the Court, 26 September 2002, case C-351/98, para 64; case C-372/97, para 57; *Administración del Estado v Xunta de Galicia*, Judgment of the Court, 21 July 2005, case C-71/04, ECLI:EU:C:2005:493, para 43.

[26] See case C-351/98, para 51.

[27] See case C-351/98, para 52.

several times *to interpret* the *de minimis* aid regimes and have never considered them to be in breach of the Treaties;[28] nor have the parties to the respective cases claimed the illegality of these regimes.[29] In other words, in some judgments, both in theory and in practice, it is *expressly*[30] or *implicitly*[31] accepted that "*the small amounts of aid granted to an undertaking over a given period of time mean that, in a number of economic sectors, trade between Member States is not affected*".[32] This rule, which, according to the Court of Justice, "allows the European Commission, in the communications and frameworks which it has drawn up, to take the view that, in accordance with the Treaty and by virtue of the discretion which it enjoys in assessing the possible economic effects of aid, *except in certain sectors characterised by special conditions of competition, aid of less than a certain amount does not affect trade and therefore is not caught by Articles 92 and 93 of the Treaty*".[33]

---

[28] Sometimes it turns out that the aid does not fall within the scope of a *de minimis* regime—but this cannot mean that the regime is inadmissible. In case C-280/00, it is clarified that "*Subsequently, the Commission notice of 6 March 1996 on the de minimis rule for State aid (OJ 1996 C 68, p. 9) does not cover the transport sector, as is clear from its fourth paragraph. Similarly, Commission Regulation (EC) No 69/2001 of 12 January 2001 on the application of Articles 87 and 88 of the EC Treaty to de minimis aid (OJ 2001 L 10, p. 30) does not apply to that sector, as is clear from its third recital and Article 1(a)*" (para 80). In case C-172/03, the Court reaffirms *in abstracto* the rule that there is no value below which aid does not affect trade between MS. Notwithstanding the above, the Court of Justice considers the 1996 Notice to be applicable, and the *de minimis* rule set out therein is not applicable in the specific case, since it does not appear from the file that the amount of aid granted would be less than the amount set out in that Notice.

[29] See case C-351/98, para 51 and case C-172/03, para 35.

[30] In CJEU: case C-351/98, para 52, and *Kingdom of Spain v Commission of the European Communities*, Judgment of the Court, 13 February 2003, case C-409/00, ECLI:EU:C:2003:92, it assumes the existence of the *de minimis* rule; and decides, having regard to the *de minimis* regime applicable to the case *sub judice*, to which aid that regime *is* or *is not* applicable. In CJEU, *Istituto nazionale per l'assicurazione contro gli infortuni sul lavoro (INAIL) v Zennaro Giuseppe Legnami Sas di Zennaro Mauro & C*, its Judgment of the Court, 28 October 2020, case C-608/19, ECLI:EU:C:2020:86, in which a request for a preliminary ruling was concerned with the interpretation of Articles 3 and 6 of Regulation (EU) No 1407/2013, the Court clarified that "*Articles 3 and 6 of Regulation No 1407/2013 must be placed in the general context of that regulation, which is intended to permit derogation, as regards State aid of a limited amount, from the rule that all aid must, prior to being granted, be notified to the Commission*". It further clarified that: "*with regard to the objectives of Regulation No 1407/2013, it should be noted that the de minimis regulation aims to simplify the administrative burden on undertakings, the Commission and the Member States (see, to that effect, Judgment of 7 March 2002, Italy v Commission, C-310/99, EU:C:2002:143, paragraph 94), on the basis of the principle, recalled in recital 3 of that regulation, that aid of an amount not exceeding the de minimis ceiling does not affect trade between Member States and is not liable to distort competition.*"

[31] This is why some legal authors argue that the *de minimis* regimes have been implicitly approved, see Nyssens 2008, p. 412. See also CJEU: *Eric Libert and Others v Gouvernement flamand*, Judgment of the Court, 8 May 2013, case C-197/11, and *All Projects & Developments NV and Others v Vlaamse Regering*, case C-203/11, para 81.

[32] See case C-351/98, para 51.

[33] See CJEU: *Kingdom of Spain v Commission of the European Communities*, Judgment of the Court, 13 February 2003, case C-409/00, ECLI:EU:C:2003:92, para 69. Emphasis added.

The above shows openness to admitting the *de minimis* rule, emphasizing the discretionary power of the European Commission in the provision of guidelines.

On the other hand, the understanding of the *de minimis* rule should take into account that the grounds for its acceptance are not only the original ones: (i) *of not affecting competition and the internal market*, (ii) *but also the need to reduce the administrative burden of the European Commission and the MS with the non-control of such aid*, freeing the European Commission to control the aid of higher value and/or with a greater impact on competition and the internal market. Moreover, *de minimis* regimes evolved without prejudice to the case-law that does not expressly admit the *de minimis* rule.

Furthermore, as far as aid is concerned, the *de minimis* principle is the result of balancing several concerns. At the same time that it seeks to address a prevailing concern that the competition rules with regard to State aid are effectively supervised—which is why it is important to free the European Commission from analysing *bagatelle nature* aid—it caters to the need of streamlining administrative management and increasing transparency, legal certainty (the need to ensure consistent application of exceptional State aid frameworks within the Union).

It should be noted that a realistic perspective must not overlook the aid control *management* dimension,[34] not only in view of the option of freeing the European Commission to control higher value aid, but also in view of the option—assumed in several regulations—of imposing monitoring obligations on MS.

2.3 The Role of the European Commission and the Role of the Member States

The European Commission's main role in relation to State aid is to examine whether the aid measures planned are compatible with the internal market,[35] based on the criteria set out in Article 107(2) and (3) TFEU, as required by Article 108(1) TFEU. This compatibility assessment falls within the exclusive purview of the European Commission, controlled by the European Courts. The European Commission's purview also falls outside the scope of European Courts' case-law, since national courts lack jurisdiction to declare a State aid measure compatible with Article 107(2) or (3) TFEU,[36] according to the Court of Justice's settled case-law.

Under Article 108(2) TFEU, the European Commission plays a very important role in the recovery of unlawful aid, by seeking, in its recovery decisions, to identify the recipients of the incompatible aid and quantify the aid to be recovered. If this proves impossible, the European Commission must describe in the recovery decision

[34] See Piernas Lopez 2015, pp. 205–206.

[35] See Quigley 2015, pp. 3 et seq.

[36] See, among others, CJEU, *Centre d'exportation du livre français (CELF) and Ministre de la Culture et de la Communication v Société internationale de diffusion et d'édition (SIDE)*, Judgment of de the Court, 12 February 2008, case C-199/06, ECLI:EU:C:2008:79, para 38.

how MS are to identify the recipients and determine the amount of aid to be recovered. Lastly, it should be noted that the European Commission assists the MS concerned in the implementation of the recovery decision under the principle of loyal cooperation.

This is the European Commission's role when State aid is involved, but the question is whether the role of the European Commission is the same when *de minimis* aid is involved. In other words, it remains to be seen what role the European Commission and the MS play in the control of the *de minimis* aid regimes. The question arises because *de minimis* aid is not State aid, not really.

Without prejudice to what will be said below about the role of the European Commission and the MS in the recovery of unlawful *de minimis* aid, the general guidance offered by European legislation in connection with *checking* the fulfilment of the *de minimis* rules' requirements seems to point to such control/monitoring lying with the MS. In other words, the system foreseen for the implementation and monitoring of *de minimis* regimes is different to that foreseen for the monitoring of State aid. Moreover, as the European Commission's role diminishes, the role of the MS increases.

As already mentioned, MS play a crucial role in implementing the *de minimis* regime, as control is left to them. In other words, unlike State aid that is, as a rule, notified to the European Commission for its review, *de minimis* aid is only controlled by MS—*de minimis non curat European Commission*! In this regard, it should be noted that as is often emphasized by the European Commission, monitoring the *de minimis* regimes is one of the most important and most difficult aspects of its practical application—this task is left to the MS.

The role of MS regarding *de minimis* regimes is mainly to confirm, before granting any *de minimis* aid, that its ceiling will not be exceeded by the new *de minimis* aid. This *ex-ante* control by MS is particularly important because it does not require the European Commission to be notified of *de minimis* aid, which means that the European method of monitoring *de minimis* aid granted to undertakings is dependent on the MS. MS do not control whether aid affects or threatens to affect competition, *but rather check compliance with the requirements of the de minimis regulations concerned.* Thus, the *de minimis* regulations relieve the European Commission of an important workload, which falls on the MS.

This conclusion runs somehow counter to the Union's understanding of exclusive authority as regards competition policy—Article 3(1)(b) TFEU—at least in practice (since the European Commission will not monitor in the first place). But not just in practice, because the MS monitoring *de minimis* is an exclusive task of the MS[37]—since we are not dealing with State aid under Article 107(1) TFEU. The possibility

[37] Berghofer 2007, p. 17.

of the European Commission monitoring/controlling did not result from Regulation (EC) 994/98[38] nor from Regulation (EU) 2015/1588.[39]

Tasking MS with such monitoring is not without risk, including different interpretations of the *de minimis* regulation by national authorities, thereby increasing the potential for breach of the European Union law uniform interpretation principle.[40]

It is important to remember that, according to this principle, European Union law must apply in the same way and with the same meaning in every MS, otherwise—in the matter of interest to this study—the unity of the internal market[41] and the competition rules may be jeopardized.

MS are usually vested with administrative powers[42] to perform their *de minimis* aid monitoring role. But in practice, such control goes far beyond legal control: technical economic and financial control is often required.

One of the most difficult requirements to control is concretely determining whether a group of companies should be considered as a "*single undertaking*".

The interpretation of the "single undertaking" concept is highly relevant both from the point of view of the potential aid recipients and of healthy competition. In other words, a wrong classification of the single undertaking concept impacts both the undertaking in question (which may *or may not* be the aid recipient based on such classification) and competition and the trade market (which *may* or *may not* be violated, depending on the incorrect or correct classification).

This is a fragile system for ensuring the effectiveness of EU competition law—which may be understandable given the reasons cited for admitting this type of aid—but may, however, specifically compromise the European Commission's real control of competition.

Although this aid is of low value, in *hard cases* the situation may change: consider, e.g., the award of aid to a single undertaking where there is doubt as to whether

---

[38] Council Regulation (EC) No 994/98 of 7 May 1998 on the application of Articles 87 and 88 (former Articles 92 and 93) of the Treaty establishing the European Community to certain categories of horizontal State aid, as amended by Regulation (EU) No 733/2013 of 22 July 2013 amending Regulation (EC) No 994/98 on the application of Articles 92 and 93 of the Treaty establishing the European Community to certain categories of horizontal State aid, OJ L 204, 31 July 2013, pp. 11–14.

[39] Council Regulation (EU) 2015/1588 of 13 July 2015 on the application of Articles 107 and 108 of the Treaty on the Functioning of the European Union to certain categories of horizontal State aid (OJ L 248, 24 September 2015, pp. 1–8), as amended by Council Regulation (EU) 2018/1911 of 26 November 2018 amending Regulation (EU) 2015/1588 on the application of Articles 107 and 108 of the Treaty on the Functioning of the European Union to certain categories of horizontal State aid, *OJ L 311, 7 December 2018, pp. 8–9.*

[40] It should be noted that, as mentioned in the Temporary Framework [see § 1.3.b)], "*unfair competition would also exacerbate regional inequalities within the EU*".

[41] Ramos 1999, p. 99.

[42] This does not concern the powers vested in national courts to check compliance with the *de minimis* regimes.

the "universe" of the group of companies—e.g. 1000—constitutes a "single undertaking" or, alternatively, 1000 independent companies. In other words, in quantitative terms, the value of the aid which may be involved, over three financial years, is €200,000,000 (1000 × €200,000). Therefore, if each of the 1000 independent companies is wrongly allocated to a single undertaking, the single undertaking will unduly benefit from €199,800,000 (€200,000,000–€200,000), with obvious damage to the proper functioning of the internal market and healthy competition.

This weaker monitoring is compounded by the fact that *de minimis* control relies on the undertakings' declarations. Although there is an advantage to the undertakings taking on responsibility upon signing the declaration, the fact remains that the undertakings receiving *de minimis* aid have a private interest in the aid that may be at odds with the public interest of controlling competition and trade market. Because the undertakings are usually SMEs, they may not have the human resources or the capacity to hire resources that would allow them to fill out their declaration in an accurate and informed manner.

Even where MS have implemented a *de minimis* control system, i.e., a central *de minimis* register, it is not easy to exercise effective control: not just because it is difficult to make the single undertaking concept operational, but also because of the need to control the cumulation of *de minimis* aid with State aid and other *de minimis* aid. This becomes even more challenging if the entity responsible for controlling the general *de minimis* aid is not the same as the one that controls the special *de minimis* aid.

It should be noted that the European Union law uniform interpretation principle and the European Union law effectiveness principle would tend to approximate the monitoring means set out above or even lead to a single regime[43] (preferably European). However, the creation of a central European register to monitor *de minimis* aid is not without legal and, above all, practical/operational difficulties.[44]

Within existing MS's *de minimis* monitoring options, the special de *minimis* regime for the agricultural sector requires mandatory administrative control—specifically a central *de minimis* register.[45] Under this regime, the use of a central register becomes necessary in those MS opting for a higher individual ceiling and a higher national ceiling, because the sectoral ceiling, which is a prerequisite for that option, requires even closer monitoring of the aid granted. It is therefore mandatory to establish and maintain a central register of all *de minimis* aid granted, which enables checking that neither the individual nor the sectoral or national ceiling are exceeded.

---

[43] The admission of a *de minimis* national central register has been one of the most problematic issues for MS, see Nicolaides 2014.

[44] See European Commission 2013, p. 59.

[45] Commission Regulation (EU) 2019/316 of 21 February 2019 amending Commission Regulation (EU) No 1408/2013 on the application of Articles 107 and 108 of the Treaty on the Functioning of the European Union to *de minimis* aid in the agriculture sector, OJ L 51I, 22 February 2019, pp. 1–6.

2.4 Certain Problematic Topics of the General *De Minimis* Regime

Despite the improvements introduced by the current general *de minimis* regime, certain topics of the previous *de minimis* regime remain problematic in the new regime, which also brought additional problems.

Furthermore, some of these problematic topics have been echoed in the practical application of the regime under consideration, as arises from the European Commission's analysis of the result of the consultation on the application of certain *de minimis* regimes. For this point, we will rely on the general *de minimis* regime since the same problems tend to replicate themselves in the other *de minimis* regimes.

The *de minimis* aid received by a "single undertaking" may be cumulated with other *de minimis* aid granted by any public authority within the *same* MS. It should be noted that the previous Regulation did not spell out that the €200,000 ceiling was per MS.[46] In short, each MS is only responsible for controlling *de minimis* aid granted within its borders.

The provision—Article 3(2)—limiting aid control to the territory of the MS is in line with the control that some MS have implemented to monitor the *de minimis* aid and spares MS the huge challenge of controlling *de minimis* aid granted to the same "single undertaking" with subsidiaries in another MS.[47,48]

But we should keep in mind that the "single undertaking" concept as set out in the general *de minimis* regulation admits such situations as the existence of "subsidiaries" based in other MS. This opens the door for a "single undertaking" to benefit from *de minimis* aid above the €200,000 ceiling[49]—considering any potential *de minimis* amounts received in different MS—and the relevant aid runs the risk of not being "good aid". The opportunity is there to breach the *de minimis* regimes in the different MS.

As for recipients, complying with this rule is very demanding in practice, particularly for SMEs when they belong to a group of companies present in several MS, insofar as this will have to make its *de minimis* control (document-based) in each MS. Compliance with this obligation tends to result in a bureaucratic burden that is often disproportionate to the size of the company.

It should be noted, as the doctrine the previous regime, that the *simplification* of some of the concepts used by the general *de minimis* regulation to make the *de minimis* regime operational, namely the notion of "single undertaking", is not without risks[50]

[46] As underlined by legal authors: Nyssens 2008, p. 441, and Nicolaides 2014.

[47] Van de Casteele 2016, p. 240.

[48] Sinnaeve 2014, p. 266.

[49] See in this connection the CJEU, *Netherlands v Commission*, Judgment of the Court, 13 June 2002, case C-382/99, ECLI:EU:C:2002:363.

[50] One of the characteristics of *de minimis* regulation has always been its *apparent* or even *putative* simplification. See Bär-Bouyssière 2005, p. 188; Berghofer 2007, p. 20, and Sinnaeve 2014, p. 261.

and poses practical application challenges that are not always easy overcome by the authorities that grant the aid or by the entities tasked with monitoring.

The concept of "single undertaking" is difficult to apply, especially when the public entities that grant *de minimis* aid are local authorities that are not very familiar with European competition law or when the monitoring bodies still have some difficulties in accurately assessing the single undertaking under analysis. The problem becomes more acute when some MS rely on the *legal concept* of undertaking for monitoring[51]exposing a huge gap between the concept under the *de minimis* regime and its practical application.

It is worth highlighting some of the main concerns expressed by the different players—*maxime*, public entities and undertakingsin the consultation carried out by the European Commission in 2019 on the application of the general *de minimis* regime[52] (i) undertakings and the entities responsible for the central *de minimis* register have a very hard time understanding the term "single undertaking" as "it stands next to the very similar definition of 'associated enterprise' in the SME definition and can hardly be put into practice"; (ii) the concept of dominant influence, as a criterion to qualify as single undertaking, "is particularly unclear and not defined"; (iii) it is "difficult to understand just how many levels are checked when making sure an SME is not, relative to another company, actually a large company".

These criteria are sometimes difficult to apply in practice. For instance, if the "dominant influence" is exercised exclusively through an arrangement (whose existence is not reflected in the company's articles of incorporation or articles of association) that is deliberately concealed from third parties, there is a possibility that the companies involved (and their related entities) cannot be identified as a "single undertaking".

Checking the "single undertaking" concept sometimes imposes a heavy administrative burden: each individual *de minimis* aid requires investigating and checking not just the applicant undertaking itself, but all affiliated companies in the group of companies, and if they have received *de minimis* support in the past three years. In this context, calculating the cumulation of *de minimis* aid at a "group level" translates into an administrative burden.

Unlike its predecessor, this general *de minimis* Regulation applies to *firms in difficulty*[53] (except for aid granted in the form of loans and guarantees).

[51] European Commission 2013, p. 50.

[52] See European Commission 2019.

[53] The notion of a *firm in difficulty* is taken from Article 2.1 of the Communication from the Commission—Community guidelines on State aid for rescuing and restructuring firms in difficulty (2004/C 244/02), OJ C 244, 1 November 2004, pp. 2–17, as last extended by the Commission Communication extending the Community guidelines on State aid for rescuing and restructuring firms in difficulty of 1 October 2004 (2012/C 296/02), OJ C 296, 2 November 2012, p. 3. See also von Donat 2010, pp. 216–221.

De minimis aid is a further support instrument available to the most vulnerable enterprises—in line, moreover, with the public policies for SMEs put forward by the Union in the *Small Business Act for Europe.*[54]

The flip side of the coin, however, is that the *rule* of state intervention to rescue a firm in difficulty cannot be upheld.[55] Consequently, the Commission's policies in this area are geared towards excluding firms in difficulty from all other State aid regulations and Commission guidelines (with the exception of the rescue and restructuring guidelines), because aid to firms in difficulty is one of the most distortive types of State aid.

The problem lies in the *contradiction* between the *strict* conditions under which State aid for the restructuring of firms in difficulty[56] is permissible and the *ease* with which *de minimis* aid can be granted to such firms.

This contradiction is all the more obvious in view of the difficulties faced by MS in determining the "difficulty" of the firm and determining its gross grant equivalent.[57] For these reasons, the *de minimis* rule laid down for SGEI does not apply to firms in difficulty.[58]

While, on the one hand, firms in difficulty can now benefit from a more relaxed instrument for granting aid, on the other, given that the rehabilitation of firms in difficulty has a high rate of failure, an instrument that enables misusing public money may have been created that is difficult for the MS to control and is not monitored by the Commission.[59]

And let us not forget the *moral hazard* created by the aid—firms anticipating that they are likely to be rescued when in difficulty may be inclined to adopt excessively risky and unsustainable business strategies. Furthermore, the prospect of rescue and restructuring aid to a given company may artificially lower its cost of capital, giving it an undue competitive advantage in the market.

The challenge of identifying the *single undertaking* adds to the challenge of determining what a *firm in difficulty* is, the need to recognise whether firms are really in difficulty and who effectively has control over them making the whole process even harder for MS granting *de minimis* aid.

---

[54] See Communication from the Commission to the Council, the European Parliament, the European Economic and Social Committee and the Committee of the Regions—"Think Small First"—A "Small Business Act" for Europe {SEC(2008) 2101} {SEC(2008) 2102} /* COM/2008/0394 final */.

[55] See recital 4 of the Communication from the Commission—Community guidelines on State aid for rescuing and restructuring firms in difficulty, JO C 244, 1 November 2004, pp. 2–17.

[56] The '*one-time, last time' principle* applies, so that companies are not kept artificially alive because of State aid.

[57] This was, moreover, the justification in the previous Regulation (see recital 7) for excluding firms in difficulty from the *de minimis* aid regime.

[58] Commission Regulation (EU) No 360/2012 of 25 April 2012 on the application of Articles 107 and 108 of the Treaty on the Functioning of the European Union to *de minimis* aid granted to undertakings providing services of general economic interest, OJ L 114, 26 April 2012, pp. 8–13.

[59] The Commission's desire for control can be seen in European Commission 2013, pp. 21 et seq. It should not be forgotten that, according to Article 108(1) TFEU, the Commission shall, in cooperation with the MS, keep under constant review all systems of aid existing in those MS.

This whole scenario could result in MS failing to apply EU law uniformly and instead apply the regulation under review differently,[60] due to a potentially incorrect consideration of the *de minimis* regime.

Lastly, and as was the case with the previous general *de minimis* regulation, there is no doubt that failure to comply with the *substantive* conditions laid down in Articles 1–5 of the general *de minimis* regulation entails the unlawfulness of such aid.

There is doubt, however, as to how to treat breaches of *procedural* conditions and monitoring obligations. This doubt remains unaddressed, i.e., it remains to be seen what the sanction will be in the event of failure to comply with the procedural rules laid down in the general *de minimis* Regulation.

This doubt is mirrored in the *different interpretations* allowed by the analysis of Article 3(1) of the general *de minimis* regulation, which states: "*Aid measures shall be deemed not to meet all the criteria of Article 107(1) of the Treaty and shall therefore be exempted from the notification requirement of Article 108(3) of the Treaty, if they fulfil the conditions laid down in this Regulation*".

On the one hand, the text of this Article may lead to the interpretation that the violation of procedural rules is not automatically illegal.[61]

On the other hand, this doubt was even more salient in the past, because the relevant wording of Regulation (EC) No 1998/2006[62] was different to Regulation (EC) No 875/2007[63] and, therefore, the literal element of interpretation (different in the two regulations) concurred in the sense of admitting different interpretative results. Moreover, the fact that a special *de minimis* regulation expressly included procedural rules as *de minimis* conditions could only lead to the conclusion that the reason for including this rule in a special regime was precisely because such interpretation did not already result from the general *de minimis* regime. If that were the case, there would be no need for such specification in a special regime. However, the wording of the regulations that replaced the two aforementioned regulations (respectively No 1407/2013[64] and No 717/2014[65]) is exactly the same. The literal element of the interpretation has therefore lost that argumentative weight.

On the other hand, it is also arguable that the wording of Article 3(1) of the general *de minimis* regulation, which refers to the *conditions* laid down in this regulation, leaves no room for doubt, insofar as it makes no distinction between the

---

[60] European Commission 2013, p. 24.

[61] The doubt is also raised by certain legal authors, see Nyssens 2008, pp. 443 and 444.

[62] Commission Regulation (EC) No 1998/2006 of 15 December 2006 on the application of Articles 87 and 88 of the Treaty to *de minimis* aid, OJ L 379, 28 December 2006, pp. 5–10.

[63] Commission Regulation (EC) No 875/2007 of 24 July 2007 on the application of Articles 87 and 88 of the EC Treaty to *de minimis* aid in the fisheries sector and amending Regulation (EC) No 1860/2004, OJ L 193, 25 July 2007, pp. 6–12.

[64] Commission Regulation (EU) No 1407/2013 of 18 December 2013 on the application of Articles 107 and 108 of the Treaty on the Functioning of the European Union to *de minimis* aid, OJ L 352, 24 December 2013, pp. 1–8.

[65] Commission Regulation (EU) No 717/2014 of 27 June 2014 on the application of Articles 107 and 108 of the Treaty on the Functioning of the European Union to *de minimis* aid in the fishery and aquaculture sector, OJ L 190, 28 June 2014, pp. 45–54.

type of conditions—and therefore does not authorise the interpreter to make such a distinction.

The guidelines in Court of Justice case-law for the removal of this doubt are also unclear.

Based on case-law that addressed the consequences of the absence or insufficiency of information provided by a MS, with regard to the control of the cumulation of *de minimis* aid,[66] the following should be highlighted: (i) that failure to comply with such information obligation may definitively condition the Commission's analysis, namely by not allowing the proper control of the permitted ceilings and (ii) that the non-compliant MS may not challenge the validity of a Commission decision by relying on the elements not conveyed to the European Commission during the administrative procedure.

In view of the above, the conclusion to be drawn *prima facie* can only be that there is *ipso facto* illegality[67] due to the non-fulfilment of certain procedural conditions (namely the failure to comply with the obligation of MS to provide the European Commission, whenever requested, with information on *de minimis aid*, or the provision of such information in an incomplete form). First of all, because such information was key for the Court of Justice to determine the real recipients of the aid and, consequently, to check that there is no prohibited cumulation of aid; in view of this failure to comply, the aid must be recovered.

However, from the aforementioned case-law one cannot extract the *ratio decidendi* that the sanction will *always* be the same for the violation of *any* and *all* procedural conditions—simply because such jurisdictional decision *only* addresses the obligation to *provide information.*

The extension, *per se*, of that *ratio decidendi* to *all* the procedural conditions may lead to situations of untenable disproportionality. Let us, for the sake of argument, consider that the *de minimis* ceilings (*organisation of control, duration and amount*) have been satisfied but not the obligation to refer expressly to the general *de minimis* regulation, or that its title or the reference to its publication in the *Official Journal of the European Union* have not been mentioned—should such aid be unlawful?

A *broad and theoretical* answer is inadequate, both for automatic illegality and non-legality. The answer must necessarily be found in the light of each specific case, in line with the functional nature of the case-law of the Court of Justice and, above all, in accordance with the principle of proportionality, which is often invoked by the Court[68] and which must be invoked in the light of the nature of the aid in question—*de minimis*—which necessarily differs from the system of State aid.

---

[66] See case C-382/99.

[67] The reason for this interpretation is that the European Commission depends on the MS to obtain information on aid measures.

[68] See, *inter alia*, CJEU, *The Queen, on the application of Alliance for Natural Health and Nutri-Link Ltd v Secretary of State for Health and Alliance for Natural Health v Secretary of State for Health and National Assembly for Wales*, Judgment of the Court, of 12 July 2005, joined cases C-154/04 and C-155/04, ECLI:EU:C:2005:449.

References

Bär-Bouyssière B (2005) Les règlements d'exemption en matière d'aides d'Etat [State aid exemption regulations]. In: Dony M, Smits C (eds) Aides d'État. Éditions de l' Université de Bruxelles, Brussels, pp 170–193

Berghofer M (2007) The New *De Minimis* Regulation: Enlarging the Sword of Damocles? European State Aid Law Quarterly 6: 11–23

Estoa Pérez A (2007) La regulación de las ayudas de MINIMIS en el derecho comunitario: comentario al reglamento (CE) No 1998/2006 [The regulation of MINIMIS aid in Community law: commentary on regulation (EC) No 1998/2006]. Revista de derecho comunitario europeo 11: 623–636

European Commission (2013) Commission Staff Working Document Impact Assessment - accompanying the document - commission regulation (EU) no …/… - on the application of articles 107 and 108 of the Treaty on the Functioning of the European Union to *de minimis* aid - {c(2013) 4448 final} {swd(2013) 522 final} - Brussels, 18 July 2013, swd(2013) 521 final. untitled (europa.eu). Accessed 20 April 2020

European Commission (2019) Targeted consultation to stakeholders on the *De minimis* Regulation. 2019 de minimis (europa.eu). Accessed 20 April 2020

Hofmann H C H (2016) The Legal Framework of Subsidies and State Aid Review. In: Hofmann HCH, Micheau C (eds) State Aid Law of the European Union. Oxford University Press, Oxford, pp 36–62

Hojnik J (2013) *De Minimis* Rule within the EU Internal Market Freedoms: Towards a More Mature and Legitimate Market?". European Journal of Legal Studies 6: 26–27

Nicolaides P (2014) The New Rules on De minimis Aid for 2014-2020: Regulation 1407/2013. The New Rules on De minimis Aid for 2014-2020: Regulation 1407/2013 - Free State Aid blog article - Read now (lexxion.eu). Accessed 4 April 2018

Nyssens H (2008) *De minimis* Part 2 – Chapter 8. In: Mederer W, Pesaresi N, Van Hoof M (eds) EU Competition Law: Volume IV: Book One, State Aid. Claeys and Casteels, Leuven, pp 409–449

Piernas Lopez J J (2015) The Concept of State Aid Under EU Law: From Internal Market to Competition and Beyond. Oxford University Press, United Kingdom

Quigley C (2015) European State Aid Law and Policy, 3rd edn. Hart Publishing, Oxford/Portland, Oregon

Ramos R M G M (1999) Das comunidades à União Europeia: estudos de direito Comunitário [From the Communities to the European Union: studies in Community law], 2nd edn. Coimbra Editora, Coimbra

Sinnaeve A (2014) The Complexity of Simplification: The Commission's Review of the *de minimis* Regulation. European State Aid Law Quarterly 13: 261-276

Van de Casteele K (2016) *De minimis* aid. In: Hancher L, Ottervanger T, Slot PJ (eds) E.U. State Aids, 5th edn. Sweet & Maxwell, London, pp. 235–244

von Donat C (2010) Rescue and Restructuring Aid. In: Heidenhain M (ed) European State Aid Law. Verlag C.H. Beck, Munich, pp 211–240

Zuleger V (2010) *De minimis* Aid. In: Heidenhain M (ed) European State Aid Law. Verlag C.H. Beck, Munich, pp 61–72

Chapter 3
De Minimis Regimes: General and Special

Contents

Abstract This chapter deals with the *de minimis* regimes. It starts with a historical overview of such *de minimis* regimes, goes on to analyse their common aspects, and closes with an analysis of each individual *de minimis* regimes. The chapter highlights the most relevant aspects of the general *de minimis* regime as well as the specificities of the *de minimis* aid to road freight transport. It is also focused on each individual special *de minimis* regimes, i.e., the *de minimis* regime for the agriculture sector, *de minimis* regime for the fishery and aquaculture sector and the *de minimis* regime for the financing of undertakings that provide SGEI.

Keywords *De minimis* regimes · General and special regimes · Road freight transport · Agriculture sector · Fishery and aquaculture sector · SGEI

3.1 Introduction

We mentioned by way of introduction that *de minimis* aid is aid which, in principle, affects the market in a negligible manner, given, in general (but not always, since *de minimis* can be granted to large undertakings with a significant market share) the recipients' very limited importance on the market for the products concerned[1] and the fact that the amount concerned is deemed too low to have a significant effect on

[1] See CJEU, *Voelk v Vervaecke,* Judgment of the Court, 9 July 1969, case 5/69, ECLI:EU:C:1969:35.

© T.M.C. ASSER PRESS and the author 2022

R. Pedro, *De Minimis Aid Under EU Law*,
https://doi.org/10.1007/978-94-6265-543-0_3

trade between MS and competition, being therefore fully and legally exempted from prior notification to the European Commission.

To sum it up, one could argue that it is not State aid for the purposes of Article 107(1) TFEU, but aid of little to no import to the internal market, which is admitted and characterized by the European Commission—which means that the legal presumption that *de minimis* measures have no effect on the internal market and on competition remains.[2]

Although it is not an easy task to set forth a notion of *de minimis* aid, a few characteristic features can be identified with a fair degree of certainty, namely: (i) a *specific regime* taking account of the low amount concerned; (ii) a regime *seeking to strike the balance* between streamlining and non-distortion of competition within the internal market; (iii) *small-scale aid*, subject *to minimum conditions* and involving *low administrative costs* when compared to State aid; (iv) aid benefiting from a rebuttable *legal presumption* of being compatible with the internal market,[3] which may therefore be granted subject to less stringent conditions than those laid down for State aid.

However, it should be made clear that the *de minimis* regime is not binding on the Court of Justice, or in the words of this Court: "(…) *It follows that, although those rules, setting out the approach which the Commission proposes to follow, certainly help to ensure that it acts in a manner which is transparent, foreseeable and consistent with legal certainty, they cannot bind the Court.*"[4] But as the Court of Justice also acknowledges: "(…) *However, they may form a useful point of reference*".[5]

De minimis are not *ex novo* regimes, but have a few forerunner provisions: (i) Community guidelines on State aid for Small- and Medium-sized Enterprises (SMEs) of 1992;[6] (ii) Commission notice on the *de minimis* rule for State aid of 1996;[7] (iii) Article 2 of Council Regulation (EC) No 994/98 of 7 May 1998 on the application of Articles 87 and 88 (former Articles 92 and 93) of the Treaty establishing the European Community to certain categories of horizontal State aid, as amended by Regulation (EU) No 733/2013 of 22 July 2013 amending Regulation (EC) No 994/98 on the application of Articles 92 and 93 of the Treaty establishing the European Community to certain categories of horizontal State aid;[8] (iv) Commission Regulation (EC) No 69/2001 of 12 January 2001 on the application of Articles 87 and 88 of the EC

[2] On this theme, see Bär-Bouyssière 2005, pp. 187 et seq.; Berghofer 2007, p. 17; Estoa Pérez 2007, pp. 631 et seq; Nyssens 2008, pp. 435 et seq.; Zuleger 2010, pp. 64 et seq.; Nicolaides 2014; Pedro 2015, pp. 77 et seq.; Costachescu 2016, pp. 7 et seq; Wolf 2016, pp. 325–327; Van de Casteele 2016, pp. 235–244 and on SGEI, see Wolf 2016, pp. 325–327.

[3] See European Commission 2013, p. 40.

[4] See CJEU, *Italy v Commission,* Judgment of the Court, 7 March 2002, case C-310/99, ECLI:EU:C:2002:143.

[5] See CJEU, *Commission v Greece,* Judgment of the Court, 4 July 2000, case C-387/97, ECLI:EU:C:2000:356.

[6] OJ C 213, 19 August 1992, pp. 2–8.

[7] OJ C 068, 6 May 1996, pp. 9–10.

[8] OJ L 204, 31 July 2013, pp. 11–14.

Treaty to *de minimis* aid,[9] and (v) Commission Regulation (EC) No 1998/2006 of 15 December 2006 on the application of Articles 87 and 88 of the Treaty to *de minimis* aid.[10]

Presently, it should be borne in mind that Article 109 TFEU empowers the Council to set the categories of aid exempt from the obligation to notify the aid to the European Commission and that, pursuant to these powers, the Council, under Regulation (EC) No 994/98—meanwhile replaced by Regulation (EU) No 2015/1588[11]—decided that *de minimis* aid could be one of those categories.

Lastly, the European Commission has approved Regulation (EU) No 1407/2013[12] under review herein, which provides for aid compatible with the internal market. This aid benefits from a *full exemption*, as already mentioned, *no prior notification to the European Commission being required.*[13] The general *de minimis* regulation represents an evolution from previous regulations, amends some rules and maintains other previous rules and practices.[14]

In addition to these developments, the evolution of the types of "legal" instruments drawn upon to regulate *de minimis* aid should also be considered. In other words, *de minimis* aid *'legal rules'* have evolved towards *being increasingly more binding.* Although at first *de minimis* aid was governed by *soft law instruments,*[15] it has come to be governed by *hard law instruments*, in particular by *Regulations.*[16] The *de minimis* regulations under review reveal the continued choice of a Regulation.

3.2 Legal Framework: A Few General Aspects

Considering the general aid theory, the form taken by *de minimis* aid is irrelevant, but its *substance and its effects are crucial.* That is, *de minimis* aid applies only to aid in respect of which it is possible precisely to calculate the gross grant equivalent of the aid *ex ante.*

The legal or administrative "support" adopted to grant the aid is also considered irrelevant, i.e., it does not matter whether it is a contract, a law, an administrative act or otherwise. *De minimis* aid may also be granted as an individual (*ad hoc*) measure or in the context of aid schemes.

---

[9] OJ L 10, 13 January 2001, pp. 30–32.

[10] OJ L 379, 28 December 2006, pp. 5–10.

[11] OJ L 311, 7 December 2018, pp. 8–9.

[12] OJ L 352, 24 December 2013, pp. 1–8.

[13] See Bär-Bouyssière 2005, p. 171.

[14] See Pedro 2015, pp. 66 et seq.

[15] As was the case with the Commission notice on the *de minimis* rule for State aid, OJ C 68, 6 March 1996, p. 9.

[16] This change was brought about by Regulation (EC) No 69/2001, which sought to create a proper and solid *de minimis* aid rule, see Berghofer 2007, p. 13.

Since it is impossible to summarize all the forms that *de minimis* aid can take, some examples are put forward: loan, capital injection, guarantee, financing measures in the form of equity and quasi-equity investment, credit or tax exemption and subsidy or subsidy interest.

Lastly, it should be stressed that the different forms of *de minimis* aid must be expressed in terms of cash subsidy and gross value net of any tax deduction.

As regards the source of funding, on the one hand, there is no distinction between the source of the public funding, so *the general de minimis regulation applies regardless of whether the source is based on national funds or European funds.*[17] On the other hand, it is also irrelevant that the aid is granted by the State (strictly speaking), by other public entities or by third parties, such as the central, regional, local government or other state-controlled bodies, such as state enterprises.

What matters is that it is aid.[18] In that regard, the Court of Justice sustains that "*Community law cannot permit the rules on State aid to be circumvented merely through the creation of autonomous institutions charged with allocating aid*".[19]

The amount of the aid should not be predicated on the risk profile of the recipient. For this reason, a calculation method should be used that is adequate to determine the precise amount of the aid to ensure transparency, equal treatment and effective monitoring by means of limit instruments. There can only be transparency if it is possible to calculate accurately the gross grant equivalent of the aid *ex ante* without any need for a risk assessment.[20]

The general *de minimis* regulation sets out various calculation methodologies in Article 4, clarifying that certain aid must be considered transparent. However, it is a non-exhaustive list comprising:[21] (i) aid included in grants or interest subsidies; (ii) aid included in loans, the gross grant equivalent being calculated on the basis of the reference rate applicable at the time of granting the aid; (iii) aid included in capital

[17] See also already present in the *General Block Exemption Regulation*: Commission Regulation (EC) No 800/2008, meanwhile repealed by Commission Regulation (EU) No 651/2014 of 17 June 2014 declaring certain categories of aid compatible with the internal market in application of Articles 107 and 108 of the Treaty (OJ L 187, 26 June 2014, pp. 1–78), amended by Commission Regulation (EU) 2017/1084 of 14 June 2017 amending Regulation (EU) No 651/2014 as regards aid for port and airport infrastructure, notification ceilings for aid for culture and heritage conservation and for aid for sport and multifunctional recreational infrastructures, and regional operating aid schemes for outermost regions and amending Regulation (EU) No 702/2014 as regards the calculation of eligible costs, OJ L 156, 20 June 2017, pp. 1–18.

[18] According to certain legal authors, the application of this element implies the realization of two "tests", one related to "*imputability to the State*" and the other related to "*weight in the public budget*", see Soltész 2016, pp. 154 et seq.

[19] See CJEU, *France v Commission,* Judgment of the Court, 16 May 2002, case C-482/99, ECLI:EU:C:2002:29.

[20] The transparency element was already required by Regulation (EC) No 1998/2006, as well as the case-law of the Court of Justice, namely the *Wolfgang Heiser v Finanzamt Innsbruck,* Judgment of the Court, 3 March 2005, case C-172/03, ECLI:EU:C:2005:130.

[21] The non-exhaustive character is confirmed by the provisions of Article 4(7), of the general *de minimis* regulation.

injections; (iv) aid included in risk finance measures; (iv) aid included in guarantees; (v) aid included in other instruments, which will be considered as transparent *de minimis* aid, if the instrument provides for a limit ensuring that the relevant ceiling is not exceeded.

Intensive *ex-ante* administrative control effectively complies with aid rules and the MS's duty to cooperate with the European Commission in this respect.[22] In other words, MS must check and ensure that the legally permitted ceiling will not be exceeded by the new aid to be granted before granting any *de minimis* aid.

For this purpose, and as better developed below, there are two possible alternatives:[23] (i) create a central *de minimis* aid register or (ii) obtain a written declaration from the undertaking concerned.

The general *de minimis* regulation entered into force on 1 January 2014, applies until 31 December 2023[24] and is fully binding and directly applicable in all MS. However, the immediately preceding regime, to which this regulation follows, provides in Article 5(3) that, on expiry, *de minimis* aid fulfilling the conditions laid down therein may be validly applied by an additional period of six months, i.e. until the end of June 2014—giving MS sufficient time to adapt to the new regulation.

Of the transitional rules provided for by that regulation, it should be noted that all individual *de minimis* aid granted under the two previous regulations does not fulfil all the criteria set out in Article 107(1) TFEU and is therefore exempt from the notification requirement of Article 108(3) TFEU.

Lastly, as is already common in this type of regulation, the general *de minimis* regulation provides that, for its duration, all *de minimis* aid regimes fulfilling the conditions laid down therein remain in force for an additional period of six months.

3.3 General Regime and Special Regimes: Common Aspects

Despite the different treatment that characterizes each special regime when compared to the general *de minimis* regulation, the *different de minimis* regimes have some common aspects, such as:

[22] See Consolidated version of the Treaty on European Union (TEU), OJ C 326 de 26 November 2012, pp. 13–390, Article 4.

[23] A third alternative, which has already been pointed out by the European Commission, is a creation of a *mandatory central European register*. However, this proposal has not progressed, and the Commission intends to study this possibility. See European Commission 2013, p. 59.

[24] The general *de minimis* regulation originality applies until 31 December 2020, but later the Commission Regulation (EU) 2020/972 of 2 July 2020 amending Regulation (EU) No 1407/2013 as regards its prolongation and amending Regulation (EU) No 651/2014 as regards its prolongation and relevant adjustments, OJ L 215, 7 July 2020, pp. 3–6. The reason is to provide predictability and legal certainty. So, Article 8, the second paragraph of the general *de minimis* regulation was amended and replaced by the following: '*It shall apply until 31 December 2023*'.

(i) *de minimis* regimes must not apply to aid whose amount is set in accordance with the price or quantity of products purchased or placed on the market (albeit with sectoral particularities);
(ii) *de minimis* regimes must not apply to export aid and aid favouring domestic over imported products;
(iii) the three-year period to be taken into account for the purposes of *de minimis* regimes should be assessed on a rolling basis, so that for each new grant of *de minimis* aid the total amount of *de minimis* aid granted during the fiscal year concerned and the two previous fiscal years should be taken into account;
(iv) where the undertakings concerned operate in different economic sectors that may fall within the scope of different *de minimis* regimes, the respective *de minimis* regime must apply to the extent that MS ensure by appropriate means such as the separation of activities or the distinction of costs;
(v) rules are laid down to ensure that the maximum aid intensities laid down in specific regulations or European Commission decisions and other cumulation rules cannot be circumvented (although these may vary depending on the *de minimis* regime concerned);
(vi) *de minimis* regimes must only apply to aid for which it is possible to calculate precisely, *ex ante,* their gross grant equivalent without any need for a risk assessment ('transparent aid');
(vii) *de minimis* aid must be considered as granted when the undertaking becomes entitled to receive the aid under the applicable national framework;
(viii) exceeding the respective ceilings or failing to comply with the relevant requirements entails the non-application of the respective *de minimis* regime and, consequently, the application of the State aid framework;
(ix) for control/monitoring purposes, MS should put in place the necessary tools to ensure that the total amount of *de minimis* aid granted to the same undertaking does not exceed the authorized ceiling;
(x) the principle of irrelevance of the form taken by *de minimis* aid applies;
(xi) the amount of aid payable in several instalments is its discounted value as at the time of grant;
(xii) transitional provisions are laid down stating that it applies to *de minimis* aid granted before its entry into force, provided that such aid meets the requirements in the relevant *de minimis* regime and that, on expiry of the relevant regulation, *de minimis* aid meeting the conditions laid down therein may be validly applied for an additional period of six months.

3.4 *De Minimis* Aid to Road Freight Transport

Although there is no autonomous regulation dedicated to the *de minimis* regime concerning a single undertaking performing road freight transport for hire or reward, it should be noted that the general *de minimis* regulation acknowledges a certain material autonomy of what could be called a fifth type of *de minimis* aid. As such, it must be stressed that the general *de minimis* regime establishes a lower quantitative ceiling for a single undertaking performing road freight transport for hire or reward, namely €100,000.

Therefore, the total amount of *de minimis* aid granted by a MS to a single undertaking performing road freight transport for hire or reward must not exceed €100,000 over any period of three fiscal years. This *de minimis* aid cannot be used for the acquisition of road freight transport vehicles.

The provision of integrated services including actual transport, such as postal or courier, or waste collection or treatment services, shall not be considered as a transport service.

Lastly, if an undertaking engages in road freight transport operations for hire or reward and also carries out other activities to which the ceiling of €200,000 applies, this ceiling will apply to the undertaking, provided that the MS concerned ensure, by appropriate means such as segregation of activities or of costs, that activities in the road freight transport sector do not receive more than €100,000 in aid and that no *de minimis* aid is used for the acquisition of road freight transport vehicles.

3.5 Special *De Minimis* Regimes

3.5.1 De Minimis *Regime in the Agriculture Sector*

This regime is laid down in the regulation on *de minimis* aid for the agriculture sector.[25]

To better understand how this regime evolved, albeit in very brief terms, it should be noted that the quantitative ceiling in this area has been increasing.

That is, until the date of approval of the current regime, i.e., under the immediately preceding regulation,[26] it was considered that aid not exceeding €7500 per recipient over a period of three fiscal years would not distort or threaten to distort competition during three fiscal years, nor would a ceiling of 0.75% of the value of agricultural production established for each MS.

Under the (current) *de minimis* regulation for the agriculture sector, applicable from 1 January 2014, the quantitative ceiling was raised to €15,000 over a period of three fiscal years and the upper threshold to 1% of the value of agricultural production for each MS.

Commission Regulation (EU) 2019/316 of 21 February 2019 amending Regulation (EU) No 1408/2013 on the application of Articles 107 and 108 of the Treaty on

---

[25] Commission Regulation (EU) No 1408/2013 of 18 December 2013 on the application of Articles 107 and 108 of the Treaty on the Functioning of the European Union to *de minimis* aid in the agriculture sector, OJ L 352, 24 December 2013, pp. 9–17.

[26] See Commission Regulation (EC) No 1535/2007 of 20 December 2007 on the application of Articles 87 and 88 of the EC Treaty to *de minimis* aid in the sector of agricultural production, OJ L 337, 21 December 2007, pp. 46–48.

the Functioning of the European Union to *de minimis* aid in the agriculture sector[27] later *changed* the maximum amount of aid to be granted to a single undertaking over a three-year period to €20,000 and the national ceiling increased to 1.25% of annual production.

Additionally, Article 3(3) of the regulation imposes a ceiling at MS level, i.e., the cumulative amount of *de minimis* aid granted by MS to undertakings active in the primary production of agricultural products over any period of three fiscal years shall not exceed the national ceiling set out in Annex I to that Regulation. According to the wording of new paragraph 3A of Article 3, this ceiling can be raised to €25,000 if the additional conditions laid down therein are met. Lastly, it should also be borne in mind that, for the new paragraph 3A of Article 3 to operate, there must be a higher national ceiling, which is set out in Annex II to the regulation in question.

The *de minimis* regulation for the agriculture sector came into force on 1 January 2014 and originally applied until 31 December 2020. Commission Regulation (EU) 2019/316 was later amended and Article 8, second paragraph, was reworded as follows: "*It shall apply until 31 December 2027*".

From a sectoral point of view, under Article 1, the regulation applies to aid granted to undertakings active in the primary production of agricultural products, with three exceptions:

(i) aid the amount of which is fixed on the basis of the price or quantity of products put on the market;[28]
(ii) aid to export-related activities towards third countries or MS, namely aid directly linked to the quantities exported, to the establishment and operation of a distribution network or to other current expenditure linked to the export activity. However, according to recital (7), aid towards the costs of participating in trade fairs, or of studies or consultancy services needed for the launch of a new or existing product on a new market in another MS or a third country does not normally constitute export aid;
(iii) aid contingent upon the use of domestic over imported goods.

In order to clarify the *exclusions* from the scope of the *de minimis* regime under consideration, it is also necessary to take into account, given its interpretative nature, recital (5) which clarifies that processing and marketing of agricultural products are included in the scope of the general *de minimis* regulation.

The quantitative ceiling per undertaking is now €20,000, and the time limit of three fiscal years and the organizational ceiling (based on the concept of "single undertaking") remain.

Article 3(3) imposes an additional limit at MS level, i.e., the cumulative amount of *de minimis* aid granted per MS to undertakings active in the primary production

[27] OJ L 51, 22 February 2019, pp. 1–6.

[28] On the rationale for this exclusion, see recital (6) which clarifies that once the Union has legislated for the establishment of a common organisation of the market in a given sector of agriculture, MS are under an obligation to refrain from taking any measure, which might undermine or create exceptions to it.

of agricultural products over any period of 3 fiscal years cannot exceed the national ceiling set out in Annex I.

According to the wording of new Article 3(3A), this ceiling can be raised to €25,000 if the additional conditions laid down therein are met, and a higher national ceiling is provided for in Annex II.

The *de minimis* regime under consideration imposes several requirements, the cumulation rules standing out:

(i) *de minimis* aid cannot be cumulated with State aid in relation to the same eligible costs or with State aid for the same risk finance measure, if such cumulation exceeds the highest relevant aid intensity or aid amount set in the specific circumstances of each case by a block exemption regulation or a decision adopted by the European Commission;

(ii) *de minimis* aid which is not granted for or attributable to specific eligible costs may be cumulated with other State aid granted under a block exemption regulation or a decision adopted by the European Commission;

(iii) aid under this *de minimis* regime may be cumulated with activities under the general *de minimis* regime up to the relevant ceiling laid down in Article 3(2) of Regulation (EU) No 1407/2013,[29] provided that the MS concerned ensures, by appropriate means such as separation of activities or distinction of costs, that the primary production of agricultural products does not benefit from *de minimis* aid granted in accordance with the general *de minimis* regime;

(iv) aid under this regime may be cumulated with activities under the *de minimis* regime for the fishery and aquaculture sector up to the ceiling laid down in that regime, provided that the MS concerned ensures, by appropriate means such as separation of activities or distinction of costs, that the primary production of agricultural products does not benefit from *de minimis* aid granted in accordance with the *de minimis* regime for the fishery and aquaculture sector.

3.5.2 De Minimis *Regime in the Fishery and Aquaculture Sector*

This regime is laid down in the *de minimis* regulation for the fisheries and aquaculture sector[30] and, unlike in the agriculture sector, no distinction is made between the primary sector, processing and marketing.

The *de minimis* regulation for the fisheries and aquaculture sector came into force on 1 July 2014 and was originally applicable until 31 December 2020. Commission Regulation (EU) 2020/2008 of 8 December 2020 amending Regulations (EU) No 702/2014, (EU) No 717/2014 and (EU) No 1388/2014, as regards their period of

[29] OJ L 352, 24 December 2013, pp. 1–8.

[30] Commission Regulation (EU) No 717/2014 of 27 June 2014 on the application of Articles 107 and 108 of the Treaty on the Functioning of the European Union to *de minimis* aid in the fishery and aquaculture sector, OJ L 190, 28 June 2014, pp. 45–54.

application and other relevant adjustments[31] later amended their period of validity until 31 December 2022.

From a sectoral point of view, under its Article 1 this regulation applies, as a rule, to aid granted to undertakings in the fisheries and aquaculture sector. For this purpose, "*fisheries or aquaculture sector*" means the sector of the economy which includes all activities of production, processing and marketing of fisheries or aquaculture products.[32]

However, there are *eleven exceptions* (the first three general and the remaining specific to the fisheries and aquaculture sector), which we transcribe for ease of reference: (i) aid the amount of which is fixed on the basis of price or quantity of products purchased or put on the market; (ii) aid to export-related activities towards third countries or MS, namely aid directly linked to the quantities exported, to the establishment and operation of a distribution network or to other current expenditure linked to the export activity;[33] (iii) aid contingent upon the use of domestic over imported goods; (iv) aid for the purchase of fishing vessels; (v) aid for the modernisation or replacement of main or ancillary engines of fishing vessels; (vi) aid to operations increasing the fishing capacity of a vessel or equipment increasing the ability of a vessel to find fish; (vii) aid for the construction of new fishing vessels or importation of fishing vessels; (viii) aid to the temporary or permanent suspension of fishing activities unless specifically provided for in the Regulation (EU) No 508/2014;[34] (ix) aid to exploratory fishing; (x) aid to the transfer of ownership of a business; (xi) aid to direct restocking, unless explicitly provided for as a conservation measure by a Union legal act or in the case of experimental restocking.

In general, the (i) quantitative ceiling per recipient is €30,000; (ii) the time limit is three fiscal years and (iii) the organizational ceiling is based on the concept of "single undertaking", and (iv) a ceiling at MS level is imposed.

In addition, it should be borne in mind that it is a general principle of particular relevance in this regard that no aid should be granted if EU law, in particular the rules of the Common Fisheries Policy, is not complied with. This principle also applies to *de minimis* aid.

Lastly, we must take into account that specific rules on cumulation are provided for:

---

[31] OJ L 414, 9 December 2020, pp. 15–18.

[32] See Article 5(d) of the Regulation (EU) No 1379/2013 of the European Parliament and of the Council of 11 December 2013 on the common organisation of the markets in fishery and aquaculture products, amending Council Regulations (EC) No 1184/2006 and (EC) No 1224/2009 and repealing Council Regulation (EC) No 104/2000, OJ L 354, 28 December 2013, pp. 1–21.

[33] However, aid towards the costs of participating in trade fairs, or of studies or consultancy services needed for the launch of a new or existing product on a new market in another MS or a third country does not normally constitute export aid.

[34] Regulation (EU) No 508/2014 of the European Parliament and of the Council of 15 May 2014 on the European Maritime and Fisheries Fund and repealing Council Regulations (EC) No 2328/2003, (EC) No 861/2006, (EC) No 1198/2006 and (EC) No 791/2007 and Regulation (EU) No 1255/2011 of the European Parliament and of the Council, OJ L 149, 20 May 2014, pp. 1–66.

(i) *de minimis* aid granted for activities in the fishery and aquaculture sector in accordance with this Regulation *may be cumulated* with *de minimis* aid granted in respect of the latter sector(s) or activities up to the relevant ceiling laid down in Article 3(2) of Regulation (EU) No 1407/2013, provided that the MS concerned ensures, by appropriate means such as separation of activities or distinction of costs, that the activities in the fishery and aquaculture sector do not benefit from *de minimis* aid granted in accordance with Regulation (EU) No 1407/2013;

(ii) *de minimis* aid granted in accordance with Regulation (EU) No 1408/2013 *may be cumulated* with *de minimis* aid in the fishery and aquaculture sector in accordance with this Regulation up to the ceiling laid down therein, provided that the MS concerned ensures, by appropriate means such as separation of activities or distinction of costs, that the primary production of agricultural products does not benefit from *de minimis* aid granted in accordance with this Regulation;

(iii) the *de minimis* aid under consideration shall not be cumulated[35] with State aid in relation to the same eligible costs or with State aid for the same risk finance measure, if such cumulation would exceed the highest relevant aid intensity or aid amount fixed in the specific circumstances of each case by a block exemption regulation or a decision adopted by the European Commission;

(iv) *de minimis* aid which is not granted for or attributable to specific eligible costs *may be cumulated* with other State aid granted under a block exemption regulation or a decision adopted by the European Commission.

3.5.3 **De Minimis** ***Regime for the Financing of Undertakings Providing SGEI***

A special regime is currently foreseen for the financing of undertakings providing SGEI which is already in the form of a regulation.[36]

According to this regulation, aid up to €500,000 per undertaking over a period of three fiscal years is exempt from European State aid rules if it is granted as consideration for the provision of SGEI. The basis for the law to accept this kind of consideration is the fact that the amounts concerned are too low to distort competition.

However, the quantitative ceiling is higher than the ceilings of the general *de minimis* regime as the grant is supposed to measure the balance, at least in part, of the higher costs incurred for the provision of public services.

---

[35] It should be noted that the regulation under analysis contains an oversight, as, indeed, happened with the general *de minimis* regulation. However, the general *de minimis* regulation was rectified and the former was not. To summarize, the word "no" was deleted by mistake or oversight. The oversight remains in the Portuguese version, but not, e.g., in the English version.

[36] Commission Regulation (EU) No 360/2012 of 25 April 2012 on the application of Articles 107 and 108 of the Treaty on the Functioning of the European Union to *de minimis* aid granted to undertakings providing services of general economic interest, OJ L 114, 26 April 2012, pp. 8–13.

E.g., public utilities such as the drinking water service may receive up to €500,000 in aid over a three-year period without the need for notification to and analysis by the European Commission.

In addition to the conditions common to the various *de minimis* regimes, the main features of the *de minimis* aid regime for the financing of SGEI[37] are set out below. One should stress from the outset that this aid must be granted in writing (to ensure that only SGEI benefit from this regime).

Only aid which does not exceed €500,000 over a period of three fiscal years is allowed (this amount is assessed on a rolling basis and fractioning the aid is prohibited). It should be noted that if the amount exceeds the relevant ceiling, that amount may not benefit from this *de minimis* regime, even for a fraction not exceeding that ceiling.[38]

The *de minimis* regime for the financing of undertakings providing SGEI, as a rule, applies to all undertakings providing SGEI, although it is a rule with the following *exceptions* and therefore not applicable to aid:

(i) granted to undertakings active in the fisheries and aquaculture sector;
(ii) granted to undertakings active in the primary production of agricultural product;
(iii) granted to undertakings active in the processing and marketing of agricultural products when the amount of the aid is fixed on the basis of the price or quantity of such products purchased from primary producers or put on the market by the undertakings concerned and/or when the aid is conditional on being partly or entirely passed on to primary producers;
(iv) granted to export-related activities towards third countries or MS (namely aid directly linked to the quantities exported, to the establishment and operation of a distribution network or to other current expenditure linked to the export activity);
(v) contingent upon the use of domestic over imported goods;
(vi) granted to undertakings active in the coal sector;[39]
(vii) granted to undertakings performing road freight transport for hire or reward;
(viii) granted to undertakings in difficulty.

The regulation in question sets out several cumulation rules, providing that *de minimis* aid to undertakings providing SGEI:

---

[37] Alternatively, the financing of undertakings providing SGEI can be based on the general *de minimis* regulation, on the terms set out in recital (14) of the *de minimis* regulation on the financing of undertakings providing SGEI.

[38] See CG, *Regione autonoma della Sardegna and others v Commission,* Judgment of the Court, 20 September 2011, joined cases T-394/08, T-408/08, T-453/08 and T-454/08, ECLI:EU:T:2011:493.

[39] The following definition should be taken into account: *"coal" shall mean high-grade, medium-grade and low-grade category "A" and "B" coals as defined by the United Nations Economic Commission for Europe's classification in the International Coding System for Coals.* See 2010/787/EU, Council Decision of 10 December 2010 on State aid to facilitate the closure of uncompetitive coal mines, OJ L 336, 21 December 2010, pp. 24–29.

(i) cannot be cumulated with State aid in respect of the same eligible costs if such cumulation would result in an aid intensity exceeding that stipulated in the specific circumstances of each case by a block exemption regulation or decision adopted by the European Commission;
(ii) may be cumulated with *de minimis* aid under other *de minimis* regulations up to the ceiling of €500,000;
(iii) may not be cumulated with any compensation in respect of the same service of general economic interest, regardless of whether it constitutes State aid.[40]

The regulation entered into force on April 29 of 2012 and expired on December 31 of 2018. Commission Regulation (EU) 2020/1474 of 13 October 2020 amending Regulation (EU) No 360/2012 as regards the extension of its period of application and a time-bound derogation for undertakings in difficulty to take into account the impact of the COVID-19 pandemic[41] later extended the period of application until 31 December 2023.

References

Baldi CE (2016) La disciplina comunitaria degli aiuti di Stato: manuale critico ad uso delle amministrazioni e delle imprese [The Community framework for State aid: a critical handbook for administrations and enterprises]. Santarcangelo di Romagna (Rimini), Maggioli

Bär-Bouyssière B (2005) Les règlements d'exemption en matière d'aides d'Etat [State aid exemption regulations]. In: Dony M, Smits C (eds) Aides d'État. Éditions de l' Université de Bruxelles, Brussels, pp 170–193

Berghofer M (2007) The New *De Minimis* Regulation: Enlarging the Sword of Damocles? European State Aid Law Quarterly 6: 11–23

Costachescu A (2016) The Comparative Analysis between the Minimis Aid/The Regional State Aid. Romanian Competition Journal 1–2:1–37 https://doi.org/10.2139/ssrn.2894819

Estoa Pérez A (2007) La regulación de las ayudas de MINIMIS en el derecho comunitario: comentario al reglamento (CE) No 1998/2006 [Regulation of de MINIMIS aid in EU law: commentary on regulation (EC) No 1998/2006]. Revista de derecho comunitario europeo 11: 623–636

European Commission (2013) Commission Staff Working Document Impact Assessment - accompanying the document - commission regulation (EU) no .../... - on the application of articles 107 and 108 of the Treaty on the Functioning of the European Union to *de minimis* aid - {c(2013) 4448 final} {swd(2013) 522 final} - Brussels, 18 July 2013, swd(2013) 521 final. untitled (europa.eu). Accessed 20 April 2020

Nicolaides P (2014) The New Rules on *De minimis* Aid for 2014–2020: Regulation 1407/2013. The New Rules on De minimis Aid for 2014-2020: Regulation 1407/2013 - Free State Aid blog article - Read now (lexxion.eu). Accessed 4 April 2018

Nyssens H (2008) *De minimis* Part 2 – Chapter 8. In: Mederer W, Pesaresi N, Van Hoof M (eds) EU Competition Law: Volume IV: Book One, State Aid. Claeys and Casteels, Leuven, pp 409–449

Pedro R (2015) Auxílios *de minimis* 2014-2020: Notas à luz do Regulamento (UE) n.º 1407/2013 [*De minimis* aid 2014-2020: Notes in the light of Regulation (EU) No 1407/2013]. Revista de Concorrência e Regulação 17: 65–95

[40] To understand some critical points of this regime, see Baldi 2016, p. 409.
[41] OJ L 337, 14 October 2020, pp. 1–2.

Quigley C (2015) European State Aid Law and Policy, 3rd edn. Hart Publishing, Oxford/Portland, Oregon
Soltész U (2016) Part II B - The definition of State Aid. In: Säcker FJ, Montag F (eds) European State Aid Law: A Commentary. Verlag C.H. Beck, Munich, pp 154–174
Van de Casteele K (2016) *De minimis* aid. In: Hancher L, Ottervanger T, Slot PJ (eds) E.U. State Aids, 5th edn. Sweet & Maxwell, London, pp 235–244
Wolf M (2016) Services of General Economic Interest. In: Säcker FJ, Montag F (eds) European State Aid Law: A Commentary. Verlag C.H. Beck, Munich, pp 295-381
Zuleger V (2010) *De Minimis* Aid. In: Heidenhain M (ed) European State Aid Law. Verlag C.H. Beck, Munich, pp 61–72

Chapter 4
Scope of the General *De Minimis* Regime

Contents

Abstract This chapter deals with the definition of the *de minimis* regimes’ scope, namely the material scope and the personal scope, and the case-law for the general *de minimis* regime. The scope of *de minimis* regimes needs to be understood if one is to enforce them properly; to this end, we assess the notion of “single undertaking”, both from the perspective of the legal frameworks and from the perspective of CJEU case-law. Since the *de minimis* regimes are often applied in the context of European funding, in particular European, Structural and Investment Funds frameworks, the

© T.M.C. ASSER PRESS and the author 2022

R. Pedro, *De Minimis Aid Under EU Law*,
https://doi.org/10.1007/978-94-6265-543-0_4

concept of "single undertaking" needs to be reviewed against the concept of "beneficiary" of such funds. "Firms in difficulty" is another relevant notion that needs to be assessed within the scope of application of *de minimis* regimes to determine which *de minimis* aid may or may not be granted to "firms in difficulty". Lastly, we review the *de minimis* aid regime related to mergers, acquisitions, or spin-offs of undertakings.

Keywords *De minimis* aid · Undertaking · Single undertaking · Beneficiary · Firms in difficulty · Mergers and acquisitions

4.1 Material and Personal Scope: General

4.1.1 Material Scope

Although *de minimis* aid has historically been developed to benefit Small- and Medium-sized Enterprises and, in practice, it is in fact SMEs that are the main recipient group of such aid,[1] the general *de minimis* regulation ultimately applies to both SMEs and large undertakings, as it does not distinguish between the two. The notion of SMEs can be taken from European soft law, namely the Commission Recommendation of 6 May 2003 on the definition of micro, small and medium-sized enterprises (2003/361/EC).[2]

In addition, the general *de minimis* regime applies, as a rule, to undertakings across all sectors except certain sectors of activity listed therein, which is to say that, on the one hand, less consideration is given to the recipient and more to the nature of the business to which the support is granted[3] and, on the other hand, considering all exceptions, the interpreter is to understand that all other sectors must be included.

This means that a given legal entity may receive low-amount aid for various businesses, provided that they meet the relevant requirements as arising from a combination of the different *de minimis* regulations.

The issue of *mixed/hybrid entities,*[4] i.e., certain recipients of aid that carry out both economic and non-economic activities, must also be discussed in connection with the material scope, which raises the question of whether *de minimis* aid only includes support provided to economic activities or whether it also allows for support provided to non-economic activities.

The question is also relevant in terms of State aid. That is, considering the specific nature of certain activities, namely culture and heritage conservation, it should be

[1] See Pedro 2015, p. 70.

[2] Commission Recommendation of 6 May 2003 concerning the definition of micro, small and medium-sized enterprises C (2003) 1422), OJ L 124, 20 May 2003, pp. 36–41.

[3] See Baldi 2016, p. 136.

[4] See GC, *POA v Commission*, Judgment of General Court, 8 February 2018, case T-74/16, ECLI:EU:T:2018:75, paras 83 and 84.

taken into account that these may be organised in a non-commercial way and therefore be of a non-economic nature. Public funding may therefore not constitute State aid.[5]

However, where an entity carries out both economic and non-economic activities it would seem appropriate to accept the rule that any public funding it receives will be covered by State aid rules only insofar as it covers the economic activities' costs.[6] The entity is therefore required to keep separate accounts for the different funding received in order to exclude any risk of "cross-subsidisation" of its economic activities by the public funds it receives for its non-economic activities.

Lastly, as far as *de minimis* aid is concerned, according to the position of the Court of Justice,[7] the rule laid down for State aid seems to be accepted, i.e., that only the advantages which the mixed entity—carrying out both economic and non-economic activities—has derived from any economic activities may be taken into account for the purposes of calculating the required quantitative ceiling, since non-economic activities must be excluded from this calculation.

4.1.2 Personal Scope

With regard to the personal scope, it should be stressed, as legal authors do for the previous regime, that some of the concepts used by the regulations to implement the *de minimis* regimes, namely that of "*single undertaking*" and "*firms in difficulty*"' are simplified to a fault and therefore not without risk[8]—creating practical application problems that are not always easy to overcome, either by the granting authorities or by the entities responsible for monitoring them.

The concept of a *single undertaking* proves difficult to apply, mainly because it is an *autonomous* concept of European Competition Law and economic in character.

The problem becomes more acute when MS build their monitoring on the *legal concept of undertaking*[9]—creating a large gap between the concept provided for in the *de minimis* regime and its practical application.

---

[5] Moreover, the European Commission considers that public funding of a cultural or heritage conservation activity which is accessible to the public free of charge fulfils a purely social and cultural function which is non-economic in nature. See Commission Notice on the notion of State aid as referred to in Article 107(1) of the Treaty on the Functioning of the European Union (2016/C 262/01), OJ C 262, 19 July 2016, pp. 1–50.

[6] See Commission Notice on the notion of State aid as referred to in Article 107(1) of the Treaty on the Functioning of the European Union (2016/C 262/01), OJ C 262, 19 July 2016, pp. 1–50.

[7] See case T-74/16, paras 83 and 84.

[8] One of the characteristics of *de minimis* regulation has always been its apparent or even putative simplification. See, among many, Bär-Bouyssière 2005, p. 188; Berghofer 2007, p. 20 and Sinnaeve 2014, p. 261.

[9] European Commission 2013, p. 50.

4.2 Material Scope: Economic Activity Sectors

4.2.1 In General

Considering the rule that the general *de minimis* regulation applies to all sectors except those sectors which are expressly excluded, it is therefore necessary to identify and analyse the excluded sectors. Article 1(1) of the general *de minimis* regulation sets forth that activities in the following sectors are excluded from the general *de minimis* regime.

In other words, special *de minimis* rules are laid down for the fishery, aquaculture, and agriculture sectors on the grounds that the amounts provided for in the general *de minimis* regulation, if applied to those sectors, could distort or threaten to distort competition.

4.2.2 Exclusions

Article 1(1)(a) of the general *de minimis* regulation excludes from the scope of the regulation aid granted to undertakings active in the fishery and aquaculture sector, as covered by Council Regulation (EC) No 104/2000. This regulation has since been *repealed* by Regulation (EU) No 1379/2013.[10]

According to Article 5 of the above cited act: (i) "'*Fishery and aquaculture sector*' *means the sector of the economy which comprises all activities of production, processing and marketing of fishery or aquaculture products*" [subparagraph (d)]; (ii) "'*Fishery products*' *mean aquatic organisms resulting from any fishing activity or products derived therefrom, as listed in Annex I*" [subparagraph (a)]; (iii) "'*Aquaculture products*' *mean aquatic organisms at any stage of their life cycle resulting from any aquaculture activity or products derived therefrom, as listed in Annex I*" [subparagraph (b)].

Article 1(1)(b) of the general *de minimis* regulation excludes from the regulation aid granted to undertakings active in the agricultural products primary production sector.

According to Article 2(1)(a), "'*Agricultural products*' *means the products listed in Annex I to the Treaty, with the exception of fishery and aquaculture products covered by Regulation (EC) No 104/2000*". However, Annex I to the Treaty covers both primary products (live animals, cereals, etc.) and processed products (wine, oil, olive oil, etc.).[11]

---

[10] Regulation (EU) No 1379/2013 of the European Parliament and of the Council of 11 December 2013 on the common organisation of the markets in fishery and aquaculture products, amending Council Regulations (EC) No 1184/2006 and (EC) No 1224/2009 and repealing Council Regulation (EC) No 104/2000, OJ L 354, 28 December 2013, pp. 1–21.

[11] See Baldi 2016, p. 139.

Agricultural products seem therefore to be defined by "what they are not" instead of by "what they are", i.e., their definition is the result of comparing this particular definition and the definition of *'Processing of agricultural products '*, as set out in Article 2(1)(b) of the general *de minimis* regulation, which is: "*any operation on an agricultural product resulting in a product which is also an agricultural product, except on-farm activities necessary for preparing an animal or plant product for the first sale*".

Pursuant to Article 1(1)(c), aid granted to undertakings active in the sector of processing and marketing of agricultural products is excluded in the following cases: (i) where the amount of the aid is fixed on the basis of the price or quantity of such products purchased from primary producers or put on the market by the undertakings concerned,[12] or (ii) where the aid is conditional on being partly or entirely passed on to primary producers.

The concept of *processing* of agricultural products in this context is, as can be seen from the immediately preceding point, offered by Article 2(1) (b) of the regulation under consideration and the notion of *'Marketing of agricultural products'* is set forth in subparagraph (c) and means "*holding or display with a view to sale, offering for sale, delivery or any other manner of placing on the market, except the first sale by a primary producer to resellers or processors and any activity preparing a product for such first sale; a sale by a primary producer to final consumers shall be considered as marketing if it takes place in separate premises reserved for that purpose*".

In the context set out above, this regulation could apply to the processing and marketing of certain agricultural products.[13] This option is justified by the fact that such products have moved away from regulation of the primary production sector to a more traditional regulation of services and industry characterized by the open market.[14]

Therefore, as stated in recital (7) of the general *de minimis* regulation, considering the similarities between the processing and marketing of agricultural products and of non-agricultural products, this regulation should apply to the processing and marketing of agricultural products, provided that certain conditions are met. Neither on-farm activities necessary for preparing a product for the first sale, such as the harvesting, cutting and threshing of cereals, or the packing of eggs, nor the first sale

[12] The rationale for this exclusion is found in the case-law of the Court of Justice when clarifying in the CJEU *France v Commission,* Judgment of the Court, 12 December 2002, case C-456/00, ECLI:EU:C:2002:753, para 31: "*(...) where there is a regulation on the common organisation of the market in a given area, the Member States are under an obligation to refrain from taking any measures which might undermine or create exceptions to it*". For this reason and as explained in recital (8) of the general *de minimis* regulation, "*this Regulation should not apply to aid the amount of which is fixed on the basis of the price or quantity of products purchased or put on the market. Nor should it apply to support which is linked to an obligation to share the aid with primary producers*". In short, for the protection of the aforementioned common market organization, these exclusions were provided for.

[13] Bacon 2017, p. 404.

[14] Nyssens 2008, p. 419.

to resellers or processors should be considered as processing or marketing in this respect.

Exclusion of export aid to third countries (e.g. trade fair costs and costs of launching a product). The basis for this exclusion is found in the agreements the Union has in place with the World Trade Organization[15] and the fact that this type of aid tends to affect the market more intensively than other aid.[16]

In particular, aid granted directly on the basis of quantities exported, the establishment and operation of a distribution network or other current expenditure relating to export activity is excluded—such aid is prohibited *per se.*[17] However, according to recital (9), aid towards the costs of participating in trade fairs, or of studies or consultancy services needed for the launch of a new or existing product on a new market in another MS or a third country does not normally constitute export aid.

Lastly, it should be borne in mind that aid contingent on the use of domestic over imported goods is excluded.

4.2.3 Undertakings Active in Sectors Excluded and Not Excluded Under the General **De Minimis** *Regime*

The exclusion list suggests that there are undertakings active in various sectors, some of which are excluded from this regulation while others are not.

Thus, despite these exclusions, if these undertakings are active in non-excluded sectors or activities, the general *de minimis* regulation should apply to these sectors or activities if the MS ensures appropriate separation of activities or costs from different activities or sectors not excluded.[18]

4.2.4 General **De Minimis** *Regime in Action*

In order to determine the material scope, i.e., to identify the sectors of economic activity which are included in and excluded from the scope of the general *de minimis* regulation, it is important to understand how they are implemented in the national context.

Strictly speaking, the problem arises in the specific determination of the excluded sectors, since the regulation under consideration generally applies to "*aid granted*

[15] Van de Casteele 2016, p. 237.

[16] Nyssens 2008, p. 417.

[17] Ibid, p. 418.

[18] However, if an undertaking receives aid under a specific *de minimis* regime and under this regulation, the *de minimis* ceiling provided for in this regulation must consider both. See Nyssens 2008, p. 422.

to undertakings in all sectors, with the exception of" aid listed in the different subparagraphs of Article 1(1), as provided for therein.

That is, the problem is to determine, in practical terms, which sectors of activity are excluded from the *de minimis* regime.

However, and despite the immediate conclusion that can be drawn simply by reading the above rule, the fact is that the review of the different subparagraphs of Article 1(1), in particular subparagraphs (d) and (e), leads to the conclusion that, in order to understand them, it may not be sufficient to determine the sector of economic activity concerned, but it may also be necessary to identify *paradigmatic types of aid which are highly likely to affect competition*, such as export aid and for the promotion of domestic products. For, although Article 1(1)(a), (b) and (c) are part of a sectoral logic, this is not the case with the other subparagraphs.

In practical terms, the application of this regime may involve three operations: (i) specifically determining the activities of a particular sector [that is the case with subparagraphs (a), (b) and (c)] and, in some situations, once the previous task is complete; (ii) establishing if there are other requirements, such as whether "*the amount of the aid is fixed on the basis of the price or quantity of such products purchased from primary producers or put on the market by the undertakings concerned*" or whether the aid is "*conditional on being partly or entirely passed on to primary producers*" [which is the case with subparagraph (c)] and (iii) assessing whether such aid is intended for export-related activities [that is the case of subparagraph (d)] or to favour domestic products [that is the case of subparagraph (e)].

In short, one needs to make a *case-by-case* assessment according to the above-mentioned parameters as provided for by Article 1(1).

In addition, the practical application of the rules in the general *de minimis* regulation requires that, on top of the interpretation of the legal hypothesis included in each subparagraph, legal/technical notions/descriptions related to certain products and product lists be considered, in particular to understand the scope of *agricultural products* set out in Article 38 TFEU and the list of products included in Annex I TFEU.

The practical problem arises, *inter alia*, with regard to "agricultural products" which, under the general *de minimis* regulation, are the "*products listed in Annex I TFEU, with the exception of fishery and aquaculture products covered by Regulation (EC) No 104/2000*".[19] In other words, it is necessary to determine in particular the products included in Annex I TFEU.

In view of the correct determination of the scope of the products included in Annex I TFEU, the eight-digit Combined Nomenclature (CN)[20] can be drawn upon,

[19] Regulation (EU) No 1379/2013 of the European Parliament and of the Council of 11 December 2013 on the common organisation of the markets in fishery and aquaculture products, amending Council Regulations (EC) No 1184/2006 and (EC) No 1224/2009 and repealing Council Regulation (EC) No 104/2000, OJ L 354, 28 December 2013, pp. 1–21.

[20] Council Regulation (EEC) No 2658/87 of 23 July 1987 on the tariff and statistical nomenclature and on the Common Customs Tariff, OJ L 256, 7 September 1987, pp. 1–675.

although it is not always easy to determine whether a given product is included or not.[21]

Also, according to certain legal authors,[22] other instruments (in some way) useful for the interpretation of Annex I TFEU should be considered, even if only as mere guides/auxiliaries and not exhaustive, such as: (i) Regulation (EU) No 1308/2013 of the European Parliament and of the Council of 17 December 2013 establishing a common organisation of the markets in agricultural products and repealing Council Regulations (EEC) No 922/72, (EEC) No 234/79, (EC) No 1037/2001 and (EC) No 1234/2007[23] and (ii) Regulation (EU) No 510/2014 of the European Parliament and of the Council, of April 16, 2014, laying down the trade arrangements applicable to certain goods resulting from the processing of agricultural products and repealing Council Regulations (EC) No 1216/2009 and (EC) No 614/2009.[24]

In practice, to establish whether the *de minimis* rules for the agriculture sector or the general *de minimis* rules will apply to a given project, the analysis should not be limited to the recipient (*maxime*, single undertaking) but rather encompass the purpose of the incentive.

In summary, in light of the *de minimis* regimes, the core business activities of the undertaking (in abstract) and the classification of its economic activity are not relevant, but rather the specific activity for which the incentive is requested. Consequently, if the investment relates to the primary activity (*e.g.* a tractor), the *de minimis* rule for the agriculture sector applies; however, if an expense is involved for processing (*e.g.* grape press) or marketing (*e.g.* refrigerator to keep unripe fruit intended for direct sale to the public) activity, the general *de minimis* rules apply.[25]

---

[21] Foszczynski and Stobiecka-Kuik 2008, p. 1512.

[22] Ibid, p. 1512.

[23] OJ L 347, of 20.12.2013, pp. 671–854. The doctrine referred to the date of Regulation (EEC) No 827/68 of the Council of 28 June 1968 on the common organisation of the market in certain products listed in Annex II to the Treaty, which was *repealed* by Council Regulation (EC) No 1234/2007 of 22 October 2007 establishing a common organisation of agricultural markets and on specific provisions for certain agricultural products (Single CMO Regulation), which in turn was *repealed* by Regulation (EU) No 1308/2013 of the European Parliament and of the Council of 17 December 2013 establishing a common organisation of the markets in agricultural products and repealing Council Regulations (EEC) No 922/72, (EEC) No 234/79, (EC) No 1037/2001 and (EC) No 1234/2007 OJ L 347, 20 December 2013, pp. 671–854.

[24] OJ L 150, 20 May 2014, pp. 1–58. The doctrine referred to the date of Annex B of Council Regulation (EC) No 3448/93 of 6 December 1993 laying down the trade arrangements applicable to certain goods resulting from the processing of agricultural products, which was *repealed* by Regulation (EC) No Council Regulation (EC) No 1216/2009 of 30 November 2009 laying down the trade arrangements applicable to certain goods resulting from the processing of agricultural products, which in turn was *repealed* by Regulation (EU) No 510/2014 of the European Parliament and of the Council of 16 April 2014 laying down the trade arrangements applicable to certain goods resulting from the processing of agricultural products and repealing Council Regulations (EC) No 1216/2009 and (EC) No 614/2009, OJ L 150, 20 May 2014, pp. 1–58.

[25] Such a solution shall be valid provided that the other requirements of Article 1(1)(c) of the general *de minimis* rule are met.

4.3 Personal Scope: Notion of "Single Undertaking"

4.3.1 Notion of "Undertaking" for the Purpose of Applying the State Aid Regime

The Treaties do not include a notion of "*undertaking*", leaving it to the Court of Justice to develop. This Court has developed a case-law concept from a functional perspective,[26] that is, based on the economic activity, encompassing "*any entity engaged in an economic activity, regardless of its legal status and the way in which it is financed*",[27] and "*that any activity consisting in offering goods and services on a given market is an economic activity*"[28] and not from a subjective/legal perspective (otherwise the effectiveness of EU law would be contingent on the classification made by each MS).[29]

The Court of Justice has consistently defined '*undertakings*' as entities engaging in an economic activity, irrespective of their legal status and how they are financed. That is, it has developed an approach focused on the notion of economic activity.[30] The only relevant criterion is whether such an entity carries on an economic activity.

The classification of an entity as an undertaking is therefore entirely predicated on the nature of its activities. Therefore: (i) the status of the entity under national law is not decisive; (ii) it becomes irrelevant whether or not it is a for-profit entity;[31] (iii) if an entity engages in both economic and non-economic activities, it is considered as an undertaking only to the extent of its economic activities.

European case-law has already made it clear that the concepts of undertaking and economic activity are identical in all spheres of competition law, regardless of whether they are addressed to undertakings or States, since all these provisions have a common purpose, namely that provided for in Article 3(1)(b) TFEU, i.e., to establish a system ensuring that competition in the internal market is not distorted.[32]

---

[26] Quigley 2015, p. 54.

[27] See CJEU, *Höfner and Elser v Macrotron,* Judgment of the Court, 23 April 1991, case C-41/90, ECLI:EU:C:1991:161, and, *AOK-Bundesverband and others,* Judgment of the Court, 16 March 2004, joined cases C-264/01, C-306/01, C-354/01 and C-355/01, ECLI:EU:C:2004:150.

[28] See, among others, CJEU, *Commission v Italy,* Judgment of the Court, 18 June 1998, case C-35/96, ECLI:EU:C:1998:303, and, *Pavlov and others,* Judgment of the Court, 12 September 2000, joined cases C-180/98, C-181/98, C-182/98, C-183/98 and C-184/98, ECLI:EU:C:2000:428.

[29] See, among others, CJEU, case C-41/90 and *Cassa di Risparmio di Firenze and others,* Judgment of the Court, 10 January 2006, case C-222/04, ECLI:EU:C:2006:8.

[30] Santer 2016, pp. 74 et seq.

[31] See, among others, CJEU, *MOTOE v Elliniko Dimosio,* Judgment of the Court, 1 July 2008, case C-49/07, ECLI:EU:C:2008:37.

[32] See CG, *Freistaat Sachsen and others v Commission,* Judgment of the Court, 24 March 2011, joined cases T-443/08 and T-455/08, ECLI:EU:T:2011:117, and CJEU, *Mitteldeutsche Flughafen and Flughafen Leipzig-Halle v Commission,* Judgment of the Court, 19 December 2012, case C-288/11 P, ECLI:EU:C:2012:821.

However, the Court of Justice has already determined that the concept of *"economic unity"* in State aid may differ from that applicable in other areas of competition law.[33] In other words, from the case-law of the Court of Justice one derives, on the one hand, a *functional approach*[34] and, on the other, an approach focused on the notion of *economic activity.*[35]

As regards the *first approach*, an "undertaking" does not depend on national undertakings and partnerships legislation or on national provisions on commercial activities (commercial / companies' law), but only on State aid.

The internal legal configuration is therefore irrelevant and national law cannot change the understanding of the concept of 'undertaking' for the purposes of applying the State aid regime.

As regards the *second approach*—focusing on the notion of economic activity—it should be noted that one of its practical effects is the possibility of considering groups of entities (e.g. groups of undertakings[36] or holdings[37]) as a single undertaking. See, by way of example, the Dutch petrol stations case, where it was decided to treat more than 600 petrol stations and one oil company as one single undertaking.[38]

Underlying that qualification operation is the reasoning that several separate legal entities can be regarded as forming an economic unit for the purposes of applying the State aid rules. That economic unit is then considered to be the relevant undertaking.

In this regard, the Court of Justice finds it relevant that there is a *controlling interest*[39] and other *functional, economic, and organic links,*[40] which constitute an *industrially and financially coherent whole.*[41]

---

[33] See CJEU, *AceaElectrabel Produzione v Commission,* Judgment of the Court, 16 December 2010, case C-480/09 P, ECLI:EU:C:2010:787.

[34] See, among others, Quigley 2015, p. 54; Santer 2016, pp. 74 et seq.

[35] See Santer 2016, pp. 74 et seq.

[36] See Quigley 2015, pp. 55 et seq.

[37] Ibid, p. 57.

[38] See CJEU, *Netherlands v Commission,* Judgment of the Court, 13 June 2002, case C-382/99, ECLI:EU:C:2002:363.

[39] On the one hand, such control can take place regardless of whether the aid recipient has direct contact with the market or not: *"However, that may be the case both of an operator in direct contact with the market and, indirectly, of another entity controlling that operator as part of an economic unit which they together form"*. See CJEU, *Cassa di Risparmio di Firenze and others,* Judgment of the Court, 10 January 2006, case C-222/04, ECLI:EU:C:2006:8, para 110.

[40] See case C-480/09 P, para 51: *"What may reveal that it is possible to exercise functions relating to control, direction and financial support—going beyond the simple placing of capital by an investor—and illustrate the existence of organic and functional links between an entity owning a controlling shareholding in a company and the controlled company itself, is the fact that members of the management committee and the controlling body of that entity are appointed to the equivalent bodies of the controlled company (see, to that effect, Cassa di Risparmio di Firenze and Others, paragraphs 116 and 117)"*.

[41] See case C-480/09 P, para 48: *"The former company and the new operating companies can form an economic unit, inter alia, where the restructuring carried out constitutes an indivisible*

In addition, the notion "*single economic entity*" arises from several Court of Justice judgments in application of competition law.

However, as the Court of Justice underlines, it is a concept of variable geometry, i.e., the concept of *economic unity* in State aid may differ from that which applies in other areas of competition law.[42]

From the point of view of secondary European law, it should be noted that it establishes procedures and thresholds for considering that a group of undertakings should qualify as a "single undertaking" (see GBER[43] and some *de minimis* regimes).

Lastly, it should be noted that the rules of secondary European law cannot render the rules of primary European law on State aid ineffective but must be interpreted in such a way as to guarantee the effectiveness of primary law. This means that undertakings that do not formally have one or any of the other relationships described in secondary law may still be considered as a "single undertaking" by the Court of Justice.[44]

In summary, the underlying justification for overcoming the concept of legal entity in favour of a concept that is more economic and factual in character is the effectiveness of European Union law.

---

whole, from an industrial and economic point of view (see, to that effect, Intermills v Commission, paragraph 12)".

[42] See case C-480/09 P.

[43] Commission Regulation (EU) No 651/2014 of 17 June 2014 declaring certain categories of aid compatible with the internal market in application of Articles 107 and 108 of the Treaty, OJ L 187, 26 June 2014, pp. 1–78.

[44] See CJEU, *HaTeFo GmbH v Finanzamt Haldensleben,* Judgment of the Court, 27 February 2014, case C-110/13, ECLI:EU:C:2014:114 paras 34 and 35: "*Therefore the fourth subparagraph of Article 3(3) of the Annex to the SME Recommendation must be interpreted in the light of that objective, so that enterprises which do not formally have one or other of the relationships referred to in paragraph 28 above, but which, because of the role played by a natural person or group of natural persons acting jointly, nevertheless constitute a single economic unit, must also be regarded as linked enterprises for the purposes of that provision, since they engage in their activities or in part of their activities in the same relevant market or in adjacent markets (see, by analogy, Italy v Commission, paragraph 51). 35 Moreover, the condition that natural persons are acting jointly is satisfied where those persons work together in order to exercise an influence over the commercial decisions of the enterprises concerned which precludes those enterprises from being regarded as economically independent of one another. Whether that condition is satisfied depends on the circumstances of the case, and that is not necessarily conditional on the existence of contractual relations between those persons or even a finding that they intended to circumvent the definition of an SME*".

4.3.2 *Notion of "Single Undertaking" for the Purposes of Applying the General* De Minimis *Regime*

The most relevant novelty of the *de minimis* discipline in force results from the concept of a "single undertaking",[45] i.e., roughly the possibility that a group of undertakings can be considered as a single subject for the purposes of allocating aid.

It is in the context referred to above that the notion of 'single undertaking' *can be* understood and *must be* understood. However, the evolution of this concept in *de minimis* aid and its configuration in the light of the current framework must be considered.

As will be explained in more detail below, in order to benefit from the *de minimis* regime, the aid must take into account three elements (or thresholds), including the fact that its recipient must be a single undertaking. In other words, an organizational threshold for an undertaking must be abided by.

However, it should be stated that the general *de minimis* regulation, while referring to the single undertaking, does not contain a definition of undertaking.

Regarding the notion to be considered, it should be borne in mind that it has been the subject of "evolutionary" treatment, for lack of a better expression.

Thus: (i) the concept of "*enterprise*" was used in Regulation (EC) No 69/2001,[46] and (ii) Regulation (EC) No 1998/2006 uses the term "*undertaking*". These developments were chiefly warranted by the need to ensure that Court of Justice case-law would require the European Commission to ascertain the actual recipients of the aid.[47]

These developments have (iii) moved a step forward with the current general *de minimis* regulation, which (still) refers to the concept of "*single undertaking*".

The amendment is based on the fact that the concept provided for in the previous framework is not easy to apply in practical terms, in particular for local and regional authorities.

This concept was based on the "*linked enterprises*"[48] criterion set out in Commission Recommendation 2003/361/EC[49] and the Annex to the previous GBER[50].

The option taken by the European Commission was to look for a balanced notion, i.e., a notion that could satisfy the need to apply an economic notion of undertaking,

---

[45] See Baldi 2016, p. 140.

[46] See also Nicolaides 2005, pp. 434 et seq.

[47] Van de Casteele 2016, p. 238.

[48] See European Commission 2013, p. 41.

[49] Commission Recommendation of 6 May 2003 concerning the definition of micro, small and medium-sized enterprises C (2003) 1422), OJ L 124, 20 May 2003, pp 36–41.

[50] Commission Regulation (EC) No 800/2008 of 6 August 2008 declaring certain categories of aid compatible with the common market in application of Articles 87 and 88 of the Treaty (General block exemption Regulation). OJ L 214, 9 August 2008, pp. 3–47.

on the one hand, and provide a clear definition for the purpose of checking each case, on the other hand.[51]

From these criteria, the European Commission selected those which it considered most appropriate for the purposes of applying the *de minimis* framework.

In view of the above, the general *de minimis* regulation seems to presuppose a broader concept of undertaking, which is more economic (economic group) than legal (individual entity) and identifies it with any entity engaged in an economic activity, regardless of its status legal[52] and how it is financed.[53,54]

For the purposes hereof, from the point of view of secondary European law, in particular, the general *de minimis* regime, the concept of a *"single undertaking"* should be considered, which is subject to a set of criteria for its proper identification, as described below.

4.3.3 Defining "Single Undertaking" Criteria

We need to take a closer look at the defining elements or criteria of the notion of "*single undertaking*".

Based on the case-law notion of undertaking, that is, any entity engaged in an economic activity—economic activity being understood as the supply of goods or services in a given market—and taking into account some of the criteria of the "*linked enterprise*"' concept as set out in Commission Recommendation 2003/361/EC,[55] the general *de minimis* regulation predicates its implementation on the concept of single undertaking, i.e., entities controlled by the same entity (on a legal or *de facto* basis). Joint control is a key element in the discovery of the single undertaking.

The clarification of the notion of a single undertaking must result from the balance struck between the need to apply an economic notion of enterprise and the objective of providing the public authorities with a clear definition which is not too costly to achieve in each individual case.

---

[51] Sinnaeve 2014, p. 267.

[52] Therefore, the status that the entity assumes under national law is irrelevant. Relevant is whether it carries out an economic activity.

[53] It is also irrelevant whether it is a for-profit entity or not. See, among others, case C-49/07.

[54] If a specific entity develops economic and non-economic activities, it should only be considered as an undertaking to the extent of the economic activities it carries on.

[55] Commission Recommendation of 6 May 2003 concerning the definition of micro, small and medium-sized enterprises (2003/361/CE), OJ L 124, 20 May 2003, pp. 36–41.

Article 2(2) of the general *de minimis* regulation[56] sets out several criteria for the identification of the single undertaking, and considers that it includes all enterprises (SMEs or large undertakings) having at least one of the following relationships with each other:

(i) *"one enterprise has a majority of the shareholders' or members' voting rights in another enterprise;*
(ii) *one enterprise has the right to appoint or remove a majority of the members of the administrative, management or supervisory body of another enterprise;*
(iii) *one enterprise has the right to exercise a dominant influence over another enterprise pursuant to a contract entered into with that enterprise or to a provision in its memorandum or articles of association;*
(iv) *one enterprise, which is a shareholder in or member of another enterprise, controls alone, pursuant to an agreement with other shareholders in or members of that enterprise, a majority of shareholders' or members' voting rights in that enterprise;*
(v) *Enterprises having any of the relationships referred to through one or more other enterprises shall also be considered to be a single undertaking."*

4.3.4 Case-Law on the Concept of a "Single Undertaking" Under the De Minimis *Regime*

Although the case-law on the above-mentioned subject is very scarce, there is a landmark ruling that assessed the validity of State aid and de *minimis aid*.

First of all, this Court of Justice case-law insists on a case-by-case analysis in the light of the available factual elements.[57] To this end, the Court considers that the guiding criterion must be that all entities (legally or *de facto*) controlled by the same entity should be regarded as a single undertaking.[58]

[56] This notion is also followed in (i) the *de minimis* regulation for the agriculture sector, in Article 2(2) and (ii), in Article 2(2) of the *de minimis* regulation for the fishery and aquaculture sector. However, this notion does not appear expressly in the *de minimis* regulation on the financing of undertakings that provide SGEI, which in recital (20), refers to "*same undertaking*". Despite the difficulty in offering a clear and express answer—from the outset, due to the ambiguity of the European Commission's position—, from a practical point of view, namely, in terms of the connection between the various *de minimis* regimes, a certain doctrine advocates the application of the same concept of "single undertaking" also to the *de minimis* regime concerning the financing of undertakings that provide SGEI. See Baldi 2016, pp. 156 et seq. However, another part of the doctrine understands that the notion of "single undertaking" should not be applied, but the general notion of "undertaking" should be applied. In this sense, see Sinnaeve 2014, p. 275.

[57] See case C-382/99. The CG, *Kuwait Petroleum (Nederland) v Commission,* Judgment of the Court, 31 May 2006, case T-354/99, ECLI:EU:T:2006:137 should also be considered, which, to a large extent, repeats the arguments of the Court of Justice judgment cited above.

[58] See case C-382/99.

The need to specifically establish the existence of a single undertaking is firstly warranted by the Court of Justice based on the need to avoid the risk of undue aid[59] cumulation as a result of one undertaking exercising *de facto* control over another.[60,61]

The notion of "single undertaking" seems to have a strong precedent in European case-law,[62] namely the judgment of the Court of Justice, *Kingdom of the Netherlands v Commission of the European Communities*, 13 June 2002, C-382/99.[63]

In very brief terms, the facts underlying the case were the following: the Kingdom of the Netherlands adopted a temporary regulation on subsidies payable to service stations located near the German border. The regulation provided for the grant of a subsidy of NLG 0.10 per litre of petrol to operators located within 10 km of the border between the Netherlands and Germany, and of NLG 0.05 per litre of petrol to operators located between 10 and 20 km from that border.

The regulation (i) provided that in the event of an increase in the German excise duties, the disparity in the excise duties levied, which was the reason for the aid scheme, would decrease; (ii) set a ceiling on the subsidies equivalent to ECU 100,000 over a period of three years (from 1 July 1997 to 30 June 2000 inclusive), i.e., the ceiling laid down in the European Commission's Notice; and (iii) established that the aid was aid per applicant, which covered any natural or legal person, or successor in title thereto, on whose behalf, or at whose risk, one or more service stations were operated.

Subsequently, the European Commission was notified of a draft amendment to the scheme, establishing that the subsidy would no longer be granted per applicant but per service station. The aim of the draft amendment was to remove the imbalance between service stations in respect of the level of subsidies received.

In its arguments, the Court of Justice submitted the following ideas:

(i) "*real recipient*", stating in recital (32): "*According to the Commission, in order to verify that there is no cumulation of aid, the real recipient of the aid must be identified. In the present case, the recipient could be a service station but it could also be a larger economic entity such as an oil company, where, as a result of that aid, that company did not have to make compensatory payments or paid less compensation to service stations linked to it by a PMS clause, than if there had been no aid*";

(ii) "*economic entity*", stating in recital (37): "*As regards the substance of the case, it should be observed that, inasmuch as the scheme at issue provides for aid to be granted per service station, by definition it provides for the owner of several service stations, all operated by him, to receive as many grants of*

[59] See case C-382/99.

[60] See case C-382/99.

[61] The concern about the transfer of aid from one company to another warrants an investigation in case of suspicion. See Nicolaides 2005, pp. 434 et seq.

[62] See Baldi 2016, p. 140.

[63] See case C-382/99.

aid as he owns service stations. Such a system thus carries a risk of exceeding the de minimis ceiling per recipient, an outcome prohibited by the Notice";

(iii) "*risk of cumulation*", clarifying in recital (34): "*As to the obligation to state reasons, it is apparent from paragraph 74 of the Decision that, according to the Commission, for the purpose of applying the de minimis rule, it is necessary to 'determin[e] who the actual aid recipient is and whether the de minimis threshold has been complied with for each recipient'. Furthermore, in paragraph 69 of the Decision, the Commission states that there is a 'risk of aid cumulation' where 'one owner possesses several service stations' or where 'the supplier has de facto control over the dealer by virtue of an exclusive purchasing agreement'. It is also apparent from paragraph 82 of the Decision that aid cumulation of the kind prohibited by the Notice occurs in cases where 'the same company owns and operates several service stations' or where 'the same dealer has applied for aid more than once and therefore appears several times in the list of eligible recipients'*";

(iv) "*de facto control*", stating in recital (38): "*The Commission also correctly inferred that there is a similar risk of cumulation of aid where an oil company has de facto control over service-station operators, whose freedom is limited by exclusive purchasing and lease agreements. In that case, as is apparent from paragraphs 60 to 66 of this judgment, the oil company may likewise be regarded as the real recipient of the aid granted to the service stations, inasmuch as the grant of such aid renders any PMS clause redundant*".

4.3.5 Notion of "Single Undertaking" and Legal Concept of "Beneficiary" of ESIF

For a better practical understanding of this topic, it becomes relevant to collate the notion of "single undertaking" and that of "beneficiary", by reference to situations in which it is subject to the *de minimis* regime.

From a practical point of view, the proper understanding of the notion of "single undertaking" appears to be or is put to the test whenever, e.g., there is an application for registration on the electronic platform of the general *de minimis* aid of a "beneficiary", namely, of ESIF, and it becomes imperative to know if this beneficiary fulfils the requirements imposed to ensure competition (mainly, by ascertaining whether that beneficiary may or may not receive *de minimis* aid due to cumulation with any other aid).

In summary, the "beneficiary" and "single undertaking" concepts meet whenever the entity responsible for the control/monitoring of *de minimis* aid is tasked with determining whether the organizational, temporal and quantitative thresholds of any new aid financed by ESIF are met.

In other words, in practice, in view of the need to carry out the task of determining whether a specific ESIF beneficiary[64] *may* or *may not* receive a financial incentive (which implies, from the outset, the fulfilment of the material and personal conditions of eligibility on the part of the Managing Authority), the *de minimis* control entity is faced with the task of ascertaining whether that potential beneficiary of ESIF meets the *de minimis* aid requirements or not.

In short, they are distinct legal concepts, that of "beneficiary" functionally oriented towards the fulfilment of a certain financial regime (ESIF) and the second, that of "single undertaking" designed to guarantee the competition rules (*in casu, de minimis* aid).

Therefore, and taking into account that the notion of a single undertaking, has already been established, it is now important to clarify the notion of "beneficiary", which is found in the acts related to the ESIF.

At European level, the general ESIF regulation in force,[65] in terms of operational definitions, defines "beneficiary" in its Article 2(10),"*a public or private body and, for the purposes of the EAFRD Regulation and of the EMFF Regulation only, a natural person, responsible for initiating or both initiating and implementing operations; and in the context of State aid schemes, as defined in point 13 of this Article, the body which receives the aid; and in the context of financial instruments under Title IV of Part Two of this Regulation, it means the body that implements the financial instrument or the fund of funds as appropriate*".

It is important to bear in mind that, in practical terms, the concept of "beneficiary" becomes useless for the purpose of applying the *de minimis* regime, since this concept is only relevant for the purposes of applying the ESIF, as in the *de minimis* regime, it is a question of whether it has received an undue advantage, that is, whether the beneficiary is a "single undertaking".

This is easily understood since the aid can constitute a direct advantage for the formal "recipient" and an indirect advantage for other subjects of the "group", that is, for the real "recipient", as it will tend to happen with venture capital funds, consortia, groups of undertakings, etc.[66]

[64] Or rather, a potential beneficiary, since he can only be a beneficiary if he complies with the requirements imposed by the *de minimis* regimes.

[65] Regulation (EU) No 1303/2013 of the European Parliament and of the European Council of 17 December 2013 laying down common provisions for the European Regional Development Fund (ERDF), the European Social Fund (ESF) and the Cohesion Fund, the European Agricultural Fund for Rural Development (EAFRD) and the European Maritime and Fisheries Fund (EMFF), which are necessary to ensure the effectiveness of the ESI Funds and the coordination of the Funds with one another and with other Union instruments, OJ L 347, 20 December 2013, pp. 320–469.

[66] Baldi 2016, p. 33.

4.3.6 *Application of the Concept of "Single Undertaking" by a Member State*

De minimis aid received by a "single undertaking" can be cumulated with other *de minimis* aid granted by any public authority in the same MS. That is, Article 3(2) of the general *de minimis* regulation made it clear that the €200,000 ceiling applies per MS.[67,68]

Thus, if a recipient is part of an international group, the control of any *de minimis* aid received by another entity of the same group in another MS is not required. In short, the MS is only responsible for controlling *de minimis* aid granted within its borders.

This solution is reinforced by the fact that it is a rather difficult to control from a practical point of view.[69]

4.4 Personal Scope: Legal Concept of "Firms in Difficulty"

4.4.1 *Background and Current Regime*

The European Commission seems to be of two minds[70] regarding the possibility of firms in difficulty qualifying for *de minimis* aid: the aid was permitted under Regulation (EC) No 69/2001, then no longer permitted under Regulation (EC) No 1998/2006,[71] having resurfaced in the current general *de minimis* regulation.[72]

It should be noted that the concept of "firm in difficulty" proper has been discussed and amended to become a simpler concept, namely by removing "personal" elements and replacing them with "material" elements associated with financial ratios.[73]

---

[67] See Van de Casteele 2016, p. 240.

[68] The previous general *de minimis* regulation was not clear, see Nyssens 2008, p. 431; Nicolaides 2014.

[69] See Sinnaeve 2014, p. 266.

[70] See Van de Casteele 2016, p. 237.

[71] See CG, *Heitkamp BauHolding v Commission*, Judgment of the Court, 4 February 2016, case T-287/11, ECLI:EU:T:2016:60.

[72] On the positions taken by the MS in the preparation of the general *de minimis* regulation in force, see Baldi 2016, p. 137. The solution sought to reduce administrative control costs, see Sinnaeve 2014, p. 268.

[73] See Soltész and Lyons 2017, p. 424.

4.4.2 De Minimis *Aid that May Be Granted to "Firms in Difficulty"*

In light of the above developments, the European Commission has reverted to its original position,[74] namely that aid to firms in difficulty is once again not excluded from the scope of the general *de minimis* regulation.

In short, there is a rule that allows the grant of *de minimis* aid to firms in difficulty. However, that rule must take into account the exception which prohibits the granting of *de minimis* aid comprised in loans or guarantees. That is, as is clear from Article 4(3) and (6) of the general *de minimis* regulation,[75] aid comprised in loans and guarantees is considered as transparent *de minimis* aid if *"the beneficiary is not subject to collective insolvency proceedings nor fulfils the criteria under its domestic law for being placed in collective insolvency proceedings at the request of its creditors"*. Therefore, *a contrario sensu*, in the event of insolvency, such aid will not be considered transparent and, under Article 4(1) of the general *de minimis* regime[76], will not be eligible for this *de minimis* regime.

4.4.3 De Minimis *Aid that Cannot be Granted to "Firms in Difficulty"*

According to the *de minimis* regulation on the financing of undertakings providing SGEI, the framework established therein should not apply to firms in difficulty within the meaning of the Community Guidelines on State aid for rescuing and restructuring firms in difficulty,[77] since it is not appropriate to grant operating aid to firms in difficulty outside a restructuring context and it is difficult to determine the gross grant equivalent of aid granted to such undertakings.

It should also be noted that even if there is a situation where the *de minimis* regime allows aid to be granted to a firm in difficulty, such support may be prohibited by another legal regime, as is the case with Regulation (EU) No 1301/2013 of the European Parliament and of the Council of 17 December 2013 on the European Regional Development Fund, on the European Regional Development Fund and on specific provisions concerning the Investment for growth and jobs goal and repealing Regulation (EC) No 1080/2006 ("ERDF").[78]

---

[74] See Van de Casteele 2016, p. 237.

[75] This rule is replicated in (i) Article 4(3) and (6), of the *de minimis* regime for the agriculture sector and in (ii) Article 4(3) and 6, of the *de minimis* regime for the fishery and aquaculture sector.

[76] This rule is replicated (i) in Article 4(1) of the *de minimis* regime for the agriculture sector and (ii) in Article 4(1) of the *de minimis* regime for the fishery and aquaculture sector.

[77] OJ C 244, 1 October 2004, p. 2. Subsequently, in 2014, the Communication from the Commission—Guidelines on State aid for rescuing and restructuring firms in difficulty (2014/C 249/01) was approved. OJ C 249, 31 July 2014, pp. 1–28.

[78] OJ L 347, 20 December 2013, pp. 289–302.

In view of the wording of Article 3(3)(d) of the above regulation, which provides that the ERDF does not support undertakings in difficulty, as defined under Union State aid rules,[79] certain legal authors make it clear that this rule should also apply to *de minimis* aid financed by that fund,[80] i.e., funding through the ERDF is prohibited even if a *de minimis* regime permits it.

4.4.4 Issues in Connection with the Legal Concept of "Firms in Difficulty"

The European Commission's policy in this area is that firms in difficulty are excluded from the State aid regulations and European Commission guidelines (with the exception of the rescuing and restructuring guidelines), since aid to firms in difficulties is among the most distortive types of State aid.

In a way, state intervention to save a company in difficulty is forbidden as a rule.[81]

The admission of aid to firms in difficulty brings to light the paradox that exists between the *strict* conditions under which State aid for the restructuring of firms in difficulty[82] may be granted and the *ease* with which *de minimis* aid may be granted to undertakings in those conditions.

This contradiction becomes more obvious in view of the problems encountered by MS in determining the difficulty in which the firm finds itself as well as its gross grant equivalent.[83]

For these reasons, the *de minimis* regime for financing SGEI undertakings does not apply to firms in difficulty.

If, on the one hand, firms in difficulty can now benefit from an easier aid instrument, on the other hand, given the high rate of failure to rehabilitate firms in difficulty, an instrument may have been created that enables the misuse of public money and is very difficult to control by MS, and not controlled at all by the European Commission.[84]

---

[79] A similar solution can be found with regard to the Cohesion Fund. See Article 2(2)(e) of Regulation (EU) No 1300/2013 of the European Parliament and of the Council of 17 December 2013 on the Cohesion Fund and repealing Council Regulation (EC) No 1084/2006, OJ L 347, 20 December 2013, pp. 281–288.

[80] See Costachescu 2016, p. 23.

[81] See recital 4 of the Communication from the Commission—Community guidelines on State aid for rescuing and restructuring firms in difficulty, OJ C 244, 1 October 2004, p. 2.

[82] Using the *principle of single aid*, in order to avoid that, because of State aid, undertakings are artificially in operation.

[83] In fact, this was the reason in the previous general *de minimis* regulation (recital 7) for excluding firms in difficulty from the *de minimis* aid regime.

[84] However, the European Commission's desire for control can be seen in European Commission 2013, pp. 21 et seq.

There is also concern regarding the *moral hazard* created by aid to such undertakings[85]—undertakings that predict that they are likely to be helped when they are in difficulty may tend to adopt overly risky and unsustainable business strategies.

Moreover, the prospect of rescue and restructuring aid for a given undertaking may artificially reduce its cost of capital, affording it an undue competitive advantage on the market.

In addition, in the context of *de minimis* regimes, the difficulty in determining what is a "firm in difficulty" adds to the complexity of identifying the "single undertaking", i.e., MS find themselves in deeper trouble at the time of granting *de minimis* aid due to the need to recognize if undertakings are really in "difficulty" and who actually has "control" over them.

4.4.5 Guiding Elements of the Legal Concept of "Firms in Difficulty"

It must be clarified from the outset that there is no *"firm in difficulty"* concept to be found in primary European Union law,[86] even though the General Court has already held that the evidence relating, *inter alia*, to the level of losses and financial debts is capable of demonstrating *per se* the character of the firm in difficulty.[87]

In addition, the *Commission Notice—Guidelines on State aid for rescuing and restructuring non-financial firms in difficulty*[88] provides, in paragraph 24, that some references in the field, in particular of State aid, therefore prohibit undertakings in difficulty from receiving aid.

For such purposes, and save as otherwise provided for therein, paragraph 24 (a) defines "firms in difficulty" as undertakings in difficulty within the meaning of paragraph 20 of these guidelines, i.e. "*(...) a company is considered in difficulty when, without intervention by the State, it will almost certainly be condemned to going out of business in the short or medium term*".

Paragraph 20 provides for a relatively objective "test"[89] which considers that a firm is in difficulty if at least one of the following circumstances occurs:

"*(a) In the case of a limited liability company, where more than half of its subscribed share capital has disappeared as a result of accumulated losses. This is the case when deduction of accumulated losses from reserves (and all other elements generally considered as part of the own funds of the company) leads to a negative cumulative amount that exceeds half of the subscribed share capital;*

---

85 See Quigley 2015, p. 403.

86 Ibid, p. 405.

87 See, among others, CG, *Corsica Ferries France v Commission,* Judgment of the Court, 15 June 2005, case T-349/03, ECLI:EU:T:2005:221, and *Région Nord-Pas-de-Calais v Commission,* Judgment of the Court, 12 May 2011, joined cases T-267/08 and T-279/08, ECLI:EU:T:2011:209.

88 OJ C 249, 31 July 2014, pp. 1–28.

89 See Soltész and Lyons 2017, p. 424.

(b) In the case of a company where at least some members have unlimited liability for the debt of the company, where more than half of its capital as shown in the company accounts has disappeared as a result of accumulated losses;

(c) Where the undertaking is subject to collective insolvency proceedings or fulfils the criteria under its domestic law for being placed in collective insolvency proceedings at the request of its creditors;

(d) In the case of an undertaking that is not an SME, where, for the past two years: (i) the undertaking's book debt to equity ratio has been greater than 7,5 and (ii) the undertaking's EBITDA interest coverage ratio has been below 1,0."

4.5 Personal Scope: Mergers, Acquisitions, or Spin-Offs of Undertakings

4.5.1 Mergers and Acquisitions

In response to the questions raised by stakeholders and MS, the general *de minimis* regulation clarified the rules applicable in the case of mergers and acquisitions.[90]

That is, for the first time, *de minimis* regimes regulate the different mergers and acquisitions scenarios. Article 4(8) of the general *de minimis* regime sets forth that all prior *de minimis* aid granted to any of the merging undertakings will be taken into account in determining whether any new *de minimis* aid to the new or the acquiring undertaking exceeds the relevant ceiling.

De minimis aid lawfully granted before the merger or acquisition remains lawful.[91]

Clearly, the concern regarding the proper application of the *de minimis* regime in the event of mergers, acquisitions or spin-offs of undertakings did not slip the European Commission's attention when preparing the *current de minimis* regime.[92,93]

However, contrary to what might be expected, State aid law has not paid much attention to the subject of mergers and acquisitions: despite, among other things, its relevance to the application of *de minimis* regimes, State aid law does not offer a definition of merger and acquisition.[94]

---

[90] See Soltész 2016, p. 232.

[91] It should be noted that this regime is repeated in relation to the *de minimis* regime for the agriculture sector and in relation to the *de minimis* regime for the fishery and aquaculture sector. However, this is not the case for the *de minimis* regime for the financing of undertakings that provide SGEIs. Despite the silence of the law, a certain doctrine believes that it applies, see Sinnaeve 2014, p. 275.

[92] See European Commission 2013, p. 29.

[93] It should be noted that the previous regime did not provide for any regime on these topics.

[94] The concern with both the legal approach and the economic approach is mainly related to "*the alteration, or not, of the control rights over a undertaking or part of it, more than the existence, or not, of a single legal personality, the most important thing is that assets previously subject to an*

4.5.2 *Spin-off of an Undertaking into Two or More Separate Undertakings*

As with mergers, the general *de minimis* regime is also innovative in respect of the spin-off of one undertaking into other undertakings. Article 4(9) sets forth that if one undertaking spins off into two or more separate undertakings, *de minimis* aid granted prior to the spin-off will be allocated to the undertaking that benefited from it, which is in principle the undertaking taking over the activities for which the *de minimis* aid was used.

If such an allocation is not possible, the *de minimis* aid will be allocated proportionately on the basis of the book value of the equity capital of the new undertakings at the effective date of the spin-off.

Although the Article is unclear on whether *de minimis* aid lawfully granted before the spin-off remains lawful, certain legal authors hold that this principle should also apply to these situations.[95]

In this context, it is important not to overlook the case-law of the Court of Justice[96] which has drawn attention to the fact that, even in the event of a de *jure spin-off*, a control relationship may remain, that is, a mere spin-off may not mean, in the long run, that the undertakings concerned do not continue to receive the aid.

In this regard, it should also be borne in mind that: (i) "*49 It is also apparent from the Court's case-law that an entity which, owning controlling shareholdings in a company, actually exercises that control by involving itself directly or indirectly in the management thereof must be regarded as taking part in the economic activity carried on by the controlled undertaking (Case C-222/04 Cassa di Risparmio di Firenze and Others [2006] ECR I-289, paragraphs 112 and 118)*" and (ii): "*50 If that is not the case, the simple separation of an undertaking into two different entities, the first of which pursues directly the former economic activity and the second of which controls the first, being fully involved in its management, would be sufficient to deprive the rules of the European Union relating to State aid of their practical effect. It would enable the second entity to benefit from subsidies or other advantages granted by the State or by means of State resources and to use them in whole or in part for the benefit of the former, in the interest, also, of the economic unit formed by the two entities (Cassa di Risparmio di Firenze and Others, paragraph 114)*".

---

independent economic rationality center, after a certain operation, become dependent on a single economic rationality center". In this sense, see Matos and Rodrigues 2000, p. 21.

[95] See Baldi 2016, p. 153.

[96] See case C-480/09 P, paras 49 and 50.

References

Bacon K (2017) European Union law of State aid, 3rd edn. Oxford University Press, Oxford

Baldi CE (2016) La disciplina comunitaria degli aiuti di Stato: manuale critico ad uso delle amministrazioni e delle imprese [The Community framework for State aid: a critical handbook for administrations and enterprises]. Santarcangelo di Romagna (Rimini), Maggioli

Bär-Bouyssière B (2005) Les règlements d'exemption en matière d'aides d'Etat [State aid exemption regulations]. In: Dony M, Smits C (eds) Aides d'État. Éditions de l' Université de Bruxelles, Brussels, pp 170–193

Berghofer M (2007) The New *De Minimis* Regulation: Enlarging the Sword of Damocles? European State Aid Law Quarterly 6: 11–23

Costachescu A (2016) The Comparative Analysis between the Minimis Aid/The Regional State Aid. Romanian Competition Journal 1–2:1–37 https://doi.org/10.2139/ssrn.2894819

European Commission (2013) Commission Staff Working Document Impact Assessment - accompanying the document - commission regulation (EU) no .../... - on the application of articles 107 and 108 of the Treaty on the Functioning of the European Union to *de minimis* aid - {c(2013) 4448 final} {swd(2013) 522 final} - Brussels, 18 July 2013, swd(2013) 521 final. untitled (europa.eu). Accessed 20 April 2020

Foszczynski A, Stobiecka-Kuik F (2008) Chapter 15 - Part 4. In: Mederer W, Pesaresi N, Van Hoof M (eds) EU Competition Law: Volume IV: Book Two, State Aid. Claeys and Casteels, Leuven, pp 1511–1558

Matos P V, Rodrigues V (2000) Fusões e aquisições: motivações, efeitos e política [Mergers and acquisitions: reasons, effects and policy]. Principia, S. João do Estoril

Nicolaides P (2005) Puzzles of State Aid: Structural Funds, Cumulation and *De Minimis*. European State Aid Law Quarterly: 3: 433–440

Nicolaides P (2014) The New Rules on *De minimis* Aid for 2014–2020: Regulation 1407/2013. The New Rules on De minimis Aid for 2014-2020: Regulation 1407/2013 - Free State Aid blog article - Read now (lexxion.eu). Accessed 4 April 2018

Nyssens H (2008) *De minimis* Part 2 – Chapter 8. In: Mederer W, Pesaresi N, Van Hoof M (eds) EU Competition Law: Volume IV: Book One, State Aid. Claeys and Casteels, Leuven, pp 409–449

Pedro R (2015) Auxílios *de minimis* 2014–2020: Notas à luz do Regulamento (UE) n.º 1407/2013 [*De minimis* aid 2014–2020: Notes in light of Regulation (EU) No 1407/2013]. Revista de Concorrência e Regulação 17: 65–95

Quigley C (2015) European State Aid Law and Policy, 3rd edn. Hart Publishing, Oxford/Portland, Oregon

Santer W (2016) The Notion of Undertaking. In: Hofmann HCH, Micheau C (eds) State Aid Law of the European Union. Oxford University Press, Oxford, pp 74–83

Sinnaeve A (2014) The Complexity of Simplification: The Commission's Review of the *de minimis* Regulation. European State Aid Law Quarterly 13: 261–276

Soltész U (2016) Part II B The definition of State Aid. In: Säcker FJ, Montag F (eds) European State Aid Law: A Commentary. Verlag C.H. Beck, Munich, pp 228–243

Soltész U, Lyons B (2017) Rescue and Restructuring Aid. In: Werner P, Verouden V (eds) EU State Aid Control: Law and Economics. Kluwer Law International, The Netherlands, pp 415–437

Van de Casteele K (2016) *De minimis* aid. In: Hancher L, Ottervanger T, Slot PJ (eds) E.U. State Aids, 5th edn. Sweet & Maxwell, London, pp 235–244

Chapter 5
Quantitative, Temporary Ceilings and Time When the Undertaking Becomes Entitled to Receive Aid

Contents

Abstract This chapter addresses the quantitative and temporary ceilings of the different *de minimis* regimes and the time of grant. One of the main features of *de minimis* regimes is precisely their quantitative and temporal limits. While the time limit tends to be common to all *de minimis* regimes, quantitative limits are different, which means that the quantitative limits of each special *de minimis* regime need to be analysed separately. The chapter closes with an analysis of the assumed time of grant of the aid.

Keywords *De minimis* aid · Quantitative ceilings · Temporary ceilings · Principle of indivisibility · Time of grant · Fiscal year

© T.M.C. ASSER PRESS and the author 2022

R. Pedro, *De Minimis Aid Under EU Law*,
https://doi.org/10.1007/978-94-6265-543-0_5

5.1 Quantitative Ceilings

5.1.1 In General

In addition to the control of the organizational ceiling in Chap. 4, consideration should also be given to the need to control the (i) temporal and (ii) quantitative ceilings. We will elaborate on each of those ceilings below.[1]

5.2 Quantitative Ceilings: General *De Minimis*

Under the general *de minimis* regulation, to qualify under the *de minimis* regime, the aid may not, as a rule, exceed the amount of €200,000.

As made clear in the preparatory work for that regulation, finding the appropriate ceiling is one of the *key problems* of the *de minimis* regulation, because the appropriate quantitative ceiling must, on the one hand, take into account that a very low ceiling causes public authorities granting and/or monitoring the granting of aid to incur unnecessary administrative costs and, on the other hand, that a very high ceiling creates/increases the risk that the aid will distort competition.[2]

In addition, the appropriate ceiling should provide legal clarity and certainty.

As regards the quantitative ceilings, as has already been stated in the context of the analysis of each of the *de minimis* regimes, these ceilings tend to vary depending on the regime concerned.[3] Thus, as regards the general *de minimis* regime, it would appear that the general *de minimis* regulation establishes that aid may not exceed €200,000 if it is to be considered *de minimis.*

Article 3(2) provides for a separate rule for *road freight transport for hire or reward* in addition to the above rule, which applies to all sectors of activity to which the general *de minimis* regulation applies, namely that aid cannot exceed €100,000.

First and foremost, account should be taken of developments in this regard, since Article 2(2) of the former general *de minimis* regime provided that *"De minimis aid granted to any undertaking activities in the road transport sector may not exceed EUR 100,000 over a period of three fiscal years"*. That is, such a lower ceiling applied both to the road passenger transport sector and to the road freight transport for hire or reward.

[1] On this topic, see Bär-Bouyssière 2005, pp. 187 et seq.; Berghofer 2007, p. 17; Estoa Pérez 2007, pp. 631 et seq; Nyssens 2008, pp. 435 et seq.; Zuleger 2010, pp. 64 et seq.; Nicolaides 2014; Pedro 2015, pp. 77 et seq.; Costachescu 2016, pp. 7 et seq; Wolf 2016, pp. 325–327; Van de Casteele 2016, pp. 235–244 and on SGEI: Wolf 2016, pp. 325–327.

[2] The position of MS varies between those who want to increase the ceiling, namely to €500,000, and those who believe that €200,000 is adequate. European Commission 2013, pp. 19 et seq.

[3] See Chap. 3.

In order to gain a better understanding of the scope of this Article, the ancillary element offered by recital (5) of the regulation should be considered as this recital clarifies, on the one hand, that in view of the development of the road passenger transport sector, it is no longer appropriate to apply a lower ceiling to this sector, and, on the other hand, that the provision of an integrated service where the actual transportation is only one element, such as removal services, postal or courier services or waste collection or processing services, should not be considered a transport service.

As already mentioned above,[4] the extension of the *de minimis* regime to the transport sector is the result of the evolution of this sector, in particular the restructuring of many transport activities towards liberalization, and the lower limit is warranted by the need for consistency with legislative texts adopted by the European Commission on other topics (e.g. environment) and for alignment with the objectives of transport policy as regards road congestion and freight transport, and also by the small average size of the undertakings active in this sector.[5]

For these reasons and because there is overcapacity in the sector, this *de minimis* aid cannot be used for the acquisition of road freight transport vehicles.

If the undertaking also carries out other activities to which the €200,000 ceiling applies, this quantitative ceiling applies to the undertaking, provided that the MS concerned ensures, by appropriate means such as separation of activities or distinction of costs, that the benefit to the road freight transport activity does not exceed €100,000 and that no *de minimis* aid is used for the acquisition of road freight transport vehicles.

5.3 Quantitative Ceilings: *De Minimis* for the Financing of Undertakings Providing SGEI

Quantitative ceilings must also be controlled when applying the *de minimis* regime for the financing of undertakings providing SGEI. However, the amount to be considered is higher, i.e., the amount to be considered is €500,000.

The reasons for allowing an amount higher than foreseen in the general *de minimis* regulation are twofold: (i) the European Commission's experience in applying State aid rules to undertakings providing services of general economic interest within the meaning of Article 106(2) TFEU has shown that the ceiling below which the advantages granted to those undertakings can be considered as not affecting trade between MS and/or distorting or threatening to distort competition may in some cases differ from the general *de minimis* ceiling as it is likely that at least some of these advantages will offset the additional costs related to the provision of services

[4] See Chap. 3, Sect. 3.4.

[5] See European Commission 2006.

of general economic interest and (ii) many activities qualified as services of general economic interest have a limited territorial scope.

Lastly, despite the €500,000 ceiling, it should be borne in mind that, according to recital (14) of the regulation under consideration, such a regime cannot limit the application of the general *de minimis* regulation to undertakings providing services of general economic interest.

That is, MS remain free to rely on the *de minimis* regulation on the financing of undertakings providing SGEI *or* the general *de minimis* regulation for the granting of incentives to undertakings providing SGEI.

5.4 Quantitative Ceilings: *De Minimis* in the Agriculture Sector

As regards the agriculture sector, recipient and national control are both required.[6] Two types of ceilings should be monitored: (i) the maximum amount of aid that a single undertaking can receive over a period of 3 years in this sector, i.e., €20,000, and (ii) the national cap for each MS.[7,8]

These ceilings remain necessary to ensure that the measures covered by the regulation under consideration have no effect on trade between MS and do not distort or threaten to distort competition.[9]

With regard to the limit per MS, Article 3(3) of the regulation imposes a ceiling at MS level, i.e., the cumulative amount of *de minimis* aid granted by MS to undertakings active in the primary production of agricultural products over any period of three fiscal years must not exceed the national ceiling set out in Annex I to that Regulation.

The recipient ceiling, according to the wording of the new paragraph 3A of Article 3, may be raised to €25,000 if the additional conditions laid down therein are met. It should also be borne in mind that, for the new paragraph 3A of Article 3 to operate, there must be a higher national threshold, which is set out in Annex II to the regulation in question.

---

[6] See Commission Regulation (EU) No 1408/2013 of 18 December 2013 on the application of Articles 107 and 108 of the Treaty on the Functioning of the European Union to *de minimis* aid in the agriculture sector, OJ L 352, 24 December 2013, pp. 9–17 and Commission Regulation (EU) 2019/316 of 21 February 2019 amending Regulation (EU) No 1408/2013 on the application of Articles 107 and 108 of the Treaty on the Functioning of the European Union to *de minimis* aid in the agriculture sector, OJ L 51, 22 February 2019, pp. 1–6.

[7] See the Annex to the *de minimis* regime for the agriculture sector – which establishes the maximum cumulative amounts of *de minimis* aid granted per MS to undertakings in the sector of agricultural production referred to in Article 3(3).

[8] It should be noted that, in the light of recital (14) of the *de minimis* regime for the agriculture sector, "*(...) Union funding centrally managed by the Commission which is not directly or indirectly under the control of the Member State, does not constitute State aid and should not be taken into account in determining whether the relevant ceiling or the national cap is respected*".

[9] Quigley 2015, p. 434.

5.5 Quantitative Ceilings: *De Minimis* in the Fishery and Aquaculture Sector

Lastly, in the fishery and aquaculture sector, as in the agriculture sector, two types of control must take place.[10] The (i) control of the quantitative ceiling per undertaking, which in this sector is €30,000 and the (ii) control of the national cap.[11,12]

As set out in recital (3), it is appropriate to maintain the ceiling of €30,000 as the amount of *de minimis* aid that a single undertaking may receive per MS over any period of three years.

That ceiling remains necessary to ensure that measures falling under this regulation can be deemed not to have an effect on trade between MS nor distort or threaten to distort competition where the total amount of such aid granted to all fishery and aquaculture sector undertakings *over three years* is below the cumulative amount laid down for each MS representing 2.5% of the annual fisheries turnover, i.e., of catch, processing and aquaculture activities (the national cap).

5.6 Implementation of the Quantitative Ceilings: Principle of Indivisibility

It should be noted that, pursuant to Article 3(7) of the general *de minimis* regulation, Article 3(7) of the *de minimis* regulation on the agriculture sector and Article 3(7) of the *de minimis* regulation on the fishery and aquaculture sector, where the relevant ceilings would be exceeded by the grant of new *de minimis* aid, none of that new aid may benefit from the relevant regulation.

In other words, a *principle of the indivisibility of the aid underlies all those provisions,*[13] in that it cannot be fractioned,[14] namely it may not be granted even for a fraction not exceeding that ceiling.

In this context, recital (22) of the general *de minimis* regulation explains that "*Before granting any new* de minimis *aid each Member State should verify that*

---

[10] See: (i) Commission Regulation (EU) No 717/2014 of 27 June 2014 on the application of Articles 107 and 108 of the Treaty on the Functioning of the European Union to *de minimis* aid in the fishery and aquaculture sector, OJ L 190, 28 July 2014, pp. 45–54, and (ii) Commission Regulation (EU) 2020/2008 of 8 December 2020 amending Regulations (EU) No 702/2014, (EU) No 717/2014 and (EU) No 1388/2014, as regards their period of application and other relevant adjustments C/2020/8567, OJ L 414, 9 December 2020, pp. 15–18.

[11] See the Annex to the *de minimis* regime for fishery and aquaculture - which establishes the national cap as referred to in Article 3(3).

[12] It should be noted that, in the light of recital (12) of the *de minimis* regime for the fishery and aquaculture sector "*(…) Union funding centrally managed by the Commission which is not directly or indirectly under the control of the Member State, does not constitute State aid and should not be taken into account in determining whether the relevant ceiling or the national cap is respected*".

[13] See Sinnaeve 2014, p. 262.

[14] Ibid, p. 266.

the de minimis *ceiling will not be exceeded in that MS by the new* de minimis *aid and that the other conditions of this Regulation are complied with".*

On the other hand, and as regards consequences,[15] if the ceiling is breached, the remedy will tend to be the cancellation of the aid granted and/or any other measures more suited to satisfy that legal remedy.[16]

It should be noted that the aid to be cancelled will be the last aid granted (chronologically), i.e., by way of example if aid of €200,000 has been granted and it has since been found that aid of €1 had previously been granted, which had not been considered, the aid to be cancelled is €200,000 in accordance with the succession in time.

As regards the *de minimis* regime for the financing of undertakings providing SGEI, Article 2(5) of this regulation provides that where the overall amount of *de minimis* aid under this regulation granted to an undertaking for the provision of SGEI exceeds the €500,000 ceiling, that amount may not benefit from this regulation, even for a fraction not exceeding that ceiling.

In such a case, the benefit of this regulation may not be claimed for this aid measure.[17]

The aim of this rule is, as explained in recital (5), that aid exceeding the *de minimis* ceiling cannot be broken down into a number of smaller parts in order to bring such parts within the scope of this regulation.[18]

5.7 Time Ceilings

5.7.1 In General

Another essential element has to do with the duration of a certain period relevant for the consideration of the *de minimis* regime, i.e., the time ceiling. The reference for this ceiling should be the period of three fiscal years as determined in each MS.[19]

It is a technique developed to facilitate the control of *de minimis* ceilings by the recipient, the MS, and the European Commission.[20]

According to the four *de minimis* regulations under consideration, the relevant period of three years should be assessed on a rolling basis so that, for each new

[15] See Baldi 2016, pp. 149 and 150. In the case of aid that has not yet been paid, the doctrine cited immediately above advances the hypothesis that the recipient may waive one of the *de minimis* aid, see ibid, p. 150.

[16] See CJEU, *Istituto nazionale per l'assicurazione contro gli infortuni sul lavoro (INAIL) v Zennaro Giuseppe Legnami Sas di Zennaro Mauro & C*, Judgment of the Court, 28 October 2020, case C-608/19, ECLI:EU:C:2020:86.

[17] See also Wolf 2016, p. 326.

[18] Ibid, p. 326.

[19] Does not need to match the calendar year.

[20] Nyssens 2008, p. 435.

grant of *de minimis* aid, the total amount of *de minimis* aid granted in the fiscal year concerned, as well as during the previous two fiscal years, needs to be determined.

That is, account should be taken of fiscal year X, fiscal year X-1 and fiscal year X-2. Based on the €200,000 threshold, if a single undertaking received €100,000 in the fiscal year 2021, €50,000 in the year 2020 and €50,000 in the year 2019 as soon as the fiscal year of 2022 begins, the undertaking can get *de minimis* aid of €50,000.

5.7.2 *Time of Grant*

The only relevant moment for competition purposes is the time of the grant, i.e., the moment when the recipient is vested with the right to receive the incentive.[21] For this reason, according to a rule common to the different *de minimis* rules it is considered that *de minimis* aid was granted at the time when the legal right to receive the aid is vested in the undertaking under the applicable national legal framework, regardless of date of payment of the *de minimis* aid to the undertaking.

In addition, if the aid is granted in instalments, it must refer to the time of grant and the amount must be considered in full, irrespective of the payment in instalments.[22]

The date of grant is of the essence for a number of purposes,[23] in particular: (i) for the purpose of determining the applicable *de minimis* regime in time; (ii) for the purpose of calculating the loan reference rate; (iii) for the purpose of recovering unlawful *de minimis* aid, i.e., taking into account the determination of the duly applicable regulation; (iv) for the purpose of applying the notion of "single undertaking"; (v) for monitoring purposes; (vi) for the purpose of counting deadlines for the recording and compilation of all information regarding the application of the *de minimis* regulations for a period of 10 years.

This requires careful coordination between the information on the database of the central *de minimis* regime and the amounts to be granted by the entities responsible for granting the incentive.

References

Bacon K (2017) European Union law of State aid, 3rd edn. Oxford University Press, Oxford

Baldi CE (2016) La disciplina comunitaria degli aiuti di Stato: manuale critico ad uso delle amministrazioni e delle imprese [The Community framework for State aid: a critical handbook for administrations and enterprises]. Santarcangelo di Romagna (Rimini), Maggioli

---

[21] See Baldi 2016, p. 98.

[22] See: Article 3(4) of the general *de minimis* regime; Article 3(4) of the *de minimis* regime for the agriculture sector; Article 3(4) of the *de minimis* regime for the fishery and aquaculture sector; recital (12) of the *de minimis* regulation on the financing of undertakings providing SGEI. According to a certain doctrine, this is, in fact, a general principle, see Wolf 2016, p. 232.

[23] Bacon 2017, p. 22.

Bär-Bouyssière B (2005) Les règlements d'exemption en matière d'aides d'Etat [State aid exemption regulations]. In: Dony M, Smits C (eds) Aides d'État. Éditions de l' Université de Bruxelles, Brussels, pp 170–193
Berghofer M (2007) The New *De Minimis* Regulation: Enlarging the Sword of Damocles? European State Aid Law Quarterly 6: 11–23
Costachescu A (2016) The Comparative Analysis between the Minimis Aid/The Regional State Aid. Romanian Competition Journal 1–2:1–37 http://dx.doi.org/https://doi.org/10.2139/ssrn.2894819
Estoa Pérez A (2007) La regulación de las ayudas de MINIMIS en el derecho comunitario: comentario al reglamento (CE) No 1998/2006 [The regulation of MINIMIS aid in EU law: commentary on regulation (EC) No 1998/2006]. Revista de derecho comunitario europeo 11: 623–636
European Commission (2006) IP/06/1765. https://ec.europa.eu/commission/presscorner/detail/en/IP_06_1765. Accessed 20 April 2020
European Commission (2013) Commission Staff Working Document Impact Assessment - accompanying the document - commission regulation (EU) no …/… - on the application of articles 107 and 108 of the Treaty on the Functioning of the European Union to *de minimis* aid - {c(2013) 4448 final} {swd(2013) 522 final} - Brussels, 18 July 2013, swd(2013) 521 final. untitled (europa.eu). Accessed 20 April 2020
Nicolaides P (2014) The New Rules on *De minimis* Aid for 2014–2020: Regulation 1407/2013. The New Rules on De minimis Aid for 2014-2020: Regulation 1407/2013 - Free State Aid blog article - Read now (lexxion.eu). Accessed 4 April 2018
Nyssens H (2008) *De mininis* Part 2 – Chapter 8. In: Mederer W, Pesaresi N, Van Hoof M (eds) EU Competition Law: Volume IV: Book One, State Aid. Claeys and Casteels, Leuven, pp 409–449
Pedro R (2015) Auxílios *de minimis* 2014-2020: Notas à luz do Regulamento (UE) n.º 1407/2013 [*De minimis* aid 2014-2020: Notes in light of Regulation (EU) No 1407/2013]. Revista de Concorrência e Regulação 17: 65–95
Quigley C (2015) European State Aid Law and Policy, 3rd edn. Hart Publishing, Oxford/Portland, Oregon
Sinnaeve A (2014) The Complexity of Simplification: The Commission's Review of the *de minimis* Regulation. European State Aid Law Quarterly 13: 261–276
Van de Casteele K (2016) *De minimis* aid. In: Hancher L, Ottervanger T, Slot PJ (eds) E.U. State Aids, 5th edn. Sweet & Maxwell, London, pp 235–244
Wolf M (2016) Part III. In: Säcker FJ, Montag F (eds) European State Aid Law: A Commentary. Verlag C.H. Beck, Munich, pp 295–381
Zuleger V (2010) *De Minimis* Aid. In: Heidenhain M (ed) European State Aid Law. Verlag C.H. Beck, Munich, pp 61–72

Chapter 6
De Minimis Aid Cumulation

Contents

Abstract This chapter addresses the problem of accumulating *de minimis* aid with other State aid. It analyses *de minimis* regimes and details to what extent different types of *de minimis* aid can be cumulated based on the principle that an undertaking should not receive aid twice for the same goal. It is paramount to understand these rules to avoid illegal situations such as classifying as *de minimis* aid that which is really State aid, or in the worst-case scenario granting aid that will be subject to recovery.

Keywords *De minimis* aid · Aid accumulation · State aid · General *de minimis* aid · Agriculture sector · Fishery and aquaculture sector · SGEI

6.1 In General

Cumulation of aid is one of the most recurring problems for the aid enforcer,[1] given the potential for affecting the internal market and the underlying *principle that an undertaking should not receive aid twice for the same goal.*[2]

[1] See Bär-Bouyssière 2005, pp. 187 et seq.; Berghofer 2007, p. 17; Estoa Pérez 2007, pp. 631 et seq.; Nyssens 2008, pp. 435 et seq.; Nicolaides et al 2008, pp. 48 et seq.; Zuleger 2010, pp. 64 et seq.; Nicolaides 2014; Pedro 2015, pp. 77 et seq.; Costachescu 2016, pp. 7 et seq.; Wolf 2016, pp. 325–327; Van de Casteele 2016, pp. 235–244 and on SGEI: Wolf 2016, pp. 325–327.

[2] See Sinnaeve 2014, p. 271.

© T.M.C. ASSER PRESS and the author 2022

R. Pedro, *De Minimis Aid Under EU Law*,
https://doi.org/10.1007/978-94-6265-543-0_6

The problems that may arise from the cumulation of aid under one type of *de minimis* aid (which is reflected, in particular, in the need to meet certain ceilings), it is important to establish a relation between the different *de minimis* regimes which have an impact on the cumulation of aid and the relationship between *de minimis* regimes and State aid regimes.

On the one hand, *de minimis* aid for the agriculture and fishery and aquaculture sectors, which have a clear sectoral scope, ultimately reflect the corresponding exclusion from the general *de minimis* regime.

On the other hand, *de minimis* aid for the financing of undertakings providing SGEI can be cumulated with aid benefiting from the general *de minimis* regime up to the ceiling laid down in that regulation.

Lastly, rules are laid down for the cumulation of *de minimis* regimes with State aid.

6.2 Cumulation of General *De Minimis* Aid with Special *De Minimis* Aid and State Aid

In order to determine the *de minimis* aid cumulation regime with any degree of rigor, in particular where the granting of financial incentives falling within the scope of the different *de minimis* regimes is concerned, the regime of cumulation provided for in Article 5 of the general *de minimis* regime will be identified next.

The rule laid down in the general *de minimis* regime is that cumulation with *de minimis* aid in respect of the financing of SGEI is permitted up to the ceiling set out in that regime.

For other special *de minimis* regimes, cumulation up to the ceilings of the general *de minimis* regime is permitted.

With regard to *cumulation with State aid*, cumulation with State aid in relation to the same eligible costs or with State aid for the same risk finance measure is prohibited, if such cumulation would exceed the highest relevant aid intensity or aid amount fixed in the specific circumstances of each case by a block exemption regulation or a decision adopted by the European Commission. The rationale, as set out in recital (12) of the general *de minimis* regime, is to lay down rules to ensure that it is not possible to circumvent maximum aid intensities laid down in specific regulations or European Commission decisions. Notwithstanding the above rule, doctrine nevertheless warns that this is a more theoretical matter, since *de minimis* aid is not linked to eligible costs.[3]

However, *de minimis* aid which is not granted for or allocated to specific eligible costs can be combined with other State aid granted under a block exemption regulation or a decision adopted by the European Commission.

[3] Van de Casteele 2016, p. 242.

It is now necessary to indicate the rules for the cumulation of *de minimis* aid for each of the special *de minimis* regimes.

6.3 Cumulation of *De Minimis* Aid for the Agriculture Sector with Other Aid

A kind of conditional cumulation authorization is established in Article 5 for the same undertaking, i.e., aid for the primary production sector of agricultural products may be cumulated with:

(i) aid relating to other sectors or activities provided for under the general *de minimis* regime provided that the MS concerned ensures, by appropriate means such as separation of activities or distinction of costs, that the primary production of agricultural products does not benefit from general *de minimis* aid; and
(ii) aid granted for activities in the fishery and aquaculture sector, provided that the MS concerned ensures, by appropriate means such as separation of activities or distinction of costs, that the primary production of agricultural products does not benefit from *de minimis* aid for the fishery and aquaculture sector.

Lastly, a rule prohibiting cumulation with State aid in respect of the same eligible costs or with State aid for the same risk financing measure is laid down, if such cumulation leads to an aid intensity higher than that fixed or the amount of aid fixed, depending on the specific circumstances of each case, by a block exemption regulation or decision adopted by the European Commission.[4]

However, it is accepted that *de minimis* aid which is not granted for specific eligible costs or cannot be allocated to such costs may be cumulated with other State aid granted under a block exemption regulation or a European Commission decision.

6.4 Cumulation of *De Minimis* Aid for the Fishery and Aquaculture Sector with Other Aid

In this rule too, a conditional cumulation authorization is established for the same undertaking, i.e., Article 5 allows the cumulation of aid in the fishery and aquaculture sector with:

(i) aid in respect of other sectors or activities provided for under the general *de minimis* rule, provided that the MS ensures, by appropriate means such as

[4] Relevant for the purposes hereof, see 2013/665/EU: Commission Decision of 17 July 2013 on State aid SA.33726 (11/C) [ex SA.33726 (11/NN)]—granted by Italy (deferral of payment of the milk levy in Italy) (notified under document C(2013) 4046), OJ L 309, 19 November 2013, pp. 40–48.

separation of activities or distinction of costs, that the activities in the fishery and aquaculture sector do not benefit from general *de minimis* aid; and

(ii) aid for sectors of primary production of agricultural products provided, that the MS ensures, by appropriate means such as separation of activities or distinction of costs, that the primary production of agricultural products does not benefit from *de minimis* aid for fishery and aquaculture.

Lastly, as in the abovementioned rule, a rule is also laid down prohibiting cumulation with State aid in relation to the same eligible costs or with State aid for the same risk finance measure, if such cumulation would exceed the highest relevant aid intensity or aid amount fixed in the specific circumstances of each case by a block exemption regulation or a decision adopted by the European Commission.

However, it is accepted that *de minimis* aid which is not granted for or attributable to specific eligible costs may be cumulated with other State aid granted under a block exemption regulation or a decision adopted by the European Commission.

6.5 Cumulation of *De Minimis* Aid for Financing Undertakings Providing SGEI with Other Aid

De minimis aid granted in accordance with the *de minimis* regime for the financing of undertakings providing SGEI may, in accordance with Article 2(7), be cumulated with other *de minimis* aid up to the ceiling provided for in the relevant *de minimis* aid regulation. This regulation sets forth a quantitative ceiling of €500,000.

On the one hand, in Article 2(6) and (8), two rules prohibiting cumulation are laid down:

(i) in order to avoid circumvention of the maximum aid intensities laid down in various Union instruments, *de minimis* aid must not be cumulated with State aid in respect of the same eligible costs if such cumulation would result in an aid intensity exceeding that stipulated in the specific circumstances of each case by a block exemption regulation or decision adopted by the European Commission; and

(ii) cannot be cumulated with any compensation in respect of the same service of general economic interest, regardless of whether it constitutes State aid.[5]

On the other hand, Article 2(7) allows cumulation with other *de minimis* aid up to the ceiling of the *de minimis* regime for financing of SGEI.

---

[5] That is, even if this compensation is not State aid in the light of the Altmark case-law, see Bacon 2017, p. 90.

References

Bacon K (2017) European Union Law of State Aid, 3rd edn. Oxford University Press, Oxford

Bär-Bouyssière B (2005) Les règlements d'exemption en matière d'aides d'Etat [State aid exemption regulations]. In: Dony M, Smits C (eds) Aides d'État. Éditions de l' Université de Bruxelles, Brussels, pp 170–193

Berghofer M (2007) The New *De Minimis* Regulation: Enlarging the Sword of Damocles? European State Aid Law Quarterly 6: 11–23

Costachescu A (2016) The Comparative Analysis between the Minimis Aid/The Regional State Aid. Romanian Competition Journal 1–2:1–37. https://doi.org/10.2139/ssrn.2894819

Estoa Pérez A (2007) La regulación de las ayudas de MINIMIS en el derecho comunitario: comentario al reglamento (CE) No 1998/2006 [The regulation of MINIMIS aid in EU law: commentary on regulation (EC) No 1998/2006]. Revista de derecho comunitario europeo 11: 623–636

Nicolaides P (2014) The New Rules on *De minimis* Aid for 2014-2020: Regulation 1407/2013. The New Rules on De minimis Aid for 2014-2020: Regulation 1407/2013 - Free State Aid blog article - Read now (lexxion.eu). Accessed 4 April 2018

Nicolaides P et al (2008) Cumulation of *De minimis* Aid to Enterprises that Form a Single Economic Unit. European State Aid Law Quarterly 1: 48–57

Nyssens H (2008) *De mininis* Part 2 – Chapter 8. In: Mederer W, Pesaresi N, Van Hoof M (eds) EU Competition Law: Volume IV: Book One, State Aid. Claeys and Casteels, Leuven, pp 409–449

Pedro R (2015) Auxílios *de minimis* 2014-2020: Notas à luz do Regulamento (UE) n.º 1407/2013 [*De minimis* aid 2014-2020: Notes in light of Regulation (EU) No 1407/2013]. Revista de Concorrência e Regulação 17: 65–95

Sinnaeve A (2014) The Complexity of Simplification: The Commission's Review of the *de minimis* Regulation. European State Aid Law Quarterly 13: 261–276

Van de Casteele K (2016) *De minimis* aid. In: Hancher L, Ottervanger T, Slot PJ (eds) E.U. State Aids, 5th edn. Sweet & Maxwell, London, pp 235–244

Wolf M (2016) Part III. In: Säcker FJ, Montag F (eds) European State Aid Law: A Commentary. Verlag C.H. Beck, Munich, pp 295–381

Zuleger V (2010) *De Minimis* Aid. In: Heidenhain M (ed) European State Aid Law. Verlag C.H. Beck, Munich, pp 61–72

Chapter 7
Monitoring the *De Minimis* Regimes

Contents

Abstract This chapter addresses ways to monitor *de minimis* regimes. Monitoring is paramount in terms of compliance with *de minimis* regimes, in that it ensures that the aid is of low value and therefore unlikely to affect competition and the internal market. It analyses two monitoring options, their advantages and disadvantages, and the relevant role Member States play in monitoring.

Keywords *De minimis* aid · Monitoring · Central register · Declaration by the undertaking · *Ex-ante* control · *Ex-post* control

7.1 In General

The methods for keeping track of *de minimis* regimes or, in the terminology of the regulations, *monitoring,*[1] have proved rather controversial, as shown in the preparatory works for the general *de minimis* regulation.[2] The mandatory establishment of a central *de minimis* register in each MS was discussed,[3] among other things, on an initial proposal of the European Commission. The proposal would eventually fall

[1] On this, see Bär-Bouyssière 2005, pp. 187 et seq.; Berghofer 2007, p. 17; Estoa Pérez 2007, pp. 633 et seq; Nyssens 2008, pp. 441 et seq.; Zuleger 2010, pp. 64 et seq.; Nicolaides 2014; Pedro 2015, pp. 77 et seq.; Costachescu 2016, pp. 7 et seq; Wolf 2016, pp. 325–327; Van de Casteele 2016, pp. 235–244 and on SGEI: Wolf 2016, pp. 325–327.

[2] European Commission 2014.

[3] Van de Casteele 2016, p. 241.

© T.M.C. ASSER PRESS and the author 2022

R. Pedro, *De Minimis Aid Under EU Law*,
https://doi.org/10.1007/978-94-6265-543-0_7

through due to the negative reaction of several MS, whereupon the Union adopted a *voluntary regime* (freedom to establish or not establish a central register).[4]

In addition to the above, and although it could be considered *prima facie* that this is a primary concern of the European Commission—since it has a duty to ensure compliance with the rules on State aid—it should not be forgotten that, in accordance with the principle of loyal cooperation set out in Article 4(3) TEU, MS should facilitate such cooperation, creating the necessary tools to ensure that the total amount of *de minimis* aid granted to a single company does not exceed the legally permitted ceilings.

In particular, national instruments should be developed, not only because the principle of loyal cooperation requires it, but also with a view to the effective enforcement of Union law, ensuring abidance by the rule that stipulates that a MS can only grant new *de minimis* aid in accordance with the relevant regulation after it has established that, following such a grant, the total amount of *de minimis* aid granted to the undertaking concerned does not reach a level that exceeds the relevant ceilings and that all the requirements set out in the *de minimis* regulation are met.[5]

Differently put, the principle of *ex-ante* monitoring (before granting the incentive) is enshrined.[6]

7.2 Monitoring the *De Minimis* Regimes: Options

To comply with the rule that a MS may grant new *de minimis* aid only in accordance with the relevant regulations,[7] MS have two options:

(i) inform the undertaking in writing of the potential amount of aid expressed as gross grant equivalent and of its *de minimis* character, with express reference to the *de minimis* regulation concerned and citing its title and publication reference in the Official Journal of the Union. Before granting the aid, the MS must obtain from the undertaking concerned a written or electronic statement on the existence of any other *de minimis* aid to which the *de minimis* regulations apply during the previous two fiscal years and the current fiscal year or, alternatively,

(ii) may set up a central *de minimis* aid register containing full information on all *de minimis* aid granted by an authority of that MS over a period of three fiscal years. If this option is chosen, a MS may grant new *de minimis* aid only after it has ascertained that, following such a grant, the total amount of *de minimis*

[4] As already mentioned, a third option was put forward by the European Commission, which consists of a mandatory central European register. Although this proposal has not progressed, the European Commission maintains its intention to study this possibility. See European Commission 2013, p. 59.

[5] Van de Casteele 2016, p. 241.

[6] Sinnaeve 2014, p. 274.

[7] See: Article 6 of the general *de minimis* regime; Article 6 of the *de minimis* regime for the agriculture sector; Article 6 of the *de minimis* regime for the fishery and aquaculture sector; Article 3 of the *de minimis* regime on the financing of undertakings providing SGEIs.

aid granted to the undertaking concerned does not reach a level exceeding the relevant ceilings and that all the requirements set out in the relevant regulations are met.

Opting for one of these alternatives is not easy as both have advantages and disadvantages.

The first option has the advantage that such administrative costs do not exist (at least, not in the same amount), but the data lose quality and reliability, notably as a result of (possibly) false or inaccurate statements by undertakings.

The second option affords a more reliable control of the ceilings and an overview of all *de minimis* aid granted; however, the administrative costs that this solution entails must be borne.[8]

Responsibility for monitoring falls on MS[9] and compliance with that responsibility is guided by the *principle of institutional/organizational autonomy* of MS which, however, must take into account the limits set by EU law resulting from the *principle of equivalence and the principle of effectiveness*.

The principle of equivalence requires MS to set up a domestic regime that treats European rules at least as effectively as national rules. Lastly, the principle of effectiveness requires European rules to be effectively enforced by MS, leading to the creation of rules that ensure such effectiveness/efficiency and imposing the non-application of national rules that make it difficult to exercise legal positions of European Union law.

That is to say, on the basis of that assumption, it is left to the organizational discretion of each MS to determine how to ensure control of *de minimis* regimes provided that the solution to be adopted enables compliance with European State aid law.

7.3 *Ex-post* Control by the European Commission

It should be noted that, in addition to control/monitoring by national authorities, the above-mentioned *de minimis* regulations provide for the possibility of *ex-post* control by the European Commission.

This requires MS to record and compile all information concerning the application of a *de minimis* regulation for a period of 10 years. This period, as regards individual

[8] Although not the option most widely followed by MS, at least nine MS have already adopted a central control regime for *de minimis* aid. Central register systems vary greatly from MS to MS - some have information on all State aid, while others only on *de minimis*, and some have detailed information on recipients, while others do not. For further developments, see European Commission 2013, pp. 49 et seq. Depending on the quality of the data collected by the central register system, the MS and the European Commission will be in a better or worse position to assess their *de minimis* aid policy. In addition, it should be clear that this central register option favours micro-enterprises which, as a rule, have less capacity to perform administrative tasks.

[9] See Nyssens 2008, p. 435.

aid, is counted from the date of grant of the aid and, as regards records for any *de minimis* aid regime, this period must be counted from the date on which the last individual aid was granted under the relevant regime.

Lastly, the *de minimis* regulations also require MS to comply with any information requests from the European Commission, within 20 days or a longer deadline as may be established by the European Commission, to assess whether a particular aid recipient has satisfied the conditions laid down in the relevant *de minimis* regulation.[10]

References

Baldi CE (2016) La disciplina comunitaria degli aiuti di Stato: manuale critico ad uso delle amministrazioni e delle imprese [The Community framework for State aid: a critical handbook for administrations and enterprises]. Santarcangelo di Romagna (Rimini), Maggioli

Bär-Bouyssière B (2005) Les règlements d'exemption en matière d'aides d'Etat [State aid exemption regulations]. In: Dony M, Smits C (eds) Aides d'État. Éditions de l' Université de Bruxelles, Brussels, pp 170–193

Berghofer M (2007) The New *De Minimis* Regulation: Enlarging the Sword of Damocles? European State Aid Law Quarterly 6: 11–23

Costachescu A (2016) The Comparative Analysis between the Minimis Aid/The Regional State Aid. Romanian Competition Journal 1–2:1–37 http://dx.doi.org/https://doi.org/10.2139/ssrn.2894819

Estoa Pérez A (2007) La regulación de las ayudas de MINIMIS en el derecho comunitario: comentario al reglamento (CE) No 1998/2006 [The regulation of MINIMIS aid in Community law: commentary on regulation (EC) No 1998/2006]. Revista de derecho comunitario europeo 11: 623–636

European Commission (2013) Commission Staff Working Document Impact Assessment - accompanying the document - commission regulation (EU) no …/… - on the application of articles 107 and 108 of the Treaty on the Functioning of the European Union to *de minimis* aid - {c(2013) 4448 final} {swd(2013) 522 final} - Brussels, 18 July 2013, swd(2013) 521 final. untitled (europa.eu). Accessed 20 April 2020

European Commission (2014) Consultation on the first draft of the new *de minimis* regulation replacing Regulation No 1998/2006. http://ec.europa.eu/competition/consultations/2013_de_minimis/index_en.html. Accessed 12 April 2014 (no longer active)

Nicolaides P (2014) The New Rules on *De minimis* Aid for 2014–2020: Regulation 1407/2013. The New Rules on De minimis Aid for 2014-2020: Regulation 1407/2013 - Free State Aid blog article - Read now (lexxion.eu). Accessed 4 April 2018

Nyssens H (2008) *De mininis* Part 2 – Chapter 8. In: Mederer W, Pesaresi N, Van Hoof M (eds) EU Competition Law: Volume IV: Book One, State Aid. Claeys and Casteels, Leuven, pp 409–449

Pedro R (2015) Auxílios *de minimis* 2014–2020: Notas à luz do Regulamento (UE) n.º 1407/2013 [*De minimis* aid 2014–2020: Notes in light of Regulation (EU) No 1407/2013]. Revista de Concorrência e Regulação 17: 65–95

Quigley C (2015) European State Aid Law and Policy, 3rd edn. Hart Publishing, Oxford/Portland, Oregon

Sinnaeve A (2014) The Complexity of Simplification: The Commission's Review of the *de minimis* Regulation. European State Aid Law Quarterly 13: 261–276

[10] Additionally, each MS has to prepare an annual report on all State aid granted by it in the course of the year, including aid that falls under the *de minimis* rules.

Van de Casteele K (2016) *De minimis* aid. In: Hancher L, Ottervanger T, Slot PJ (eds) E.U. State Aids, 5th edn. Sweet & Maxwell, London, pp 235–244

Wolf M (2016) Part III. In: Säcker FJ, Montag F (eds) European State Aid Law: A Commentary, Verlag C.H. Beck, Munich, pp 295–381

Zuleger V (2010) *De Minimis* Aid. In: Heidenhain M (ed) European State Aid Law. Verlag C.H. Beck, Munich, pp 61–72

Chapter 8
Recovery of Unlawful *De Minimis* Aid

Contents

Abstract This chapter deals with the recovery of unlawful *de minimis* aid. As there is no framework for the recovery of *de minimis* aid, the chapter focuses on the framework for the recovery of State aid and the most relevant case-law to establish whether and to what extent such framework could apply. In this regard, the limits to recovery, the recovery decision, the relief foreseen for situations of non-recovery of State aid are analysed. Lastly, the chapter explores the framework for recovery of unlawful *de minimis* aid in view of the European Commission's understanding, Court of Justice case-law, and the duty of recovery within the framework for block exemption aid, as it is analogous to that of *de minimis* aid.

Keywords *De minimis* · Recovery of unlawful aid · State aid · Liability for damages · Principles of European Union · Deggendorf case-law

8.1 In General

Aid recovery is an issue paramount to understanding the *de minimis* aid regimes, particularly where they fail to meet the requirements warranting their admission.

Since there is no special regime for recovering *de minimis* aid, one must first review the rules for recovering State aid and then assess to which extent they apply to *de minimis* aid.

© T.M.C. ASSER PRESS and the author 2022

R. Pedro, *De Minimis Aid Under EU Law*,
https://doi.org/10.1007/978-94-6265-543-0_8

8.2 Recovery of Unlawful State Aid

8.2.1 Introduction

The recovery of unlawful State aid is greatly important both in practical terms and in connection with free competition in the European Union.[1] It should be noted, as a preliminary remark, that the *recovery of unlawful aid* seeks to restore the situation that existed on the internal market before the unlawful aid was paid out.[2,3]

The idea behind recovery of unlawful State aid is that by repaying the aid, the *recipient forfeits the advantage which it had enjoyed over its competitors*[4]*—by restoring the situation that existed on the internal market prior to the payment* (interest accrues until the date of actual recovery).[5,6]

The European Commission must establish, for such purpose, that the unlawful aid is incompatible with the internal market before ordering its recovery. The Court of Justice has made clear that the European Commission cannot order the recovery of unlawful aid without first examining whether the aid is compatible with the internal market, in accordance with the procedure laid down in Article 108(2) TFEU.[7] The Commission must then order the recovery of the aid in addition to determining its incompatibility, monitoring downstream to ensure that MS eliminate distortions of competition by recovering aid paid in breach of State aid rules.

As better detailed later, recovery decisions must be implemented *effectively*[8] and *immediately*.[9] The European Commission must order the recovery of unlawful and incompatible aid—*recovery decision* (unless it is contrary to any general EU law principle), and such aid must be recovered immediately and in accordance with *the*

---

[1] On this topic see, among many others, de Almeida 1997; Merola and Cappelletti 2011, pp. 465–468; Birnstiel 2012, pp. 645–665; Quigley 2015, pp. 577 et seq.; Mihaescu-Evans 2016, pp. 381 et seq.; Ghazarian 2016, pp. 228–234; Jouve 2017, pp. 367–376; Donzelli 2019, pp. 528–539; Rodríguez Pontón 2019, pp. 299–324; Goffart 2021.

[2] See CJEU, *Commission v Spain ("Magefesa II")*, Judgment of the Court, 11 December 2012, case C-610/10, ECLI:EU:C:2012:781.

[3] See Mihaescu-Evans 2016, pp. 381 et seq.

[4] See CJEU, *Commission v Italy*, Judgment of the Court, 4 April 1995, case C-348/93, ECLI:EU:C:1995:95.

[5] See Case C-610/10, para 105.

[6] See GC, *Siemens v Commission*, Judgment of the General Court, 8 June 1995, case T-459/93, ECLI:EU:T:1995:100.

[7] See CJEU, *France v Commission ("Boussac")*, Judgment of the Court, 14 February 1990, case C-301/87, ECLI:EU:C:1990:67.

[8] See CJEU, *Commission v Greece*, Judgment of the Court, 12 May 2005, case C-415/03, ECLI:EU:C:2005:287.

[9] See case C-415/03 and CJEU, *Commission v France*, Judgment of the Court, 5 October 2006, case C-232/05, ECLI:EU:C:2006:651.

procedures of the relevant MS's national law,[10,11] provided that any (provisional[12] or final) measures taken allow the *immediate* and *effective*[13] execution of the European Commission's decision. These measures benefit from a presumption of legality and remain binding in all respects, namely as long as the proceedings are pending before the EU courts.[14]

The aid recovery obligation is subject to a *ten years' limitation* period, which starts running on the day the unlawful aid is awarded to the beneficiary,[15] either as individual aid or as aid under an aid scheme.

Lastly, it should be noted that where a MS fails to comply with the recovery decision without demonstrating the absolute impossibility of recovery, the European Commission may initiate infringement proceedings[16] or pay a new compatible aid to the beneficiary or beneficiaries concerned contingent upon the recovery of the original aid ruled unlawful and incompatible. The other recourse available is a claim for damages based on the MS's breach of Union State aid recovery law.

The system for and the practice of recovering State aid are the result of an evolving and maturing process which began with the first decision of the Court of Justice in 1973.[17] This case-law and the Commission's practice were predominantly consolidated in the mid-1980s, mainly due to MS' increasing failure to comply with State aid rules.[18]

The 1983 Commission Communication[19] made it clear that the European Commission had decided to use all the means available to it to ensure that MS comply with their obligations under Article 88(3) [now 108(3)], including the obligation to recover incompatible aid granted unlawfully from the beneficiary.

---

[10] This requires loyal cooperation under Article 4(3) TEU and Article 9(4) of Commission Regulation (EC) No 794/2004 of 21 April 2004 implementing Council Regulation (EC) No 659/1999 laying down detailed rules for the application of Article 93 of the EC Treaty, OJ L 140, 30 April 2004, p. 1.

[11] Pursuant to the *principle of procedural autonomy of the MS*, the MS is free to choose the national procedure for the execution of a recovery decision, provided that it allows the immediate and effective execution of the recovery decision [see CJEU, *Commission v Germany*, Judgment of the Court, 11 September 2014, case C-527/12, ECLI:EU:C:2014:2193].

[12] See CJEU, *Commission v Greece*, Judgment of the Court, 14 November 2018, case C-93/17, ECLI:EU:C:2018:903.

[13] Underlining the obligation of *effectiveness of* results, see *Commission v Italy*, Judgment of the court, 29 March 2012, case C-243/10, ECLI:EU:C:2012:182.

[14] See CJEU, *Commission v France ('Lignes maritimes Marseille-Corse')*, Judgment of the Court, 9 July 2015, case C-63/14, ECLI:EU:C:2015:458.

[15] See GC, *BSCA v Commission*, Judgment of General Court, 25 January 2018, case T-818/14, ECLI:EU:T:2018:33.

[16] The European Commission may refer the matter *directly* to the Court of Justice [Article 108(2) TFEU].

[17] See CJEU, *Commission v Germany*, Judgment of the Court, 12 July 1973, case 70/72, ECLI:EU:C:1973:87, para 13.

[18] See de Almeida 1997, p. 117.

[19] OJ C 318, 24 November 1983, pp. 3–4.

In the second half of the 1980s and into the 1990s, the European Commission began to demand the recovery of unlawful and incompatible State aid more systematically.

In 1999, the basic rules on unlawful State aid recovery were consolidated in the Procedural Regulation.[20] Article 14 of the Procedural Regulation is of particular note to the extent that it confirms the settled case-law of the European Courts[21] and imposes an obligation on the European Commission to order the recovery of unlawful and incompatible aid unless this would be contrary to a general principle of Community law. In other words, the goal is to restore the situation that existed before the unlawful aid was granted.[22]

Paragraph 1 of the cited Article lays down that the MS must take all necessary measures to recover unlawful aid that is found to be incompatible, and para 2 states that the aid to be recovered will include interest accruing between the date on which it became available to the beneficiary and the date of its recovery.

Lastly, para 3 of the Article establishes that the recovery must be effected without delay and in accordance with the procedures set forth in the relevant MS's national law, provided that they allow the immediate and effective execution of the Commission's decision.

Commission Regulation (EC) No 794/2004 was later adopted,[23] introducing new provisions on the implementation of the recovery decision.

It should be noted that the 2007 Commission Communication[24] states that the Commission has demonstrated in recent years that it is prepared to take a firm stance against unlawful aid. At the time, the European Commission considered the situation of unlawful aid to be "really worrying": chief among its concerns were the lengthy recovery procedures and the obstacles to recovery found in several MS.

The European Commission has recently explained the developments in case-law and Commission practice since that date in its 2019 Commission Communication,[25] which repeals and supersedes the 2007 Communication.

The current Procedural Regulation was approved in the same year, which repealed and superseded the 1999 Procedural Regulation.

[20] Council Regulation (EC) No 659/1999 of 22 March 1999 laying down detailed rules for the application of Article 93 of the EC Treaty, OJ L 83, 27 March 1999, pp. 1–9.

[21] Köster 2016, pp. 1599 et seq.

[22] Köster 2016, p. 1600, and case C-610/10, para 105.

[23] Commission Regulation (EC) No 794/2004 of 21 April 2004 implementing Council Regulation (EC) No 659/1999 laying down detailed rules for the application of Article 93 of the EC Treaty, OJ L 140, 30 April 2004, pp. 1–134.

[24] OJ C 272, 15 November 2007, pp. 4–17.

[25] Communication from the Commission—Commission Notice on the recovery of unlawful and incompatible State aid C/2019/5396, OJ C 247, 23 July 2019, pp. 1–23.

The current *Procedural Regulation* was approved by EU Regulation No 2015/1589[26] and dedicates several of the rules to the subject of recovery of unlawful aid. Articles 16 and 17 are particularly noteworthy.[27]

It establishes that, where adverse decisions are taken in cases of unlawful aid, the Commission will decide that the MS concerned must take all necessary measures to recover the aid from the beneficiary. The recovery obligation is limited only if the recovery would be contrary to a general Union law principle.

This obligation to recover the unlawful State aid includes interest at an appropriate rate set by the Commission. Interest accrues between the date on which the unlawful aid became available to the beneficiary and the date of its recovery.

Recovery must be immediate and in accordance with the procedures established in the relevant MS's national law, provided that they allow the immediate and effective execution of the Commission's decision.

To that effect and in the event of proceedings before national courts, the MS concerned shall take all necessary steps available in their legal systems, including provisional measures, without prejudice to Union law. According to the first subparagraph of Article 13(2)(c) of the existing Procedural Regulation provisional recovery shall be put into effect as described above. To this end, the MS concerned must ensure that the beneficiary no longer enjoys the advantage linked to the unlawful and incompatible aid. The MS concerned should justify and fully describe any required interim measures to the European Commission.

Article 17 of the Procedural Regulation also establishes rules regarding the aid recovery statute of limitations, stating that the European Commission's powers to recover aid are subject to a *limitation period of ten years*, which starts to run on the day the unlawful aid is awarded to the beneficiary, either as individual aid or as aid under an aid scheme.

This period can be suspended by any action taken by the European Commission, or by a MS acting at the request of the European Commission, and every suspension resets the limitation period.

Moreover, the limitation period will be suspended for as long as the European Commission decision is the object of proceedings pending before the Court of Justice.

Lastly, any aid that becomes time-barred will be deemed to be an existing aid.

Although the TFEU does not contain any explicit provision on the recovery of unlawful State aid,[28] the Court of Justice has ruled that recovery is the corollary of the general prohibition of State aid laid down in Article 107(1) TFEU and ensures the effectiveness of the standstill obligation laid down in Article 108(3) TFEU. New

---

[26] Council Regulation (EU) 2015/1589 of 13 July 2015 laying down detailed rules for the application of Article 108 of the Treaty on the Functioning of the European Union (codification), OJ L 248, 24 September 2015, pp. 9–29.

[27] On this topic, see Köster 2016, pp. 1618 et seq.

[28] Köster 2016, p. 1601.

aid[29] implemented without notification to or approval by the Commission is therefore unlawful.[30]

Article 4(3) TEU further requires MS to facilitate the achievement of the European Union's tasks. In other words, compliance with the principle of loyal cooperation laid down therein requires that the European Union and the MS assist each other in carrying out those tasks with a view to attaining the objectives of the European Union. This principle applies to all relations between the European Commission and the MS and is particularly important for State aid recovery policy.

According to the case-law of the Court of Justice, Article 108(3) TFEU establishes a preventive supervision of new aid projects. The objective of preventive monitoring organised in this way is that only compatible aid should be implemented. To achieve that objective, the implementation of an aid project is deferred until the doubt as to its compatibility is removed by the European Commission's final decision.[31]

8.2.2 Limits to Recovery

One of the main limits to the recovery of unlawful State aid is found in the claim and evidence that recovery should not take place *because a general principle of the Union has been breached*.

It should be noted that the general principles of European Union law which may serve as a limit to the recovery of unlawful State aid are not listed in statutory law and that the situations in which such arguments are accepted are few and far between. Those principles are identified as the case-law of the General Court and the Court of Justice develops and they are, as a rule, subject to strict interpretation by these Courts.

Practice nevertheless shows that the following are the most frequently claimed principles in the context of the enforcement of the recovery obligation, whose upholding could lead to the invalidity of the recovery order:

(i) The *principle of legal certainty* is among the principles sometimes claimed to avoid European Commission's recovery orders.[32] This principle generally

---

[29] Article 1(c) of Council Regulation (EU) 2015/1589 of 13 July 2015 laying down detailed rules for the application of Article 108 of the Treaty on the Functioning of the European Union (codification), OJ L 248, 24 September 2015, p. 9.

[30] See CJEU, *Eesti Pagar AS v Ettevõtluse Arendamise Sihtasutus and Majandus-ja Kommunikatsiooniministeerium*, Judgment of the Court, 5 March 2019, case C-349/17, ECLI:EU:C:2019:172, paras 84–87. See also Tveit 2019, pp. 186–191.

[31] CJEU, *Deutsche Lufthansa*, Judgment of the Court, 21 November 2013, case C-284/12, EU:C:2013:755, paras 25, 26 and case-law referred to therein.

[32] Among others, see CJEU, *Duff and Others*, Judgment of the Court, 15 February 1996, case C-63/93, ECLI:EU:C:1996:51, para 20. On the doctrine, see Mihaescu-Evans 2016, pp. 389 et seq.

requires legal rules to be clear, precise, and their effects foreseeable, so that interested parties can determine their position in legal situations and relationships governed by European Union law.[33]

Although *in abstracto* it could be accepted that MS and beneficiaries of aid should be protected against a recovery order in the event of a breach of legal certainty, the fact is that the EU courts have interpreted this principle restrictively and accepted that recovery should be limited only in exceptional circumstances, to be assessed on a case-by-case basis.

In other words, this non-recovery ground has enjoyed little to no acceptance, being rejected from the outset because any security afforded by national law is outweighed by the principle of primacy and the principle of the effectiveness of Union law.[34]

(ii) Another principle claimed to avoid a recovery decision is the *principle of the protection of legitimate expectations.*[35] This principle must protect the justified expectations of MS and aid beneficiaries and could preclude the European Commission from ordering the recovery of the aid.

As the Court of Justice has consistently held, the right to rely on the principle of the protection of legitimate expectations presupposes that *precise, unconditional and consistent assurances, emanating from sources which are authorised and reliable, have been* given to the person concerned by an institution, body, office or agency of the Union by *the competent authorities of the Union.*[36]

The Court of Justice, having regard to the mandatory nature of the supervision of State aid by the European Commission under Article 108 TFEU, finds, first, that undertakings to which aid has been granted may not, in principle, entertain a legitimate expectation that the aid is lawful unless it has been granted in compliance with the procedure laid down in that article and, second, that a diligent economic operator must usually be able to determine whether that procedure has been complied with.

Claiming this principle as a ground for non-recovery of unlawful State aid has not been generally accepted, where aid has been granted without prior notice to the European Commission and is therefore unlawful under Article 108(3) TFEU. In sum, the Court of Justice has held that the beneficiary of the aid cannot, at that time, entertain a legitimate expectation that the aid was granted lawfully.[37]

---

[33] See case C-63/93, para 20.

[34] See Quigley 2015, pp. 581 et seq.; Mihaescu-Evans 2016, pp. 381 et seq.

[35] See CJEU, *Commission v Germany*, Judgment of the Court, 20 September 1990, case C-5/89, ECLI:EU:C:1990:320, paras 13 and 14. See also Adrien 2008, pp. 1399–1431.

[36] See CJEU, *ISD Polska and Others v Commission*, Judgment of the Court, 24 March 2011, case C-369/09 P, ECLI:EU:C:2011:175, para 123; CJEU, *Kahla Thüringen Porzellan v Commission*, Judgment of the Court, 16 December 2010, case C-537/08 P, ECLI:EU:C:2010:769, para 63; CJEU, *Masdar (UK) v Commission*, Judgment of the Court, 16 December 2008, case C-47/07 P, ECLI:EU:C:2008:726, paras 34 and 81.

[37] See CJEU, *Unicredito Italiano SpA v Agenzia delle Entrate, Ufficio Genova 1*, Judgment of the Court, 15 December 2005, case C-148/04, EU:C:2005:774, para 104, and *OTP Bank Nyrt. v*

(iii) The *principle of "res judicata"* is also claimed sometimes.[38] Pursuant to this principle, court decisions that have become *res judicata* after all available remedies have been exhausted or become time-barred can no longer be challenged.[39]

Despite the legal force of the principle of "*res judicata*" both within the legal systems of the MS and of the Union, the fact is that this principle is far outweighed by the principle of the primacy of European Union law.

In other words, EU rules on State aid take precedence, as a rule, over national court decisions whose consequence of applying the principle of "*res judicata*" would be a breach of EU rules on State aid.

(iv) Another principle to bear in mind is the *principle of the absolute impossibility of recovery.*[40] Underlying this principle is the idea that "nobody has an obligation to do the impossible". However, this principle too is interpreted restrictively by the case-law of the Court of Justice.[41]

It should be noted that any obstacles encountered cannot be a result of the national legal (administrative or technical) system or of the dire economic situation of the beneficiary and they must be proven: merely claiming legal, political, practical, or internal difficulties is not enough.

For this argument of non-recovery to be accepted the MS must prove that it has taken *all necessary steps to recover the aid* by removing all national, including legal, obstacles to the recovery.

A further argument that could prevent the recovery decision arises from the *limitation period*. The Procedural Regulation, in Article 17(1), provides for a period of 10 years. This limitation period starts to run on the day on which the unlawful aid is awarded to the beneficiary,[42] either as individual aid or as aid under an aid scheme.

In the case of an *aid scheme*, the limitation period does not start to run from the date of adoption of its legal basis, but from the moment when the individual aid is *granted* under that scheme.[43]

Magyar Állam and Magyar Államkincstár, Judgment of the Court, 19 March 2015, case C-672/13, EU:C:2015:185, para 77.

[38] See CJEU, *Commission v Slovakia ("Frucona Košice")*, Judgment of the Court, 22 December 2010, case C-507/08, ECLI:EU:C:2010:802.

[39] See case C-507/08, para 59.

[40] See CJEU; *Commission v France ('Plans de Campagne')*, Judgment of the Court, 12 February 2015, case C-37/14, ECLI:EU:C:2015:90, para 67.

[41] See CJEU, *Commission v Greece ("Larco")*, Judgment of the Court, 9 November 2017, case C-481/16, ECLI:EU:C:2017:845, para 28.

[42] See GC, *BSCA v Commission*, Judgment of the General Court, 25 January 2018, case T-818/14, ECLI:EU:T:2018:33, para 72.

[43] See CJEU, *France Télécom v Commission*, Judgment of the Court, 8 December 2011, case C-81/10 P, ECLI:EU:C:2011:811, para 80.

The limitation period is suspended by any action taken by the European Commission or by a MS, acting at the request of the European Commission, in connection the unlawful aid.

It should be noted that those limitation rules are European rules and must not be confused with national rules. Moreover, the Court of Justice has held that national rules on limitation cannot justify a failure to comply with the obligation to recover and must not be applied, if necessary.[44]

8.2.3 Recovery Decision

Following the recovery decision, an *obligation of effective recovery* on the part of the MS arises. There is a question as to the *nature* of the recovery obligation: the case-law of the Court of Justice considers that recovery should not be regarded as a penalty[45] but rather as a logical consequence of the fact that they were found to be unlawful.[46]

The fact that it is not regarded as a penalty means that the beneficiary of unlawful aid cannot be required to recover more than the amount actually received (and any interest). In other words, the amount to be recovered is equivalent to the undue advantage received and is therefore aimed at removing the cause for distortion of competition.

The duty to recover reflects a responsibility shared between the European Commission and the MS. It should be noted at the outset that the European Commission plays a very important role in the recovery decision, by adopting a decision finding the aid to be incompatible with the internal market.

This is a binding decision, since the European Commission has no discretion and must order the recovery of the aid,[47]—save where this would be contrary to a general principle of European Union law, as mentioned above. The European Commission's very important role in the identification of beneficiaries and the quantification of the amount to be recovered should also be highlighted.

The *role of the MS in the implementation of the recovery decision* also deserves to be stressed: the MS must take all necessary measures to recover the aid from the

[44] See CJEU, *Land Rheinland-Pfalz v Alcan Deutschland*, Judgment of the Court, 20 March 1997, case C-24/95, ECLI:EU:C:1997:163, paras 34 and 37.

[45] Quigley 2015, pp. 586 and 587.

[46] See CJEU, *Commission v Aer Lingus*, Judgment of the Court, 21 December 2016, case C-164/15P and C-165/15P, ECLI:EU:C:2016:990, paras 114 and 116.

[47] See CJEU, *Italy v Commission ('Employment Measures I')*, Judgment of the Court, 7 March 2002, case C-310/99, ECLI:EU:C:2002:143, para 99.

beneficiary and can choose how to perform its recovery obligation, provided that it complies with the principle of effectiveness[48] and the principle of equivalence.[49]

But the fact that recovery decisions are implemented by the MS themselves is a system weakness, since they are the ones who grant the aid and often do not give priority to its recovery.[50]

Lastly, it should be noted that the decision is addressed to the State broadly speaking (the Executive, the Judicial and Legislative Branches) and not to the beneficiary.[51]

The *obligation to repay* lies with the beneficiary of the unlawful aid. If the beneficiaries cannot be easily identified, the beneficiary of the aid must be considered within the context of the group of undertakings making up the economic unit to which the undertaking belongs.[52]

The concept of undertaking must be understood in the light of the concept of undertaking as understood by European case-law.[53]

The principle of economic unity requires that undertakings belonging to a group—even if qualified as separate legal entities under national law—which form an economic unit for the purposes of competition law and have benefited from the aid, are covered.

Furthermore, if it is established that aid has been transferred to another undertaking besides the original beneficiary, such aid must be recovered from the undertaking that effectively enjoys its advantage.[54]

The case-law of the Court of Justice allows for two ways of transferring the activities of an undertaking:

(i) the sale of all or part of its assets, after which the activity is no longer carried on by the same legal entity; and
(ii) the sale of its shares, after which the undertaking that benefited from the aid retains its legal personality and continues to carry on its activities.[55]

There are two possible hypotheses regarding the quantification of the amount to be recovered. One is that the European Commission has already quantified the amount

[48] See CJEU, *Commission v France ('Scott')*, Judgment of the Court, 5 October 2006, case C-232/05, ECLI:EU:C:2006:651, para 49.

[49] See CJEU, *Netherlands v Commission*, Judgment of the Court, 13 June 2002, case C-382/99, ECLI:EU:C:2002:363, para 90.

[50] Estoa Pérez 2008, pp. 193–211.

[51] Quigley 2015, p. 579.

[52] Se GC, *DSG v Commission*, Judgment of the General Court, 29 June 2000, case T-234/95, ECLI:EU:T:2000:174, para 124.

[53] See Chap. 4, Sect. 4.4.

[54] See GC, *Greece v Commission*, Judgment of the General Court, 13 September 2010, joined cases T-415/05, T-416/05 and T-423/05, ECLI:EU:T:2010:386, paras 143–146.

[55] See CJEU, *Germany v Commission ('SMI')*, Judgment of the Court, 29 April 2004, case C-277/00, ECLI:EU:C:2004:238, paras 78 and 84.

to be recovered. The other is that the amount has not been quantified and must be quantified by the MS.

In addition to the above amount, account must be taken of the interest to be recovered, accruing between the date on which the aid was made available to the beneficiary and the date of its recovery.

The amount of such interest must be equivalent to the financial advantage of providing the relevant principal free of charge for a certain period since the goal is to avoid incidental financial advantages.[56]

The *implementation of the recovery decision* can be final or provisional. Recovery is final as a rule, but it can be provisional in certain circumstances. The recovery decision is provisional if it is the object of legal proceedings, in which case a MS may accept provisional repayment of the aid to be recovered.

The beneficiary may, for instance, pay the full recovery amount into an escrow account by way of provisional recovery.

It should be stressed that the MS are afforded great freedom/autonomy to choose the national procedure to implement the recovery decision.

However, that autonomy is limited by the principle of effectiveness of Union law—according to the Court of Justice: "*a Member State is under an obligation to recover only if the measures it adopts are appropriate to restore normal competition conditions that have been distorted by the grant of the unlawful aid the recovery of which has been ordered*".[57]

An aid beneficiary that cannot repay the aid and the recovery interest because it became insolvent should in principle exit the market. In the case of an insolvent beneficiary, the MS may only seize the assets of the aid beneficiary and liquidate it if the latter is unable to repay the aid or take any other measure to recover the aid as provided for in its national law.[58]

If the beneficiary is already undergoing insolvency proceedings, the previous situation can be restored and the distortion of competition resulting from the aid eliminated by entering the claim related to the aid to be recovered into the table of claims within the recovery period.[59]

The recovery deadline is of particular importance for the implementation of the European Commission's recovery decision. This time-limit must be observed, failing which the MS will be deemed in breach of its recovery obligations. In other words, the MS remains in default in this instance, and the duty to recover subsists.

---

[56] See GC, *Siemens v Commission*, Judgment of the General Court, 8 June 1995, case T-459/93, ECLI:EU:T:1995:100, paras 97–101.

[57] See CJEU, *Scott SA and Kimberly Clark SAS v Ville d'Orléans*, Judgment of the Court, 20 May 2010, case C-210/09, ECLI:EU:C:2010:294.

[58] See CJEU, *Commission v Greece ('United Textiles')*, Judgment of the Court, 17 January 2018, case C-363/16, ECLI:EU:C:2018:12, para 36. See also Cock and Leroy 2018, pp. 298–304.

[59] See case C-610/10, paras 72 and 104.

There are two procedural deadlines, namely a deadline to provide information (complete information on the identity of the beneficiaries if they are not already identified in the recovery decision, the amount to be recovered and the applicable national procedure to comply with the recovery obligation) and a deadline to perform the recovery obligation.

The Commission may consider extending the deadline for the execution of the decision if the MS is having difficulties implementing the recovery decision and following the European Communication[60] of such difficulties to the European Commission, although such a practice tends to be regarded as exceptional.

8.2.4 Non-execution of the Recovery Decision: Possible Reactions

Where a MS has not complied with the recovery decision and has failed to demonstrate the absolute impossibility of recovery, it may be subject to:

(i) administrative offense proceedings,
(ii) the payment of new compatible aid to the beneficiary or beneficiaries concerned, contingent upon the recovery of the previous aid found to be unlawful and incompatible, and
(iii) civil liability proceedings against the MS based on breach of Union law.

One of the possible consequences of a Member State's failure to comply with the recovery decision and to demonstrate the absolute impossibility of recovery, is that the European Commission can initiate administrative offense proceedings pursuant to Article 28 of the Procedural Regulation.[61]

An action may be brought under Article 108(2) TFEU, which states that the European Commission may refer the matter directly to the Court of Justice if the MS concerned does not comply with the recovery decision within the recovery deadline. The decision to bring the case before the Court of Justice rests with the European Commission and is taken on a case-by-case basis based on objective reasons, the Member State's commitments and the measures already taken to implement the decision.[62]

In addition, and as a consequence, an action may be brought on the basis of Article 260(2) TFEU, which states that if the European Commission considers that a MS has failed to fulfil its obligations arising from a judgment under Article 108(2) TFEU, it may refer the matter to the Court of Justice after giving that State the opportunity to submit its observations. This procedure seeks to force a defaulting MS to comply

[60] Communication from the Commission—Commission Notice on the recovery of unlawful and incompatible State aid (C/2019/5396), OJ C 247, 23 July 2019, pp. 1–23.

[61] Quigley 2015, pp. 603 et seq.

[62] See CJEU cases C-363/16; C-481/16; C-63/14; *Commission v Germany ('Deutsche Post')*, Judgment of the Court, 6 May 2015, case C-674/13, ECLI:EU:C:2015:302.

with a previous judgment establishing a failure to fulfil its obligations, and thus to ensure the effective application of European Union law. Lastly, if the Court of Justice should find that the MS concerned has not complied with its judgment, it may impose a lump sum or penalty payment.[63]

As mentioned above, another consequence of not implementing the recovery decision (if it has not been demonstrated that recovery is absolutely impossible), is that the payment of a new compatible aid to the beneficiary or beneficiaries concerned is contingent on the recovery of the previous aid considered unlawful and incompatible: *Deggendorf principle.*[64]

In other words, according to the case-law of the Court of Justice, which has settled the above-mentioned principle,[65] if certain conditions have been fulfilled the European Commission may require MS to suspend the payment of a new compatible aid to an undertaking until the latter has reimbursed any former unlawful and incompatible aid subject to a recovery decision.

A limitation of the *Deggendorf* jurisprudence is that its effects are limited to undertakings claiming an aid while another aid is still to be recovered. If that is not the case—if no new application for aid is pending—there will be less pressure on the State and the beneficiary to recover the unlawful aid.[66]

One way to relax these limits has been for the European Commission to apply this case-law to undertakings belonging to the same *economic unit* as the beneficiary. E.g., when the aid is for a *newly* created undertaking controlled by the beneficiary of the aid that is to be rescued,[67] because the undertakings form an economic unit although they are different, it is appropriate to treat them as if they were a single undertaking for competition rules' purposes.

Lastly, it should be noted that the European Commission has ample discretion to determine whether undertakings that are part of a group are to be regarded as an economic unit for the purposes of the State aid rules.[68]

One of the remaining remedies to ensure the effectiveness of the rules on State aid can be found in the mechanism of *civil liability of MS for breach of Union law.* Despite the absence of an express reference in the Treaties, the Court of Justice has

---

[63] See CJEU: case C-93; *Commission v Italy ('Venice and Chioggia II')*, Judgment of the Court, 17 September 2015, case C-367/14, ECLI:EU:C:2015:611; *Commission v Italy ('Employment Measures II')*, Judgment of the Court, 17 November 2011, case C-496/09, ECLI:EU:C:2011:740; *Commission v Spain ('Basque fiscal aid')*, Judgment of the Court, 13 May 2014, case C-184/11, ECLI:EU:C:2014:316.

[64] See CJEU, *TWD v Commission*, Judgment of the Court, 15 May 1997, case C-355/95 P, ECLI:EU:C:1997:241, paras 25 and 26, and Estoa Pérez 2008, pp. 193–211.

[65] See CJEU, case C-355/95 P, paras 25 and 26.

[66] See Estoa Pérez 2008, p. 202.

[67] See ibid., pp. 202 et seq.

[68] See GC, *Pollmeier Malchow v Commission*, Judgment of the Court, 14 October 2004, case T-137/02, ECLI:EU:T:2004:304, and *British Airways and others and British Midland Airways v Commission*, Judgment of the Court, 25 June 1998, joined cases T-371/94 and T-394/94, ECLI:EU:T:1998:140, paras 313 and 314.

formulated the principle of patrimonial liability of MS for breach of Union law, taking into account the need to improve the effective protection of the rights of individuals and of the Union legal order itself.[69]

The principle of State liability for breaches of Union law was first expressed in the *Francovich*[70] and *Brasserie du Pêcheur*[71] judgments. In summary, such case-law confirms that MS must compensate injured individuals for any loss and damage arising from breaches of European Community law for which they are liable. To this end—although inspired by the general principles of MS civil liability—an autonomous civil liability system has been developed, based on three requirements: (i) the rule of law breached is designed to vest rights in individuals; (ii) the breach is sufficiently serious; and (iii) there is a direct causal link between the breach of the obligation incumbent upon the MS and the damage suffered by the injured parties.[72]

In the context of State aid, the civil liability of MS[73] may arise from (i) the *breach of the standstill obligation*[74] [provided for in Article 108(3) TFEU, since this is a provision of European law which is directly applicable to, and binding on all MS authorities] and (ii) the *failure of MS authorities to comply with a recovery decision adopted by the European Commission.*

The Member State's recovery obligation is designed to protect the same individual rights as the standstill obligation, and the Commission's recovery decisions do not afford national authorities any discretion. Breaches of the recovery obligation are therefore considered sufficiently serious in principle.[75]

Although the first two conditions for civil liability arising from breaches of European Union law by MS in application of State aid rules—(i) the rule of law breached is designed to vest rights in individuals; (ii) the breach is sufficiently serious[76]—may be deemed satisfied, the success of such an action remains predicated on a direct causal link between the breach of the Member State's obligation to recover and the loss or damage sustained by the injured parties.

Moreover, the Court of Justice has held that *affected third parties* may bring actions for damages under national law. National courts may consequently also be required to uphold *claims for compensation for damages caused to competitors of*

---

69 On the topic see, among many, Anagnostaras 2001, pp. 281–305; Tridimas 2001; Pedro 2016, pp. 61 et seq.

70 See CJEU, *Francovich and Bonifaci v Italy*, Judgment of the Court, 19 November 1991, joined cases C-6/90 and C-9/90, ECLI:EU:C:1991:428.

71 See CJEU, *Brasserie du Pêcheur v Bundesrepublik Deutschland and The Queen v Secretary of State for Transport, ex parte Factortame and others*, Judgment of the Court, 5 March 1996, joined cases C-46/93 and C-48/93, ECLI:EU:C:1996:79.

72 See CJEU, *Traghetti del Mediterraneo SpA v Repubblica italiana*, Judgment of the Court, 13 June 2006, case C-173/03, ECLI:EU:C:2006:391.

73 Honoré and Jensen 2011, pp. 265–86.

74 Quigley 2015, p. 654.

75 See also Quigley 2015, pp. 651 et seq.

76 Honoré and Jensen 2011, pp. 265–86.

the beneficiary and to third parties[77] *by unlawful State aid* against the State aid granting authority and under national law,[78] within their remit under Article 108(3) TFEU.

Lastly, *claims for damages* may also be brought *against the beneficiary of the unlawful aid.* In other words, the claimant may prefer to claim damages directly from the beneficiary in certain circumstances. In the *SFEI* judgment,[79] the Court of Justice expressly addressed the question whether claims for damages can be brought against the beneficiary under EU law, and concluded that EU law does not provide a sufficient legal basis for such claims,[80] since Article 108(3) TFEU does not impose any direct obligations on the beneficiary. But this in no way impairs the possibility of bringing an action for damages against the beneficiary based on national law's substantive provisions. In this context, the Court of Justice has specifically referred to the possibility of potential claimants relying on national law's non-contractual liability provisions.[81]

8.3 Recovery of Unlawful *De Minimis* Aid

In the 2007 Notice[82] the Commission clarified that in case of an unlawful and incompatible aid regime, the MS must carry out a detailed analysis of each individual aid granted under the scheme in question.

In order to determine the exact amount of aid to be recovered from each beneficiary under the scheme, it must determine the extent to which the aid has been granted to a specific project satisfying all conditions of the block exemption regulation at the time the aid was granted, or within an aid scheme approved by the European Commission.

In such cases, the MS may also apply the substantive *de minimis* criteria applicable at the time of granting the unlawful and incompatible aid subject to the recovery decision.

---

[77] See CJEU, *Centre d'exportation du livre français (CELF) and Ministre de la Culture et de la Communication v Société internationale de diffusion et d'édition (SIDE)*, Judgment of the Court, 12 February 2008, case C-199/06, ECLI:EU:C:2008:79, paras 53 and 55; *Transalpine Ölleitung in Österreich GmbH and Others v Finanzlandesdirektion für Tirol and Others*, Judgment of the Court, 5 October 2006, case C-368/04, ECLI:EU:C:2006:644, para 56; *Commission v Freistaat Sachsen*, Judgment of the Court, 11 December 2008, case C-334/07 P, ECLI:EU:C:2008:709, para 54.

[78] See CJEU, case C-199/06, para 53 and 55; case C-368/04, para 56; *SFEI and others*, Judgment of the Court, 11 July 1996, case C-39/94, ECLI:EU:C:1996:285, para 75.

[79] See case C-39/94.

[80] See case C-39/94.

[81] See case C-39/94.

[82] Notice from the Commission—Towards an effective implementation of Commission decisions ordering Member States to recover unlawful and incompatible State aid, OJ C 272, 15 November 2007, pp. 4–17.

More recently, the 2019 Communication[83] clarified the European Commission's position, namely that the MS is in principle required to recover all aid, unless it met the requirements set forth in any of the instruments below at the time it was granted:

(i) a regulation declaring certain categories of aid compatible with the internal market pursuant to Articles 107 and 108 TFEU;
(ii) a regulation determining that some public support does not meet all the criteria of Article 107(1) TFEU and is therefore exempt from notification under Article 108(3) TFEU—as is the case for *de minimis* regimes;
(iii) a different, earlier decision of the European Commission.[84]

Moreover, according to the European Commission, retroactive application of the *de minimis rule* to an aid beneficiary can be accepted subject to the following conditions:[85]

(i) the total amount of aid must be below the *de minimis* ceiling;[86] in that regard, the use of average amounts per beneficiary is not acceptable because it is not a sure way of determining whether an undertaking has not received a total aid amount exceeding that ceiling; this assertion is based on the case-law of the Court of Justice,[87] which rules out the possibility of calculating the amount of aid to be recovered by dividing the overall amount of aid in equal parts by the economic sectors indicated in the decision challenged, in order to demonstrate that the *de minimis* thresholds were not exceeded;
(ii) when retrospectively verifying the amount of *de minimis* aid granted over a period of three fiscal years, a MS must consider each period of the three fiscal years that includes the date on which the aid that should allegedly be excluded from recovery was granted; thus, if a MS claims in 2022 that an advantage granted on 31 December 2018 could be considered retrospectively as *de minimis* aid, that MS must also prove that by including that new *de minimis* aid, the ceiling is not exceeded in any of the following three-year periods: 2016–2018, 2017–2019 and 2018–2020; and
(iii) all conditions set out in the relevant regulation must be satisfied, which may apply retrospectively.

In addition to the retrospective application of the regime referred to above, it is important to take into account the instances in which aid that does not comply with

---

[83] Communication from the Commission—Commission Notice on the recovery of unlawful and incompatible State aid, C/2019/5396, OJ C 247, 23 July 2019, pp. 1–23.

[84] For instance, see Commission Decision of 11 July 2001 on the State aid scheme applied by Spain to certain newly established firms in Álava, OJ L 314, 18 November 2002, p. 1, recital 90.

[85] Communication from the Commission—Commission Notice on the recovery of unlawful and incompatible State aid (C/2019/5396), OJ C 247, 23 July 2019, pp. 1–23.

[86] See GC, *Regione autonoma della Sardegna and Others v Commission*, Judgment of the General Court, 20 September 2011, joined cases T-394/08, T-408/08, T-453/08 and T-454/08, ECLI:EU:T:2011:493, paras 310–312, and CJEU, *HGA and Others v Commission*, Judgment of the Court, 13 June 2013, case C-630/11 P to C-633/11 P, ECLI:EU:C:2013:387.

[87] See CJEU, *Commission v Belgium*, Judgment of the Court, 13 September 2017, case C-591/14, ECLI:EU:C:2017:670, para 46.

the requirements of *de minimis* rules, which must be notified under Article 108(3) TFEU. If they fail to meet those requirements, they should be considered unlawful pursuant to the rules for recovery of unlawful aid mentioned above.

The question now is whether a separate legal regime should apply in addition to the recovery regime applicable to unlawful State aid, when it is a *de minimis* regime and *in the absence of a Commission decision*, with more emphasis on the domestic law of the MS and a greater role for the national authorities.

In this context, reference is made to a recent judgment of the Court of Justice—case C-349/17[88]—which is based on the block exemption regulation adopted by Regulation No 800/2008.[89] In short, the Court of Justice was faced with the question of whether or not the conditions to apply the regulation were satisfied and of which regime should apply absent a European Commission recovery decision.

The specific issue at stake was whether the aid was requested before or after the start of the project for which the aid was intended, given that Article 8(2) of Regulation No 800/2008 required applications for aid to be made before work started so as to ensure the incentive effect of the aid.

In addition, it should also be borne in mind that the request for a preliminary ruling in question arose because the authorities of the MS had *themselves* requested the recovery of the aid unlawfully granted, which raised a few doubts regarding the interpretation and application of the legal framework to be applied in the case in question.[90]

Five questions were referred to the Court of Justice for a preliminary ruling, concerning: (i) the incentive effect of the aid; (ii) the obligation to recover the aid; (iii) the principle of legitimate expectations; (iv) the limitation period applicable to the recovery of the aid; (v) the obligation to claim interest.

In the light of the questions referred for a preliminary ruling by the national court—and for the purposes of this study—it is important to note that the Court of Justice makes clear the *importance of domestic law and the role of the national authorities in effecting the recovery of unlawful aid* where there is no recovery decision by the European Commission, primarily because the procedural regulation does not address the MS.

---

[88] See case C-349/17.

[89] Commission Regulation (EC) No 800/2008 of 6 August 2008 declaring certain categories of aid compatible with the common market in application of Articles 87 and 88 of the Treaty, OJ L 214, 9 August 2008, pp. 3–47.

[90] See *Eesti Pagar AS v Ettevõtluse Arendamise Sihtasutus and Majandus-ja Kommunikatsioonimin-isteerium*, Opinion of Advocate General, 25 September 2018, case C-349/17, ECLI:EU:C:2018:768, para 106: "*Although it may appear that the finding of the existence of such an obligation is unprecedented in the case-law of the Court of Justice, which has ruled only in the context of Commission decisions or national court cases, I agree with the Estonian Government that an obligation must be inferred from Articles 107(1) and 108(3) TFEU, and from the principle of loyal cooperation enshrined in Article 4 TEU, that the national authorities are obliged to recover unlawful aid on their own initiative*".

As regards the first and second questions, it should be pointed out that the Court of Justice recognises, first, that it is for the national authorities to check whether the requirements of the systems of exceptions to notification are met, *in this case* as provided for in Regulation No 800/2008 and, second, the direct effect and direct applicability of Article 108(3) TFEU.

In the light of the foregoing, the Court of Justice makes it clear that it is for the national courts to ensure that all the consequences of the breach of Article 108(3) are drawn in accordance with national law, in particular as regards the recovery of financial assistance granted in breach of that provision.

Moreover, the Court of Justice points out that the direct effect of those rules is binding not only on the national courts but also on the public authorities. In the light of the *present* case—*considering that the incentive effect of the aid has not been established*—the Court of Justice has held that it is for the various national authorities to recover aid which has been unlawfully granted on their own initiative, if they find that the statutory requirements for the grant of aid are not met.

As regards the third question, in the light of the present case, the Court of Justice considers that the limitation on recovery claimed by reference to the *principle of the protection of legitimate expectations* has not been observed, citing the case-law set out above.

As regards the fourth question, which *concerned the determination of the limitation period applicable to the recovery of unlawful aid*, the Court of Justice referred to the Procedural Regulation in force at that time (Regulation No 659/1999) and made it clear that regulation contains rules of a procedural nature, which apply to all State aid related administrative procedures pending before the European Commission and that it codifies and underpins the Commission's State aid examination practice. However, the Regulation is silent on the remit of the national courts, which continue to be governed by the provisions of the Treaty as interpreted by the Court of Justice. Considering the particular nature of the project (which was co-financed by a Structural Fund), the Court of Justice decided that the limitation period applicable to the recovery of unlawful aid is four years if the conditions for the application of Regulation No 2988/95[91] are satisfied, or, failing that, the period prescribed by the applicable national law.

Lastly, as regards the fifth question, the Court of Justice made it clear that Article 108(3) TFEU requires the national authority to order the aid recipient to pay interest in respect of the period of unlawfulness. As regards the rules applicable to the calculation of interest, in the absence of Union rules on the subject, unlawful aid must be recovered in accordance with the applicable rules of national law with due regard for the principle of effectiveness and equivalence. It further clarified that, in that regard, Article 108(3) TFEU requires those rules to ensure full recovery of the unlawful aid and, therefore, to order the beneficiary of that aid to pay interest on the entire period during which it benefited from that aid, at a rate equal to that which would have

[91] Council Regulation (EC, Euratom) No 2988/95 of 18 December 1995 on the protection of the European Communities financial interests, OJ L 312, 23 December 1995, pp. 1–4.

applied if it had to borrow a loan for the amount of the aid in question on the market and during that period.

One needs now to consider the application of the above case-law to the hypothesis of *de minimis* aid. In addition to the European Commission's role in matters of recovery of unlawful *State aid* and the role of the MS under the principle of loyal cooperation, there is a parallel hypothesis that the MS is responsible for recovering *de minimis* aid through the court system, in accordance with the case-law of the Court of Justice handed down under a block exemption regulation. The parallel hypothesis is that the MS is tasked with using all means to recover unlawful *de minimis* aid and apply national law in situations where there is no recovery decision by the European Commission through its Courts and administrative authorities.

The general guideline is that such assumption should be made in the light of the provisions of national law, provided that they are governed by the principle of effectiveness and the principle of equivalence.

If that case-law is to be considered valid, priority must be given to the application of national law. The main question is whether the procedural regulation applies to the national authorities of the MS. As the Advocate-General points out[92] and the Court of Justice[93] has already clarified, although Regulation No 659/1999 contains rules of a procedural nature applicable to all State aid related administrative procedures pending before the European Commission, it is clear from recital 2 and from all the provisions of that regulation that *it contains no provisions concerning the powers and obligations of national courts, which remain governed by the provisions of the Treaty as interpreted by the Court of Justice.*

This is a controversial issue; however, as the Advocate-General states,[94] it should be considered whether the Procedural Regulation should not be applied by analogy since this would be contrary to the principles of good administration, legitimate expectations (legal clarity) and legal certainty.[95]

In addition to the role already incumbent on the MS under the Procedural Regulation, it could be argued that there *should be an 'internal recovery decision'* since it is for the national authorities to ensure that all the consequences of the breach of Article 108(3) are addressed in accordance with national law, as regards the recovery of aid granted in breach of that provision. In other words, it is for the various national authorities to recover aid which has been granted unlawfully on their own initiative, if they establish that the legal requirements for the grant of aid are not met.

As regards the *recovery period*, according to the Court of Justice, the application of the ten-year period provided for in Article 15 of Regulation No 659/1999 by analogy in circumstances such as those prevailing in the present case cannot be regarded as

[92] See *Transalpine Ölleitung in Österreich GmbH and Others v Finanzlandesdirektion für Tirol and Others*, Opinion of Advocate General, 29 November 2005, case C-368/04, ECLI:EU:C:2005:724, para 78.

[93] See case C-368/04, paras 34 and 35.

[94] See Opinion of Advocate General, case C-368/04.

[95] Although the Advocate-General is only referring to the 10-year time limit set forth in the Procedural Regulation.

sufficiently foreseeable by any individual. The Court of Justice thus rules in a manner contrary to that advocated by the Notice on the application of the State aid legislation to national courts,[96] in which the Commission refers to Regulation No 659/1999 as regards the interest to be claimed, and advocates, in essence, the application by analogy of that regulation by the national courts.

Lastly, with regard to *any interest to be recovered*, the Court of Justice dismissed the application of Article 14(2) of Regulation No 659/1999 and of Articles 9 and 11 of Regulation No 794/2004, either directly or by analogy, stating that the legal basis for the calculation of interest is Article 108(3) TFEU, interpreted in conjunction with the principle of effectiveness. Consequently, absent any Union rules on the matter, the unlawful aid must be recovered in accordance with the applicable rules of national law, subject to the principles of effectiveness and equivalence.

In short, where unlawful *de minimis* aid is at issue without a recovery decision by the European Commission, it could be argued that it is for the national authorities to take all necessary steps to ensure effective and immediate recovery on their own initiative by applying national law as a rule, albeit subject to the principle of effectiveness and equivalence. In other words, these duties, which are incumbent on the authorities of the MS, relate to *compliance with the law*, without prejudice to a possible control of the *de minimis* aid as regards its compatibility with the internal market by the European Commission, under the control of the Union Courts.

Lastly, the means deployed by the MS to recover unlawful aid may be challenged and annulled before the national courts, as a corollary of the principle of effective judicial protection.

References

Adrien G (2008) A Study of the Notion of Legitimate Expectations in State Aid Recovery Proceedings: 'Abandon All Hope, Ye Who Enter Here'? Common Market Law Review 45: 1399–1431

Anagnostaras G (2001) The Principle of State Liability for Judicial Breaches: the Impact of European Community Law. European Public Law 7: 281–305

Birnstiel A (2012) Recovery of unlawful State aid: the role of Member State Courts in State aid recovery scenarios. European State Aid Law Quarterly 3: 645–665

de Almeida JJN (1997) A restituição das ajudas de Estado concedidas em violação do direito comunitário [Recovery of State aid granted in breach of Community law]. Coimbra Editora, Coimbra

De Cock W, Leroy J (2018) United Textiles: Is There a Possibility to Relaunch the Activities of Insolvent Aid Beneficiaries in State Aid Recovery Proceedings? Annotation on the Judgment of the Court of Justice of the European Union (First Chamber) of 17 January 2018 in Case C-363/16 European Commission v Greece. European State Aid Law Quarterly 17: 298–304

Donzelli S (2019) The Commission's New Recovery Notice: A Handbook for the Recovery of Unlawful and Incompatible Aid. European State Aid Law Quarterly 18: 528–539

[96] Commission Notice on the enforcement of State aid law by national courts, OJ C 85, 9 April 2009, pp. 1–22.

Estoa Pérez A (2008) La jurisprudencia Deggendorf como medio de forzar la recuperación de las ayudas ilegales [Deggendorf jurisprudence as a means of enforcing recovery of unlawful aid]. Revista de derecho comunitario europeo 29: 193–211

Ghazarian L (2016) Recovery Of State Aid: The Obligations of Member States, National Courts and National Authorities in State Aid Recovery and Recent Developments in the Case-Law of the Court of Justice of the European Union. European State Aid Law Quarterly 15: 228–234

Goffart P (2021) Der unionsrechtliche Verhältnismäßigkeitsgrundsatz als Grenze der Rückforderung unionsrechtswidriger mitgliedstaatlicher Beihilfen [The principle of proportionality under Union law as a limit to the Recovery of unlawful State aid from Member States]. Nomos, Baden-Baden

Honoré M, Jensen NE (2011) Damages in State Aid Cases. European State Aid Law Quarterly 10: 265–86

Jouve D (2017) Recovering Unlawful and Incompatible Aids by National Courts: CELF and Scott/Kimberly Clark Cases. European State Aid Law Quarterly 16: 367–376

Köster T (2016) Part X, Art. 7-30. In: Säcker FJ, Montag F (eds) European State Aid Law: A Commentary. Verlag C.H. Beck, Munich, pp 1581–1648

Merola M, Cappelletti L (2011) The Obligation to Recover Unlawful Aid. Journal of European Competition Law & Practice 2: 465–468

Mihaescu-Evans BC (2016) Recovery of Unlawful Aid and the Role of National Courts. In: Hofmann HCH, Micheau C (eds) State Aid Law of the European Union. Oxford University Press, Oxford, pp 381–398

Pedro R (2016) Responsabilidade civil do Estado pelo mau funcionamento da administração da justiça: fundamento, conceito e âmbito [State liability for the malfunctioning of the administration of justice: basis, concept, and scope]. Almedina, Coimbra

Quigley C (2015) European State Aid Law and Policy, 3rd edn. Hart Publishing, Oxford/Portland, Oregon

Rodríguez Pontón FJ (2019) Ayudas de Estado ilegales, obligación de recuperación y reclamación patrimonial: la reaparición del caso de las 'vacaciones fiscales vascas' [Illegal state aid, recovery obligation and compensation claims: the re-emergence of the 'Basque tax holiday' case]. Revista de Administración Pública 208: 299–324

Tridimas T (2001) Liability for Breaches of Community law: Growing Up and Mellowing Down. Common Market Law Review 38: 301–332

Tveit ST (2019) A New Boost to National Recovery? Case C-349/17 Eesti Pagar Annotation on the Judgment of the Court (Grand Chamber) of 5 March 2019 in Case C-349/17 Eesti Pagar AS v Ettevõtluse Arendamise Sihtasutus, Majandus-Ja Kommunikatsiooniministeerium. European State Aid Law Quarterly 18: 186–191 [illegible] (1860) La jurisprudence [illegible] [illegible]

[illegible] National [illegible] [illegible]

[illegible]

[illegible]

[illegible]

[illegible]

[illegible]

[illegible]

[illegible]

[illegible]

Conclusions: The Book in a Nutshell

This book offers a review of the *de minimis* aid and demonstrates that it is both a *sui generis* legal concept in the context of State aid and subject to a *complex framework*.

It is a *sui generis* concept in that (i) it seeks to strike a balance between simplifying the grant process and not distorting competition in the internal market, while being a tool that MS are able to apply easily: it should be easy to interpret, highly flexible and quick to implement and with low administrative costs—a goal not always achieved—and (ii) it is subject to *ex-ante* control by MS. While this solution does not require notifying the *de minimis* aid to the European Commission, it does cast some doubts on the exclusive authority of the Union for State aid matters.

The framework is *complex* in that (i) it requires determining the sectors of economic activity it applies to, which is not always easy to do; (ii) a few notions specific to the regime are not easy to understand, such as the notion of "*single undertaking*"; and (iii) it requires combining four *de minimis* regimes (one general and three special), which in turn requires reconciling those regimes with each other and with other aid, not least because of the cumulation rules. This complexity, experienced by MS in their daily monitoring, shows just how difficult it is to comply with the *de minimis* regimes and, consequently, lays bare the weakness of the system with respect to ensuring the compliance of the amounts set out in Article 107 TFEU.

Lastly, the particularities of the *de minimis* rules were also reflected in the recovery framework for unlawful *de minimis* aid.

© T.M.C. ASSER PRESS and the author 2022
R. Pedro, *De Minimis Aid Under EU Law*,
https://doi.org/10.1007/978-94-6265-543-0

Index

© T.M.C. ASSER PRESS and the author 2022
R. Pedro, *De Minimis Aid Under EU Law*,
https://doi.org/10.1007/978-94-6265-543-0

T

U

The manufacturer's authorised representative in the EU is Springer Nature Customer Service Centre GmbH, Europaplatz 3, 69115 Heidelberg, Germany. If you have any concerns regarding our products, please contact ProductSafety@springernature.com

Printed and bound by CPI Group (UK) Ltd, Croydon, CR0 4YY
28/09/2026
02224088-0020